# Walking Free

# Walking
# Free

## Munjed Al Muderis
### *with* Patrick Weaver

ALLEN&UNWIN
SYDNEY • MELBOURNE • AUCKLAND • LONDON

First published in 2014
Copyright © Munjed Al Muderis 2014

Allen & Unwin
83 Alexander Street
Crows Nest NSW 2065
Australia
Phone: (61 2) 8425 0100
Email: info@allenandunwin.com
Web: www.allenandunwin.com

Cataloguing-in-Publication details are available
from the National Library of Australia
www.trove.nla.gov.au

ISBN 978 1 76011 072 7

Internal design by Alissa Dinallo
Set in 13.5/19 pt Granjon by Post Pre-press Group, Australia
Printed and bound in Australia by Griffin Press

10 9 8 7 6 5 4 3 2 1

MIX
Paper from
responsible sources
FSC
www.fsc.org
FSC® C009448

The paper in this book is FSC® certified.
FSC® promotes environmentally responsible,
socially beneficial and economically viable
management of the world's forests.

# CONTENTS

# THE FIRST STEPS

There were tears of sheer joy in my eyes as twenty-four-year-old Rifleman Michael Swain of the 3rd British Rifle Battalion, resplendent in his midnight-blue dress uniform, marched the 20 metres towards Elizabeth II to receive his MBE at Windsor Castle on the morning of Tuesday, 15 April 2014. It was a particularly poignant moment for me, because I knew the heartbreak and courage that had brought him to this ceremony.

My elation was also mixed with anxiety. With every step, I was willing Michael to be careful. Not to slip or stumble. My concern was that he should complete that march without mishap.

# Walking Free

As Michael approached the Queen, tears rolled down his mother's cheeks. She glanced at me and whispered, 'You should be receiving that medal. It's because of you that he's walking.' In truth, seeing Michael stride so confidently and naturally to receive the MBE for his charity fundraising work was reward enough. As I reflected on his achievements, and my escape from Saddam Hussein's Iraq, I had to acknowledge this was certainly one of the proudest moments of my life.

Michael's march that day was so extraordinary because only five months earlier he was barely capable of walking. Now he was stepping confidently towards the Queen, with a perfectly normal gait, on two artificial robotic legs which, as his orthopaedic and osseointegration surgeon, I had given him a couple of months earlier in my home city of Sydney.

Five years previously, Michael's life had been hanging in the balance. Both his legs were blown away above the knee when he stepped on an improvised explosive device while serving in Afghanistan. Following the long months of tortuously slow recovery, he'd been fitted with traditional socket prostheses. But they caused so many difficulties that Michael, a young father who is full of energy, was mostly restricted to a wheelchair. That's when he started trawling the internet and discovered osseointegration and my specialist clinic.

In Michael's case, his ability to flawlessly walk up to meet the Queen at Windsor Castle more than amply demonstrated the success that can be achieved. As we shared that moment in the Waterloo Room, I had known Michael for less than six months, but we had already been through some inspiring experiences together. And we share another link. On 8 November 1999, precisely ten years before Michael stepped on the explosive device in Afghanistan, I had set foot on Australian territory for the first time.

The welcome I received was almost as hostile as Michael's reception in Afghanistan. I was treated like a criminal. I was verbally abused and constantly told I should return as soon as possible to my homeland. In fact, the government would do everything to help me get there.

There was one flaw to their argument. I couldn't go back to my homeland, Iraq. Well, not if I wanted to avoid imprisonment, torture and, probably, execution.

Happily, I survived the hateful onslaught and eventually thrived in my new country, to the extent that I can now play a significant role in helping hundreds of people transform their lives. Often I'm doing it through hip and knee replacements which restore pain-free mobility to people who have been crippled by arthritis and other joint problems. For scores more above-the-knee amputees like Michael, osseointegration has delivered an even greater transformation.

To be able to make such a huge contribution to improving people's lives is my major motivation. But when I arrived in Australia, there was absolutely no indication I would ever be in a position to make such a contribution.

A lot had unfolded over the intervening years to transport the boy from Baghdad to the man at Windsor Castle. Along the way there were confronting challenges. I was subjected to degradation I wouldn't wish on anyone. But overall the experiences have served to shape my character and have made me even more determined to help change people's lives for the better, forever.

# 1

# THE BEGINNING OF
# THE END

I was born by caesarian section at the Al-Haydari Private
Hospital in Baghdad on 25 June 1972.

My mother was aged forty-two and my father sixty-five.
They had met in Baghdad two years earlier at an exhibition
of art by the children of the primary school where, at the
time, my mother was the principal. Neither had been married
before. My mother, Kamila Al-Turck, was born in Basra, in
the south of Iraq, and was the third of ten children in a poor
family—she had five sisters and four brothers. As well as
teaching, she had raised six of her younger siblings, assuming
the role of parent and breadwinner after their mother and

father both died young. Her two older sisters and one of her younger sisters had married and left the family home. The rest relied on her.

Shortly after meeting my father, my mother was demoted from principal to teacher at the school for refusing to join the Ba'ath Party. She was forced to retire altogether when she married my father, because the Ba'athists were opposed to his political and professional affiliations. It was a strange decision; until the day she died, my mother was always a great admirer of Saddam Hussein. She just didn't want to join the party.

My father's family was at the other end of the economic, social and political spectrum. He was from one of Iraq's traditional ruling families. Through him, I am descended from the Prophet Mohammed, and my grandfather was the head of the Sunni faith in large parts of Iraq and the Moslem world. The leadership of that section of the Sunni faith is handed down through the family, but neither my father nor his older brother would accept the role when my grandfather died. Instead, it was passed to a cousin. Also through my father, I'm descended from the most traditional of Iraqi aristocracy, one of the nine families that originally ruled Baghdad.

My father, Abdul Razak Al Muderis, spent his whole life based in Baghdad. He was the second oldest of five children—he had an older brother and three younger sisters—and was an intellectual, a lawyer who rose to become a judge. Over the years, he had established a wealthy lifestyle and extensive contacts among the intelligentsia and artistic elite.

6

# The Beginning of the End

His older brother Mahmood also reached high office; he held a number of ministerial portfolios but is probably better remembered for his literary talents. At the time, he was Iraq's most revered writer of short stories. He died in his forties of a liver complaint, but has been immortalised through statues of him in Egypt, where he spent his last days.

Another of my father's siblings was also a high achiever. His youngest sister was the first female university lecturer in Iraq, teaching the Science of Human Society. As far as I'm aware, it's not a subject that is studied in Western countries, but it covers the development of society from nomadic and feudal roots to contemporary structures. Traditionally my family were high academic achievers, with many pursuing careers in law or medicine.

I was very close to my father and I admired him enormously. It was he who instilled in me the lifelong values of intellectual pursuit, study, hard work and dedication, as well as the merit of questioning conventional wisdom and charting your own course through life.

He was from another era—a dapper man who was very traditional in appearance, in a colonial kind of way. He always wore a suit, collared shirt and tie. I never once saw him casually dressed or in Arabic clothing.

He had the wisdom of a man who'd experienced a life in search of knowledge and understanding. And, as much as his appearance was very traditional, his thinking was extremely radical and independent.

Because of his age, he had finished working by the time I was growing up. Instead, he would spend his days reading. His scholarly pursuit covered almost every academic area you can think of—science, history, politics, philosophy, literature. Most evenings he would be driven to a prestigious club in the city where he would play chess with Iraq's most accomplished intellectuals and artists, discussing anything and everything.

There was only one person I can remember him refusing to discuss things with—an uncle on my mother's side who had lived in Saudi Arabia and the United States, but in more recent times had become extremely religious, to the point of fanaticism. He would often attempt to talk to my father—who had a degree in religion and had memorised large parts of The Koran before becoming an agnostic—about the Islamic faith. My father would never take the bait.

'I really don't remember anything. You know more than me,' he would say.

I asked my father why he wouldn't discuss religion with this uncle. My father told me: 'His views are upside down. He's already made up his mind. You can't educate someone who has such extreme views. He's been brainwashed and is far too passionate.'

My father always emphasised the power of logic and went to great lengths to drum the same rational approach into me. He insisted that decisions you make that are based on logic are usually right. He applied the philosophy across all facets of life, but especially religion.

# The Beginning of the End

I remember him telling me: 'If you think your action will cause damage to anyone or anything, you shouldn't do it, regardless of what The Koran says.'

And he openly questioned many of the fundamental teachings of The Koran, like eating pork. He explained to me that this teaching made sense in the old days when refrigeration didn't exist and a person could become seriously ill if they ate pork that hadn't been correctly processed and stored, but with modern equipment, 'it's not so logical now'. Similarly, he believed that even though smoking was not specifically forbidden religiously, 'It's bad for you. So it makes sense not to do it.'

I recall one day at primary school, we were told the story of god instructing Abraham to sacrifice his only son. It's the same story in The Bible and The Koran. As a kid, I was puzzled by the tale and asked my father about it.

He was very dismissive. 'It's stupid,' he said. 'Can you imagine going to sleep, having a nightmare where god tells you to kill your son and you go ahead and do it? What makes you think this is an instruction from god rather than just a straightforward nightmare? The man must have been delusional or a psychopath!'

No doubt it was his view of the world that led me to also become an agnostic.

As an example of how open-minded my father was, his best friend was the head of the synagogue in Baghdad. Not the most popular person in a state that is strongly against the existence of Israel!

Through that friendship in particular, my father developed a close interest in the conflict between Israel and Palestine. He blamed the turn of events largely on the British colonialists. Everywhere the British went, they left disaster, he believed. In Palestine, for example, the various ethnic groups had lived in some kind of harmony until the British arrived. 'Now look at it!' he would say with exasperation.

As well as being an intellectual and free thinker, my father was a chess champion, renowned for playing against ten others at the same time as he taught them the finer points of the game. Of course, he introduced me to chess, which was to be a regular comfort in moments of considerable stress in later years. Sometimes, when I was a young boy, he would take me to the club with him. I found it fascinating to watch these academic adults talk and debate all aspects of life over the chessboard.

In line with his liberal views, I don't remember my father ever smacking me. I feared him greatly, but out of respect, not terror. My father was my hero and one of my deepest regrets is that I didn't have enough time with him, because he was already getting on in years when I was born.

The Al Muderis family's political and social power had been very much tied to the establishment, so its influence declined with the overthrow of the monarchy, the emergence of the republic and particularly the rise of the Ba'ath Party and Saddam from the late 1960s.

All the same, it was a privileged family and we were financially comfortable.

# The Beginning of the End

My mother's approach to life, probably because of the family demands placed on her from an early age, was completely different. Where my father was considered, measured, calm and softly spoken, she was passionate and opinionated. She was always busy and was more interested in family and friends than academic pursuits. Our house was a meeting place for her relatives and acquaintances. One of her brothers, an artist and sculptor, lived with us most of the time, while her other siblings who lived in Baghdad would visit almost every day and stay for a meal.

My mother was much more a doer than a talker, which came in handy in later years. As time went by, she increasingly managed our assets—particularly a shop and office complex in downtown Baghdad that provided most of our income by that stage.

My father wasn't a businessman and had largely gone along with the guy who was managing the building for us. It turned out he was sub-leasing space and taking the rent for himself rather than passing it on to us. My father clearly thought the whole thing was too much of a headache to address directly, but my mother wasn't having a bar of it and took over the building management role herself.

My mother was also a much more traditional Moslem than my father. She would tell me: 'You're a Moslem, you shouldn't drink and you shouldn't smoke.'

I was born at a time of gathering turmoil. Just twenty-four days earlier, the oil fields of Iraq had been nationalised in the midst of the worldwide oil crisis, significantly antagonising the Western nations which were so heavily dependent on supplies from the Middle East.

My father went very much against the tide of public opinion in his condemnation of the move. While Iraqis were celebrating the demonstration of independence represented by the nationalisation, my father was telling my mother: 'This is a disaster. We need to find another country!'

He believed Iraq couldn't properly manage the oil industry on its own and that most of the wealth would be stolen by individuals. Which is exactly what happened. My father felt Iraq needed the expertise of the Western companies to keep things on an even keel. He was of the view that if Western companies had retained a 5 per cent share, everything would have run smoothly and everyone would have prospered.

While I was the only child of my parents' marriage, there were four of us in the family unit during my early years. Most of the time, my cousin Hamid lived with us. His father had died before Hamid was born and his mother, Amina, my mother's oldest sister, had died in labour. Hamid was sixteen years older than me, but we were like brothers and I looked up to him, as younger siblings do.

My cousin was very active, adventurous and mischievous, which is always impressive to someone who's much younger. Hamid would take me down to the Tigris River and we'd go swimming, even though it was fast-flowing in places. He did a lot of boxing training and was pretty fit, but he never actually fought a bout.

His rebellious nature did pitch him into trouble along the way. He lost his licence for drink driving after he had an accident on his motorbike with his girlfriend on the back. She broke her wrist in the accident. That didn't go down terribly well with his girlfriend or, more importantly, her family. Actually, her family were livid and determined to wreak some revenge—which meant Hamid had to go into hiding and lie low for a couple of weeks until the heat died down. He didn't get a warm welcome when he arrived home either.

Hamid worked with my mother's brother, the sculptor, Ismail Fattah Al-Turk. He was a technician and would make the casts for the bronze sculptures my uncle was producing. My cousin lived with us until 1978, when I was six years old. At the age of twenty-two, he decided it was time to branch out, so he went to the United States looking for a better life. He's still there, living in New York and working as a businessman, trading goods, importing and exporting.

Baghdad was a very safe city in those days and remained that way until the start of the war with Iran in 1980. The Iraqi capital is a city of seven million people and plenty of contrasts, split down the middle by the Tigris River, which winds through the city, from north to south, like a snake.

The old, historic centre is full of narrow streets and buildings that are two, three or four storeys tall, a mix of commercial and residential accommodation. Many of the widespread older structures are rundown and clearly in need of repair or restoration. The old city is slightly chaotic, teeming with people, and a nightmare for traffic. Some of the mosques and churches date back hundreds of years. In those days the city was protected by walls, and the ruins of some of those old structures are still in place.

The modern central business district, on the eastern bank of the Tigris, is like a commercial centre in any developed nation—clusters of newer, concrete and glass high-rise commercial buildings, unit blocks and hotels, most of them built in the 1970s and '80s. Surrounding them are older low-rise areas that aren't far short of slums. It's a busy and bustling but organised city centre. Saddam built a new road system for the city with highways and major connecting arterials to improve the traffic flow.

The banks of the Tigris are lined with restaurants, bars and clubs. It's a very social part of the city—and going out at night is enormously popular because it's the cooler time of day in what is a hot climate. The sun is very strong in Iraq and the summers long. In line with the climate, the people of Baghdad can demonstrate a fairly hot temperament. They are very proud and can be quite aggressive.

Outside the centre, most of the suburbs are low rise, with larger, mainly two-storey homes and wide areas set aside for citrus and palm trees. To the north-east of the city centre is the Army Canal, an open waterway built to take the city's sewage. On the other side is Sadr City, which has always been a lower socio-economic area, with small homes crowded together. It's renowned as a hotspot of trouble. You could always tell if there was a problem in Sadr City—the army would simply close the bridges and move in to corner the perceived trouble-makers.

Baghdad is largely laid out in a grid system, although there is a little more variation in Wazeria, one of the city's wealthiest areas, where we lived when I was a small child. Wazeria is a neighbourhood of peaceful tree-lined streets on the eastern banks of the Tigris in the north of Baghdad.

I remember little of our first house, although I know it was opposite the North Gate Cemetery, which served as the British cemetery in Baghdad. I do recall that as a child I would go for walks along the banks of the Tigris with my mother and father, taking in the parks, playgrounds and cafés along the way. There was little I could have wished for that I didn't already have.

We moved when I was about four into a large, two-storey home with a big garden in a newer, nearby suburb called Al Mustansiria. My mother loved flowers, so there were extensive garden beds filled with fragrant plants during spring and summer. Much of the rest of the garden was covered with fruit trees—lemons, oranges, four or five date palms, a couple of grapefruit trees.

Iraqi houses tend to be constructed to a similar design. They're usually two-storey, rectangular structures with flat roofs. They're built with clay bricks but some are finished with the bare brickwork while others are rendered on the outside and painted, usually white or beige. Inside the rooms tend to be about 4 by 5 metres. Usually there's a covered area outside to protect cars from the powerful sun. It's typical for a house to be surrounded by a garden as well as a high wall or fence for privacy.

Our house met all these measures. It included a large living area, a guest area, a kitchen and three bedrooms on the ground floor. Another two bedrooms were upstairs. And there was a garage large enough to accommodate five cars. My father's favourite vehicle was a Volvo, while, for a long time, my mother used to drive an MG sports car. She eventually gave it up and switched to a Volkswagen Beetle. Quite a change of direction— from the sporty to the subdued. Unlike my mother, my father never drove himself. We employed a regular driver in addition to a nanny and a housekeeper.

The rest of the household was made up of at least one cat and a dog. The cats were always kept indoors, because, believe it or not, the sun outside was too hot for them. The dogs, on the other hand, were confined to the garden where they kept guard against trespassers.

When I was a young lad, every day during the school year my father would take me, in the chauffeur-driven car, to the First of June Primary School—it was named for the date that commemorated the nationalisation of the Iraqi oil fields. We'd leave home about seven each morning to start lessons at eight.

# The Beginning of the End

School finished at two in the afternoon. Children had to go to school six days a week—Saturday through Thursday, with the Moslem holy day on Friday as a day off. I remember a lot of homework so, while school was finished by early afternoon, there was plenty of studying to keep me occupied at home.

I went through all my school years, from the start of kindergarten to the end of high school, with two particularly close friends, Manaf and Ayser.

Manaf's father was number two in the police force in Baghdad and his mother was a teacher at our primary school. Manaf was Sunni, tall and slim, not terribly academic and hopeless at sport. But a good bloke. I think he lives in Sweden these days.

Ayser's father owned a cloth factory and his mother was a lecturer. They were the complete opposite of my parents—strict and deeply religious Shi'ites. The front door of their home was locked at six o'clock every night, and woe betide Ayser if he wasn't home by then. There was never any question of him drinking or smoking—well, in his parents' minds anyway. Ayser, however, was as rebellious as most young people and he drank and smoked—he just made sure he wasn't caught! As far as I know, Ayser is still in Baghdad.

My family was also fortunate enough to spend a number of months each year travelling overseas. In winter we would stay in Baghdad, but in summer the world was our oyster. My father would take us off to the United States or Europe—the United Kingdom, Germany, France, Italy, the Netherlands, the old Soviet Union, Greece, Turkey, Poland, Bulgaria, Hungary and what were then Czechoslovakia and Yugoslavia.

I recollect bits and pieces from most of the places we visited. We would stay in comfortable hotels and become involved in all the traditional tourist activities. Italy left a particular mark on me, because I recall it as being very dangerous, especially crossing the road in Rome. Athens lingers in the memory as well—partly because of The Acropolis, but mostly because, as a youngster, I was struck by what a dirty city it was.

One incident in Bulgaria especially stays with me. We were in the resort town of Varna on the Black Sea. I went shopping with my mother and we came back to find my father in the shopping plaza, surrounded by women who were obviously prostitutes trying to tap into the needs of a wealthy older man. It was hilarious, because it was the exact antithesis of my father. He was amused and, I guess, a little flattered, but there is absolutely no way he would have been interested in a Bulgarian prostitute and I recall him explaining to them that he was far too old to be worried about anything like that. Even in that situation, he was unerringly polite.

We went to the United States six or seven times, including a number of trips to New York and also to what I considered horrible cities like Detroit and Cleveland, where we visited relatives. Detroit struck me as being industrial and dirty, while Cleveland was dull because my cousin there was an odd character and would actively discourage us from venturing far from his home. We were in the United States on 22 September 1980, when Iraq invaded Iran.

My father was decisive in his response and said we had to go straight back to Baghdad. He obviously sensed the magnitude of what was to unfold over the next eight years—and looking back, he was right. Quite simply, it was the beginning of the end for the way of life we had known. As it was for many Iraqis, for that matter.

Our family flew out of the United States on the first available plane, bound for a brief stopover in Athens before heading to the Iraqi capital. All was going to plan until we were on the final leg from Athens. In mid-flight, there was an announcement over the loudspeaker system that Baghdad Airport had been bombed and then closed. That meant a hurried—and rather nerve-wracking—change of plans as we were diverted to Amman in Jordan.

All flights into Baghdad had been cancelled. So, while we were much closer to home than we had been in New York or Athens, we still didn't have any direct air access. This meant an uncomfortable night at the ramshackle Amman Airport, attempting to sleep on drooping plastic chairs. From there, we had to make arrangements to take a bus back to our home city.

Waiting around for a bus was particularly tedious—but things got worse when it actually arrived. The bus was more like a truck. We were bundled aboard and sat on bench seats for the tortuous overnight drive on the rugged roads to Baghdad. It was less than a week since the start of the war with

Iran so the lights on all vehicles had to be dimmed. Drivers were ordered to paint the top of the headlights blue so they couldn't be seen from the military aircraft that may have been flying above.

The first night back at home should have been an opportunity to rest and recover from the journey. But it turned out to be nothing of the sort. Baghdad was being bombed and I had no sooner gone to bed than the air-raid siren sounded.

The next day, the Iraqi media reported that seventy Iranian aircraft had been shot down. But, as always, the first casualty of war is the truth and you have to wonder what the real tally was. Nevertheless, that offers some idea of the intensity of the bombing at that stage of the conflict. The air raids continued like that for the first couple of weeks of the war, but gradually, over time, they slowly diminished and petered out.

Quite clearly, though, the comfort of my early years had come to a sudden and, from my seven-year-old point of view at least, unexpected end. The turmoil had begun.

# 2

# THE CRADLE OF
# CIVILISATION

In one form or another, my homeland has been a focal point of human civilisation for more than 8000 years. What we now know as Iraq has a chequered history. At times it's been a haven for intellectuals and artists; in other eras, it's been a byword for destruction and exploitation.

Sadly, for the last three decades Iraq has developed a reputation as a hotbed of violence, suicide bombings, murder and mayhem, its recent history punctuated by vicious and protracted wars, arbitrary killing and torture. Certain regions are also renowned for openly supporting armed militia with close links to Al-Qaeda.

The country wasn't always like that. The fertile lands of Mesopotamia around the Tigris and Euphrates rivers—known since about 6500 BC as the Cradle of Civilisation—were for thousands of years the epicentre of educational, scientific, artistic and agricultural achievement. That same civilisation has been credited with fostering many significant skills that have become the foundation of human achievement—irrigation, the development of the wheel and the creation of cursive writing, maths and astronomy.

The Sumerian and Babylonian cultures ruled Mesopotamia from about 4000 to 500 BC. The Hanging Gardens of Babylon, one of the Seven Wonders of the Ancient World, were created by King Nebuchadnezzar near the present city of Hillah, 100 kilometres south of Baghdad, as a tribute to his wife.

By 500 BC, after the decline of Greece and before the rise of Rome, Persia was the world's strongest military power. Mesopotamia duly became part of its empire.

From then until now, the lands of Iraq have been conquered and ruled by some of the great empire builders and empires of the world. Among them were Alexander the Great, who died in Babylon; Hulagu Khan, the grandson of the Mongol leader Genghis Khan; the Turkish-based Ottoman Empire; and, from the early twentieth century, the British, who installed what was always intended as a puppet monarchy.

After decades of turbulence, in 1958 a left-wing nationalist coup led by Brigadier General Abd al-Karim Qasim took control, assassinating King Faisal II—he was machine-gunned in the courtyard of his palace—and severing the nation's ties with the British.

Various internecine grabs for power within the military resulted in a revolving door of leaders, until Saddam Hussein became prime minister in 1979. Saddam's political star had been on the rise since 1968, when the Ba'athists seized power in the 17 July Revolution and he took control of national security. He managed to keep a lid on the simmering animosity between politicians and the military and developed a reputation for ruling with an iron fist. A reputation that endured for the rest of his life.

Dissent wasn't tolerated and the consequences of questioning him or his family were horrific. At best, you'd be beaten up or maimed. At worst, you'd become a statistic—one of thousands of people who were murdered by his henchmen. How many were killed can never be known, but some sources say the number is well into the hundreds of thousands.

But there was another side to Iraq under Saddam. In the early years, he introduced a series of reforms that put Iraq at the forefront of social and economic development in the Middle East. The nation's road network was massively expanded and significant resources were ploughed into building new hospitals and schools. School was made compulsory and free education to high school level was established. Charges for medical treatment in hospitals were abolished. Industry, particularly mining, was developed, and major investment was pumped into rural areas, where most of the population lived. The nation's agricultural systems were completely overhauled—large properties were broken up and divided into smaller plots, which were handed over to family farmers. And many regional areas were connected to the electricity grid for the first time.

The first year or so of Saddam's rule was a time of prosperity in Iraq. But then came the eight-year war with Iran.

As well as the horror of the war itself, the conflict brought the Iraqi economy to its knees. Educated, hard-working people found themselves unable to make a legitimate living in their long-held professions. Some found work as tradesmen. But mostly, these people were forced to sell their belongings in a desperate attempt to keep the family fed and with a roof over their heads.

My salary when I first qualified as a doctor in Baghdad was the equivalent of one dollar a month! I would routinely blow the whole lot on a can of Coke and a mouthful of fast food within a few hours of tucking my pay packet into my trouser pocket.

Be cautious, though, when you're judging Iraq. It's not like a long-established Western nation; rather, it's a collection of disparate groups, cultures and societies with different, often competing, values and aspirations. In Iraq, loyalties are constantly divided.

From a religious point of view, the primary allegiance for the majority Shi'ite Moslem population is to the Shi'ite religion and its followers. Politically, the Shi'ite regime currently has the external support of the United States and its Western allies as well as the Shi'ite leaders of Iran, who were for so long Iraq's despised enemies.

Similarly, the main allegiance of the minority Sunni Moslems is to the Sunni faith and its adherents. Iraqi Sunnis garner political support from Saudi Arabia, a rival of Iran for leadership of the Moslem and Arab countries of the region. Saddam was a Sunni, ruling a nation of largely Shi'ite Moslems.

Then there are the geographical divisions.

In the north, the Khurds have been fighting and campaigning for decades to establish an independent nation. In the west, as demonstrated by the almost constant uprisings in Fallujah and Ramadi, Anbar Province is very much a law unto itself. Mostly desert, it is largely occupied by people who are Sunnis and who remain close to their nomadic and tribal roots. In the south, the population of Basra harbours lingering resentment against Baghdad.

And in the region, tensions between the people of today's nations of Iran and Iraq stretch back hundreds of years.

The war with Iran started when Saddam went ahead with a series of attacks on what were deemed disputed territories on the border, with his eyes on some Iranian oil fields. Iran retaliated by shelling villages inside Iraq. Within a week, Saddam announced all disputed territories had been liberated and he went on to renounce the 1975 Algiers Accord, while all the time emphatically denying any intention to go to war with Iran.

As with all such despots, actions speak louder than words. The following day Saddam ordered Iraqi forces to attack Iranian border posts as a prelude to an invasion. The weak Iranian response reinforced the impression that Iraq was poised for a swift and decisive military victory.

Later that month, Iraq launched an air and land attack, starting the disastrous full-scale conflict.

After those early air raids when we arrived back from the US, life in Baghdad became quieter and attacks on the city by the Iranian Air Force declined. In fact, I don't recall any air raids at all after 1983, although there was one incident, in 1981, which I was lucky to survive. One of my mother's younger sisters and her husband, who'd escaped the onslaught in Basra, were staying with us and one morning the air-raid sirens sounded. As soon as we heard the unfolding commotion, we did what we always did—rushed outside to watch the action! On this occasion it was a dogfight between Iraqi and Iranian aircraft over the city and therefore very exciting for an eight-year-old boy.

My uncle, full of bravado, lifted me onto his shoulders as we stood in the driveway, craning our necks to see the aerial battle over Baghdad. Then literally out of the blue, an Iranian Phantom fighter plane emerged from the skirmish in the skies, turned and came hurtling directly towards us. It fired off its rockets in a spectacular display—straight in front of us—and kept coming.

# The Cradle of Civilisation

My uncle, with me still perched on his shoulders, didn't move, transfixed by what was developing before our eyes.

Still the fighter screeched on in our direction—then the pilot started strafing the ground with machine guns. Closer and closer until the bullets were tearing up the park across the road. In an instant, the ground in front of us was exploding with machine-gun bullets. My uncle still didn't run—he just stood there, with me, at least, paralysed with fear. With the Iranian Phantom now directly ahead of us, the bullets rattled into the driveway, then they were whistling past us through the air and three actually slammed into the house.

Luckily for us, as quickly as it began, it was over—the fighter plane roared into the skies behind us and banked away into the distance. We continued to watch as it was shot down by an anti-aircraft missile. Strafing our house was probably one of the pilot's last acts.

To this day I don't know why my uncle didn't run for cover as soon as the fighter plane turned in our direction. The word stupidity springs to mind! We were sitting ducks and there was no doubt the pilot had seen us and targeted us deliberately and directly. It was purely by good fortune that we weren't ripped apart by the machine-gun bullets.

As an eight-year-old, I guess I was too immature to comprehend the potentially disastrous consequences. But my mother certainly wasn't. As soon as the fighter plane had disappeared, she raced out of the house and berated us, at the top of her voice, for being so dumb.

Afterwards, I searched our property and found two of the bullets that had hit the house. They were huge—as long as my hand and twice the width of my thumb. One ripped into the front wall, another tore into the air-conditioning unit on the roof, piercing the covering and leaving a large hole. We were lucky, though; the damage they caused wasn't extensive and was swiftly repaired. And my uncle and I were still alive!

At the end of 1980, a military stalemate was developing. Iraq's invasion had ground to a virtual halt, with Iran's air power inflicting significant damage on military equipment and supply lines. The situation had been aggravated by a combined naval and air attack that destroyed most of Iraq's navy and early-warning radar installations in the south of the country—which meant Iran could easily circumvent the Iraqi siege of the Iranian city of Abadan, just inland from the Persian Gulf. With their forces severely depleted, both countries opted to switch to a defensive strategy, holding their existing territory while rebuilding their military assets.

By early 1982, the focus of the war had altered. Now, it was Iran on the attack and the Shi'ite nation won a decisive victory in a battle that recaptured most of the southern province of Khuzestan. Over the next two months, Iran made further gains, leaving Saddam little option but to withdraw his exhausted and demoralised troops, largely to the established borders between the two countries.

To make matters worse, Syria had upped its support for Iran by closing an oil pipe line that had given Iraq access to oil tankers in the Mediterranean, delivering a powerful blow to the Iraqi economy. On the other side of the coin, Saudi Arabia was helping prop up Iraq financially. Even so, the Iraqi economy was showing signs of the pressure exerted by the war. Things were beginning to slide.

Morale in the military and in the civilian population ebbed away and there was a lot of internal migration as people flooded out of the most dangerous areas, particularly in the south, and arrived in Baghdad. Until then, the southern regions had taken the brunt of the damage—Abadan on the Shatt al-Arab waterway and Basra were both in the firing line. Meanwhile, not much had altered for us in Baghdad: the air raids had eased, there were no food shortages and supplies of petrol for industry and transport continued uninterrupted.

But in 1983, even the upmarket Baghdad district of Al Mustansiria began to change. We started to see and experience the impact of the fighting on our surroundings and lifestyle. Everyone became preoccupied with the war. That year, Iraq temporarily closed its borders, a move which brought an end, for the time being at least, to overseas travel for my family.

The situation gradually deteriorated until, two years later, with the land campaign at a stalemate, what became known as the War of the Cities started.

Iraq launched this phase of the conflict with a strategic air- and missile-bombing campaign against major Iranian cities, including its capital Tehran. Most of the raids were intercepted by Iranian air defence systems and fighter jets, but enough damage was inflicted to cause serious headaches among the ayatollahs. Later, Iraq concentrated on Scud missile attacks and even chemical warfare against Iranian targets.

In response, Iran bought its own Scud missiles from Libya and launched them at major Iraqi cities, including Baghdad. The missile attacks were accompanied by heavy shelling of cities closer to the border.

The Scud attacks were terrifying, especially because they were so random. The completely haphazard and unpredictable nature of the strikes was hugely unsettling—they would hit Baghdad at any time of the day or night. Also, the Scud wasn't a terribly accurate weapon and there were missiles flying about everywhere.

The air-raid sirens would sound as the Scud missiles approached. We'd rush downstairs, because we didn't have a bunker at home and downstairs was the safest place, protected by as much concrete as possible above us. We could hear the missiles whining and whistling overhead for two or three seconds. The noise, along with the uncertainty of not knowing where the missile would strike, was agonising. Then we'd hear the loud explosion—and be grateful the Scud had landed somewhere else.

Straight after the big bang, just like the earlier air raids by the Iranian jets, we'd head up to the roof to see where it had landed and assess the damage. I remember one missile struck a high school close to our house. Another hit a highway 2 or 3 kilometres away. Fortunately, because the Iranian Scuds weren't an advanced design and couldn't accurately strike a selected target, many of them ended up in the Tigris River, inflicting little or no damage.

The same could not be said about the Iraqi economy, which was becoming crippled by the war. By this stage the general population was beginning to suffer the war's economic effects even more than its weapons.

In 1980, Iraq had been one of the more advanced economies in the region and was a net creditor nation. But the war with Iran ended that. Oil production was cut by two-thirds in the first year, and Iraq's earnings from oil fell by more than half during the conflict. That wasn't only because of the war. Kuwait and the United Arab Emirates were both stretching their production quotas and, with increasing supplies, world prices had fallen sharply.

At the same time, military spending soared—leading the nation into economic decline. The Iraqi dinar kept sliding in value and what imports were coming into the country were vastly more expensive than they had been. As economic activity slowed, jobs were being lost and wages and salaries were, at best, staying the same. Between 1979 and 1981, the standard of living started to dive.

The impact meant educated people who had earned a comfortable living in previous years were finding themselves out of work; the more fortunate saw their incomes shrinking. They simply couldn't afford to live in an expensive suburb like Al Mustansiria any longer.

The Khurdish family who'd always lived next door sold up and moved out, as did others in our street and around the neighbourhood. The people who moved in next door were different to the polite families I grew up with—our new neighbours were truck drivers who parked their vehicles on what had been the local playground and seemed to have little regard for anyone else. The appearance of the local people changed as well. Until then, everyone had worn Western-style clothing but, as the war progressed, the new inhabitants of Al Mustansiria wore Arabic clothes and thongs.

It was indicative of the way my country and my life were changing. Entering my teenage years, I was forced to recognise that things would never be the way they had been. And I felt a deep sense of sadness at the loss of innocence.

As the years passed, I progressed to Baghdad College—a huge school with hundreds of students and grounds covering more than 10 hectares. It was highly regarded and had been set up by American Jesuits from New England in 1931 at the request of the pope of the day. Originally, it had been a private school, but in the late 1960s, the Ba'ath Party ordered the Jesuits out and took over its administration.

Quite a few things changed when that happened. The college was no longer a private school where parents paid lofty fees. Rather, it was opened up to everyone. Uniforms for the students quickly became a thing of the past. But, strangely, the teachers were still required to wear a uniform—a white coat, rather like a lab coat, with a collared shirt and tie.

I was at Baghdad College in the late 1980s, along with the children of some of the Iraqi elite of the era, most notably Qusay and Udai Hussein—Saddam's thuggish sons.

They were hoodlums even in those days and would strut around the grounds with their bodyguards, completely ignoring the rules and driving their Mercedes cars and quad bikes inside the school. Officially, all vehicles were barred from the school grounds, because there was plenty of parking available outside. But, obviously, Qusay and Udai Hussein didn't believe any rules applied to them and they drove their vehicles inside the school wherever they wanted.

I arrived after Udai had left the school, but I knew his reputation. Udai was smart, but he was a jerk. My cousin Amar hung out with Udai at school, often playing basketball with his group of devoted henchmen. Amar was an extremely good basketball player, which I guess gave him the passport into Udai's social circle. Fortunately, it didn't seem to taint Amar's future to any great extent. These days, he's an electrical engineer living in Johannesburg, South Africa.

Qusay was a contemporary of mine. Outside the classroom I purposely avoided him whenever possible because he was clearly dangerous. While Udai was regarded as being reasonably clever, Qusay was as thick as a brick. I recall him getting

4 per cent in one of his mid-term exams, which probably summed up his intellectual capabilities.

Of more immediate concern to me was Saddam's nephew Omar al-Tikriti. He sat next to me in class, making it impossible to avoid him completely. But we didn't talk and outside the classroom I kept away from him as much as possible. Omar could only be described as an ignorant, arrogant prick.

I remember on one occasion the school principal decided to stand up to Omar and his bodyguards and warned them about bringing vehicles into the school grounds. Omar responded by threatening the principal with the sack. He was very lucky to keep his job, and his life. But the whole incident had absolutely no impact on Omar and his hoodlum friends. They didn't care about school rules and just carried on as they always had.

Our history teacher in Year 9 also had a lucky escape, on the first day of the school term. He walked into the room and began his class with the words: 'I'll sum up your history in one phrase: you're all bastards!'

It was a good opening line and grabbed everyone's attention. Which, let's face it, isn't an easy task for a teacher facing a class of teenage boys for the first time. Omar wasn't impressed, though. In fact, he took deep offence, stood up and challenged the teacher.

'How dare you say that!' he roared.

At that point I saw the potential for Omar to spin completely out of control but, fortunately, the teacher seemed prepared.

# The Cradle of Civilisation

Calmly, he told Omar and the rest of us: 'I'll tell you why you're all bastards. Iraq has been invaded by almost every nation you can think of. That's why we see people from all sorts of backgrounds. Different coloured skin, blue eyes, brown eyes, black eyes.'

The teacher's clever explanation resolved what could easily have been an explosive situation and Omar sat down again, suitably bemused.

I had just one major personal clash with Omar, when we were about fifteen years old. As I was walking across the school grounds with my friend Manaf, Omar, for no reason I could ever work out, decided to throw stones at me and hit me with one. As soon as he had my attention, he shouted at me: 'Hey, you . . . what are you, Shi'ite or Sunni?'

As it happened, by this stage I had decided that I didn't believe in any religious affiliations—and, as an extremely strong sub-plot, I also wanted to avoid a conflict with Omar at all costs.

So I responded vaguely: 'I don't know what you mean.'

Omar laughed, mocking and dismissive. 'What? You don't know what you believe in? You're an idiot,' he said and walked away. Happily for me, Omar decided there was better entertainment to be had bullying more argumentative students.

But there were plenty of other incidents that illustrated Omar's view of the world and his place in it. At one stage, he was running for student representative and gathered the whole year, about 400 of us, into one of the school's large halls. Then he stood up in front of the mass of students and demanded to know: 'Who's a member of the Ba'ath Party and who's not?'

He divided us into the two groups. The Ba'ath Party members were moved to one side of the auditorium and the non-members, including me, to the other. Omar then started to gesticulate wildly and berate the non-party side, essentially telling us that we were traitors. Of course, we all knew that being classified as traitors in that regime was accompanied by potentially serious consequences.

Luckily, also in my class was another well-connected kid, Mutab Howaz al-Tikriti. Mutab was the son of the leader of Saddam's tribe from Tikrit. It would be hard to find someone who was less like Saddam's sons and the despised Omar. Mutab was a really good guy—clever and considered and from a much better social class.

As those of us who'd identified as not belonging to the Ba'ath Party quaked under Omar's mad ranting, Mutab rose to his feet and told him to shut up.

'You are misrepresenting yourself,' he said to Omar. 'You're taking the completely wrong approach. If you want people to join you, you should lead by example, not by shouting at them.'

Mutab then dismissed everyone from the auditorium and we fled into the schoolyard, relieved and grateful that someone with authority had stood up to the powerful buffoon.

Regardless, Omar went on to be elected the school representative—a position of some prestige that entailed organising various student activities—although it was through a campaign of intimidation rather than by popular vote. By gaining that position, Omar was rather more successful than his brother, Mudar, who was a couple of years older than us.

Mudar, like the others in Saddam's family, was a complete animal. His campaign—using threats and bullying—to become school representative was an utter disaster and he amassed a grand total of two votes. But Mudar wasn't going to meekly accept the democratic verdict. Instead, his body-guards beat up the winner—so viciously that they broke his back—then threw him in the river, where he was left for dead. Somehow he survived, although he was permanently paralysed and his life was shattered.

On the academic side, the school system in Iraq at the time dictated that all subjects, with the exception of religion, were compulsory. There was no exam in religion, probably because Iraq at the time was secular and there was a sizeable Christian population as well as the Moslem majority. We had to wade through everything that was thrown at us. I preferred the science subjects, hence my future choice of career. But I couldn't stand maths and it was a constant effort to persuade myself it was something of interest.

Outside the classroom, I played a lot of soccer—and was pretty good, to be honest. I was a skilful striker who scored plenty of goals. But my abilities didn't make much difference in the internal school competition, because Omar was in one of the other teams—and the only rule seemed to be that his team always won! Nonetheless, I played soccer for the school as well, with some success, and later I played for the student team at Baghdad University; there was even talk about going on to the semi-professional level. But, inevitably, I had to make a choice between soccer and studies . . . and studies won out.

The all-boys Baghdad College was twinned with an all-girls school which had a similar tradition and history. Al-Aqida High School for Girls, founded in 1928 as a prestigious Catholic college, was the educational institution of choice for the daughters of politicians, industry leaders, the judiciary and other upper echelons of society. During adolescence, our main contact with girls our own age was through the two schools. The girls would regularly use the library and laboratories in our school, and from time to time, there were joint excursions. Daily, though, the buses of both schools followed the same routes and stopped at the same places so, naturally enough, we developed friendships with the groups of girls at the bus stops.

Outside school, we'd go out for soft drinks and burgers— the interactions would have been just the same as in Western nations. And there was a reasonably relaxed approach. At that time, very few girls were covered and nearly all of them wore Western clothes. It's very different now, of course.

With the Iraqi economy in decline, there was less to go around for everyone. It even affected my family. For the whole of my life until then, I'd been used to having people around who looked after the day-to-day running of the house. It was the standard order of things, and these household employees were very much a part of the broader family set-up.

# The Cradle of Civilisation

Naturally, as a child, I hadn't been privy to the family finances, or even aware of the impact of the events going on in the region. So it was a thoroughly unpleasant surprise when we started to downsize.

I'm not sure who was first to depart, but gradually we had to let go of the driver, the live-in housekeeper and the maid. There was a feeling of emptiness when they left. But then some extremely practical issues had to be addressed.

Eventually, my mother took over the cooking duties from the housekeeper. Which wasn't great for anyone. I don't think she particularly enjoyed the role and—how do I say this politely?—cooking wasn't one of her most accomplished skills. But we did get used to the regular diet of rice, kidney beans and some form of meat! At least we knew what to expect . . . and there weren't many other aspects of our lives at that time where we could say that.

# 3

# DOWNTOWN DREAMS TO
# BOMBING IN BASRA

Some truly dreadful stories came out of the war with Iran—
even more than in the average military conflict. In fact, it was
said to be the third most destructive military confrontation of
the twentieth century, after the two world wars.

Estimates of casualties vary widely, but it's likely Iran lost
around 750,000 and Iraq about 250,000 military personnel and
civilians. Large areas of south-eastern Iraq and western Iran
were severely damaged as the armies rolled back and forth.

Iraq had used chemical weapons, in the form of poison gas,
against both the Iranian military and Iraqi Khurds. At one
point during the Battle of the Marshes in 1984, Iraq ran live

electric cables through the marsh waters specifically to electrocute Iranian soldiers who were fighting towards one of the two roads between Basra and Baghdad.

And then there was the use of child soldiers. Children as young as nine were serving in the Iranian Army. In some cases, they had volunteered with the express intent of becoming martyrs to the cause. There were stories of child soldiers being used to run through minefields in advance of the regular troops.

By early 1988, Iraq had repelled the best Iran had to offer and it was once more on the front foot. Saddam launched another wave of the War of the Cities, bombarding major Iranian population centres with missiles and using laser-targeted bombs in air attacks. Tehran and Isfahan were both being attacked on a daily basis. Iran responded, but with far fewer missiles.

Then Saddam announced he was preparing a decisive invasion of Iran using weapons of mass destruction—notably chemical weapons.

Following up the threat, Iraq bombed the town of Oshnavieh with poison gas; more than 1700 civilian casualties were reported. In July, Iraq dropped cyanide bombs on the Iranian Kurdish village of Zardan. Then a series of settlements were attacked with more poison gas.

The last straw came when the US guided-missile cruiser *Vincennes* shot down an Iranian civilian aircraft, killing all 290 passengers. The Iranian leaders took the attack as an indication that the United States was ready to declare war. That, coupled with the prospect of intensified chemical weapon attacks by Iraq, gave the Iranian leaders a strong motive to negotiate for peace.

From the middle of July, we started to hear rumours that the war was coming to an end.

At the same time as we dared hope for peace, our gathering optimism was punctured by a family tragedy—we received news that my cousin Ribal had been killed near Penjwin in the mountainous Sulaymaniyah Province in the north. He was in an army truck that received a direct hit from an Iranian mortar. Ribal, who was twenty-two years old, was one of three brothers; the others were Ali and Bassam, who was to play a crucial role in my life a few years later.

Ribal's death gave me my first experience of a Moslem funeral as part of a grieving family. I loathed the ceremonial customs it involved and thought the funeral was hypocritical and formulaic. Men and women were separated for the early stages of the funeral; the men went to the mosque, while the women stayed in the family home. The women dressed in black and, as they assembled, they would all routinely burst into floods of tears. Once the wave of wailing subsided, they'd start chatting quietly. Then someone else would walk into the house and the women would all burst into wailing and crying again.

Because he died in action, Ribal was treated as a martyr. As a result, his body wasn't washed after his death because martyrs are regarded as being clean. His coffin was also draped in the Iraqi flag, which remained at his burial site for forty days.

## Downtown Dreams to Bombing in Basra

The funeral lasted three days. In line with tradition, at the end of that time, there was a massive feast, with sheep being slaughtered and banquets prepared. Anyone from the street could come into the house, pray, eat and then leave. It can be enormously expensive for the family, but the ritual is regarded as a religious duty. My father had taught me that this tradition had roots in medieval Catholic dogma; feeding the poor in return for their prayers was thought to accelerate the passage of the wealthy deceased from purgatory to heaven. Quite ironic, since we were Moslem. I really think many were there just for the free food!

On the seventh day, there's another ceremony at the family home. This time, men and women mix together. And the tradition is repeated again on the fortieth day after the death. The women closest to the deceased person wear black until the first anniversary.

As we went through the early stages of mourning, we heard reports on the radio and TV that definitive negotiations to end the war were under way. Then, in early August 1988, the announcement was made that a peace agreement had been reached.

At the end of the war, Baghdad went into a frenzy of celebration—one long party.

Peculiarly, water was at the centre of it all. In the streets, people were firing water pistols at each other and splashing everyone around them with water from bottles. It went on like that for about ten days. I'm not sure how or why it started, but there was a story that some children had taken their water pistols up to Saddam's main palace and had fired them at the elite Republican Guards who, in return, splashed the kids with water. And it just spread from there.

Once the hostilities were over, we all thought Saddam would make a concerted effort to rebuild the economy. He didn't. In fact, it went in completely the opposite direction, with the vast majority of spending going to a renewed build-up of the armed forces. Saddam would regularly appear on TV announcing fresh military initiatives.

Clearly, this created gathering unease among the Western nations and, not least, Israel. The tensions were ramped even higher when Iranian-born, British-based journalist Farzad Bazoft, who was in his early thirties, was arrested at Baghdad Airport in late 1989 after visiting the site of an explosion at a rocket assembly plant south of Baghdad. He was imprisoned, held in solitary confinement for six weeks and tortured at the soon-to-be notorious Abu Ghraib prison. He later appeared, weak and dazed, on Iraqi television, admitting to being an Israeli spy. Which, under all the circumstances, was highly unlikely to be true.

The British Foreign Office, the European Commission and journalist organisations around the world pressed for his release—to no avail. Bazoft underwent a rushed one-day trial, was found guilty, sentenced to death and denied the right of appeal. He was hanged shortly after. Following the execution, Britain pressed for Bazoft's body to be returned to his parents. There was no response until, out of the blue, a coffin arrived at

London's Heathrow Airport with a note saying: 'Mrs Thatcher wanted him. We've sent him in a box.'

The incident underlined the barbarity of Saddam's regime and caused a massive rupture in relations between Iraq and the Western nations. As well as emphasising Iraq's isolation, it provided clear evidence to many world leaders that Saddam was dangerous and unpredictable and had the potential to create a flashpoint in the already delicate diplomatic balance in the Middle East.

It wasn't long before other events created the opportunity for the Western nations to flex their muscles.

※

I had decided in the early stages of high school that I wanted to follow in the footsteps of many family members and study medicine. It was either that or study law, like my father. The plan was that I would continue my education overseas, and I had singled out the course in medicine at New York University. Everything was in place. I had been accepted and enrolled at the university, paid the tuition fees and even booked the airline ticket to take me to the United States to start in September.

But on 2 August 1990, less than a month before I was to embark on my exciting adventure, Saddam invaded Kuwait.

Kuwait had been a strong ally of Iraq during the war with Iran and acted as a surrogate port for Iraq when the closure of the Shatt al-Arab waterway cut off Basra. Kuwait, along with the Persian Gulf monarchies, had also heavily financed Iraq's war effort—and that was where tensions began.

Iraq was in serious financial trouble and attempted to negotiate its war debts with Kuwait and its other major financial backer, Saudi Arabia. Saddam argued that Iraq had been heroic in leading the battle against the spread of Iran's influence in the Moslem world and deserved generous support from other Middle Eastern nations.

Iraq's already parlous economic position was further undermined when world oil prices dropped suddenly—at least partly because a number of Gulf States, Kuwait among them, increased oil production and exceeded the agreed quotas set by the Organization for Petroleum Exporting Countries (OPEC). After representations by Saddam's regime, OPEC raised oil prices in 1990, but suspicions between the Gulf States remained, particularly over fears that Iraq was ambitious to expand its borders and sphere of influence.

Those tensions, coupled with Kuwait's extensive oil reserves, made the tiny nation on Iraq's southern borders an enticing target for the Ba'athists in Baghdad. Saddam, however, wasn't about to admit that either of those factors were the major motivation for his expansion plans in the south and instead insisted Kuwait was a natural part of Iraq, which had been artificially partitioned off by the British when they drew the borders between the two nations early in the twentieth century.

## Downtown Dreams to Bombing in Basra

As the animosity escalated, Iraq and Kuwait became embroiled in a dispute over the Rumaila oilfield, with Iraq accusing Kuwait of horizontally drilling beneath the border to access US$2.4 billion of oil reserves it had no right to. There were heated diplomatic exchanges between the two nations, leading to a military build-up on the Kuwaiti border.

On 25 July, the US ambassador in Iraq, April Glaspie, held a meeting with Saddam and Deputy Prime Minister Tariq Aziz. It proved to be a crucial exchange. At least two transcripts of the meeting have been released, and, while they vary in detail, they agree that Glaspie told the Iraqis: 'We have no opinion on Arab–Arab conflicts.' There was also an indication that the overall situation on Iraq's southern borders 'was not associated with America'.

Saddam took this to mean that the US would not intervene if he invaded Kuwait.

As the dispute between Iraq and Kuwait became more dangerous, the Arab League stepped in, hosting a special meeting in Jeddah at the end of July 1990. After the conference, Iraq increased the pressure, demanding US$10 billion compensation from Kuwait. Kuwait made a counter-offer, which Saddam rejected. Then he promptly ordered the invasion of Kuwait.

Of course, the moment that happened, my plan to study medicine in New York fell apart. Flights in and out of Iraq were disrupted and I wasn't about to abandon my family and head to the United States at a time of such trauma and uncertainty.

To make matters worse, applications for the degree in medicine at Baghdad University had closed, so I couldn't get in there, either. That left Basra—a university with a long-established medical school, but in a town uncomfortably close to the border, and war, with Kuwait. Even so, I decided it would be my best educational opportunity. So I scrambled together an application and, as luck would have it, was accepted.

✳

Basra is Iraq's second largest city. It was founded in the seventh century and by the mid-1970s had a population of about 1.5 million. That dwindled by as much as two-thirds during the war with Iran, when the city, the centre of prolonged fighting, was frequently shelled. It was technically the wealthiest city in Iraq, because the surrounding area held more than 10 per cent of the nation's oil. The oil wealth was actually filtered back to Baghdad, though—so much of Basra's potential was unrealised.

I'd been to the southern city a few times with my family, mainly in the late 1970s. In those days, Basra was an extremely vibrant place with plenty of pubs and clubs. It was the most popular city in the Gulf, especially with Kuwaitis and Saudis, because they couldn't drink alcohol at home but they could in the bars and brothels of Basra. Remember, the United Arab Emirates was still relatively undeveloped at that time and there were no massive resorts in Dubai or Abu Dhabi to attract international tourists.

## Downtown Dreams to Bombing in Basra

By 1990, Basra had changed from the very cosmopolitan city I had known. In the recent war years, electricity, gas and water infrastructure had been all but wiped out. Electricity supplies were interrupted and blackouts had become a regular aspect of daily life. The water was poor quality, the roads had been bombed and the activities of the hospitals had been seriously depleted. Now, after only a short respite, Basra was on the front line once more.

The invasion of Kuwait was a complete mismatch. Iraq had the fourth largest army in the world; Kuwait was being defended by just 16,000 soldiers. To make matters worse, the Kuwaiti army had all been stood down from battle stations a few weeks earlier. Facing little resistance, the Iraqi war machine swept through Kuwait and stopped only when it reached the border with Saudi Arabia. It was all over in a couple of days.

Then the diplomacy resumed. On 6 August 1990, the United Nations Security Council passed resolutions condemning Iraq's action and imposing economic sanctions. These limited the amount of oil Iraq could sell and blocked all trade and financial support for Iraq, while allowing the continuing provision of medicine and some food. Over the years, those sanctions had a crippling effect on the Iraqi economy.

That was followed by the Bush administration's announcement of Operation Desert Shield and the arrival of the first United States troops in Saudi. In late November, the UN set a deadline of 15 January for Iraq to withdraw from Kuwait or face military action. Talks held in the meantime failed to achieve any breakthrough.

With little time to prepare for my last-minute enrolment at Basra University, I took the quickest travel option and flew there by plane, while a cousin drove my car south from Baghdad. The plane had obviously been confiscated during the invasion—the exterior carried the hurriedly painted livery of Iraqi Airways while the inside was unmistakably Kuwaiti Airlines décor.

When I arrived in early September, Basra was very much a city on a war footing, even though the brief battle for Kuwait was over. It was completely under the control of the Iraqi Army, which had set up checkpoints across the city centre and suburbs. The Iraqi Secret Service was very active in the city, too.

Throughout Iraq, as a matter of course, men had to carry a military service book—which looked rather like a passport and established whether you were a conscript, a reservist or had postponed military service until you finished university. You could never be without it for a moment—believe it or not, we even had to keep it with us when we went to the toilet! We also had to carry a work or university identification and a driver's licence. In Basra, we needed our citizenship papers as well.

While everything remained outwardly peaceful between September and the UN deadline of 15 January, we could sense the escalation in tension. We watched a big build-up of tanks being carried on the back of huge trucks, as well as supply vehicles and troops moving south. Iraq's forces could be mobilised very quickly because Saddam had created a wide network of highways.

I moved in with my cousin Nida and her family. Nida was fifteen years older than me and had a daughter aged fifteen and a son aged eight. Two years beforehand, her husband, who had a PhD, had been a high-ranking officer in the Iraqi Navy but fled the country as a refugee after a drunken incident on board his ship. It happened one Christmas, which was widely celebrated by Iraqis, while he was second in charge of the frigate *Ibn Khaldoun*, which served as the Iraqi Navy training vessel. They were out in the Red Sea and, after he'd had a skinful to drink, he apparently started badmouthing Saddam. Because he was a senior officer, nothing much happened at the time but when they returned to Basra, the Secret Service officer on board reported him to the authorities. Fortunately, his fellow officers warned him about being reported, so when it became obvious that unless he took drastic action he was headed for a grim end, he jumped ship and escaped to Holland. He still lives there.

After moving in with Nida's family and rushing through registration and other administrative processes, my first day at university was an eye-opener. You could easily identify the locals—they were wearing subdued colours like brown, black, grey and white, and many women covered their heads. The people from Baghdad were wearing much brighter colours, wore more Western style clothing and looked a lot happier.

At the start, the students divided into social groups based on their home city. There were about ten of us from

Baghdad—Sunnis, Shi'ites, Christians—and initially we spent most of our social time together. Gradually though, over the next few months, we started mixing with the students from Basra and it quickly became obvious that they were very friendly, although you only had to scratch the surface to unveil their resentment about their city being neglected by the government. Their hospitality was amazing and they welcomed us into their homes. Even though their living circumstances were very modest, they would still offer us all the food on their table.

Academically, signs of the disruption of war were evident. Some of the university professors had upped and left, diminishing the academic ranks, but fortunately for us, those who stayed maintained the solidly high standards the institution was known for. Although it wasn't as good as Baghdad, it remained much better than most other universities in the region.

There were two major hospitals in Basra, which were part of our medical studies. Al-Talemi Teaching Hospital was a high-rise institution on the banks of the Shatt al-Arab waterway in the east of the city, not far from the centre. It was like a hotel—with a view over the river—and was next to Saddam's palace, the two properties separated only by a wall. On the palace side of the hospital, all the window shutters had to be closed so no one could look into the grounds of Saddam's residence. Al-Talemi was about 15 kilometres from the university and housed the basic science and laboratory facilities, as well as libraries, so students in Years 1, 2 and 3 were taught there. The other hospital was the older Al-Jumhuri (The Republican

Hospital)—a two-storey building in the south-west of the city—where students in Years 4, 5 and 6, the clinical years of training, were based.

The Ba'athists weren't very active at the training hospital where I studied and people were less frightened to speak out than they were in Baghdad. You'd even hear voices of discontent—not loud, though, just rumblings beneath the surface. While Saddam's Secret Service was diligently suppressing dissent in other cities, their task in Basra was more difficult. Outside the hospitals, the city had a much stronger undercurrent of rebellion than Baghdad. Not surprisingly, later, after the withdrawal from Kuwait, Basra was where the uprising against Saddam started. The city has a strong religious base and at one stage wanted to establish a Federal Islamic Republic. In contrast, Baghdad, at that stage, wasn't a religious city at all.

❧

The feeling of unease in Basra grew as the deadline for the withdrawal of Iraqi troops from Kuwait approached. Despite the ultimatum, it became clear Saddam was going to call what he believed was a UN bluff. He did nothing.

It was the time of our mid-year university exams and we were spending most of our waking hours studying biology. When we had the chance, we were also keeping up with the unfolding events, which we found were most accurately reported on the BBC World Service, the Voice of America and Radio Monte Carlo.

Amid the uncertainty about the future, we didn't know whether to continue studying for the exams or prepare for war. The group of students from Baghdad went out for dinner to talk about the situation. We'd all been discussing the emergency with our parents and were trying to decide what we should do. The last phone call I made to my parents in Baghdad was on 16 January; it ended with them urging me to come home.

Instead, I decided to stay in Basra because I didn't want to take the chance that the war would be averted and I'd miss the biology exam. I suppose, with the benefit of hindsight, that seems trivial but, at that stage, we simply didn't know what was going to happen.

My cousin Nida chose to leave Basra. It was decided it was too dangerous to stay in the house by myself, so when she and her family had packed up and started the journey north, I locked the doors of the house and moved in with a close friend of another aunt. She had three daughters around my age and a son who was two years older than me. I spent the first night with them and kept studying for my exam until after midnight.

Around 2.30 a.m. on 17 January, we were woken by the screaming and rumbling of war planes over the city, followed by explosions. The US-led coalition had unleashed a massive aerial attack on Iraq to force its withdrawal from Kuwait. The bombardment involved 100,000 sorties by American and allied war planes, dropping nearly 90,000 tonnes of bombs.

We didn't get much sleep that night. And, conscious there would be casualties, I left the house at 6 a.m. and drove straight to the Teaching Hospital to see if I could help.

The scene when I arrived was worse than I could have imagined—absolute chaos. All the medical staff were there, including those who weren't on duty. They were frantically working on the injured, but it didn't appear that anyone was taking overall charge—so there was little coordination and it was an inefficient, everyone-for-themselves, type of approach.

The Casualty Department was overflowing with people who'd been wounded in the bombing. The further I looked, the more casualties I saw. All the procedure rooms and corridors were full—people were being treated on stretchers wherever there was space to keep them. Even at this early stage, the medical wards were being emptied to make room for bombing victims.

The majority of the casualties were civilians, many of them nightshift workers at the power stations and the Shuaba Oil Refinery in Basra, which had taken some of the worst impact of the air raids. From the high buildings, you could see the inferno as the refinery burned.

I was there, but as a rookie who'd been studying medicine for less than five months, there wasn't much I could do. I didn't even know how to put a drip in! To be honest, my main qualification for being at the hospital was the white coat I was wearing. So I went up to one of the doctors, told him I was a first-year medical student and asked him what I could do. He told me to find the senior medical students and interns, and they would allocate me a task. I ended up dealing with injuries that didn't need surgery: splinting broken bones, removing shrapnel, cleaning and dressing wounds. Most of these were injuries to legs, arms and the body, as well as lacerations of the face from flying glass.

The bombing went on all day and into the night. While I was in the hospital, I could hear the explosions around Basra and the drone of the heavy American bombers heading over the city on their way to Baghdad. I left the hospital early in the evening and drove around a few parts of the city. What I saw graphically illustrated the level of damage. At one point, I noticed gravel spread across the main road, although I couldn't see any damaged buildings. I decided to investigate further. Behind the houses lining the street was a large area of rubble which I slowly realised had been a six-storey telecommunications centre. It had been flattened. All that remained was the rubble and the gravel in the street. The complex had been an early target for the bombs.

My aunt Nida's home was just up the road and had been hit by flying debris—shrapnel in the walls and broken windows. While it was widespread, the damage was superficial rather than structural.

Downtown Basra, the city centre itself, wasn't heavily targeted and the people were so used to bombing, rocket and artillery attacks from the war with Iran that life mostly went on as normal. There wasn't much fuel around for cars because the refineries and petrol stations had been attacked. But the rest of the shops opened as usual the next morning and everyone who remained went about their daily business.

Back in Baghdad, anyone who could afford to was renting a house outside the capital to avoid the worst impact of the expected war and air raids. Mainly, they were going to Baqubah, in Diyala Province, around 50 kilometres north-east of Baghdad. At that time, it was renowned as a very peaceful area dominated by citrus farms. The wealthier people from Baghdad went there, not only to avoid the bombing but also, because it's closer to Iran, they felt it would provide a faster and easier passage over the border if the Americans invaded. Later, Baqubah became an extremely dangerous place for the Americans and was one of the breeding grounds of the suicide bombers.

My mother and father were too late to rent a house in Baqubah. So instead they looked to a town called Suwayrah, about 55 kilometres south-east of Baghdad—where former Iraqi Prime Minister Abd al-Karim Qasim, the army general who had led the coup overthrowing the monarchy in 1958, had been brought up.

A week before the war, my parents rented an eight-bedroom mansion in Suwayrah and moved in with various members of the family. My uncle, the sculptor, had sent his German-born wife back to Europe. He went to Suwayrah with their daughters Ava Jasmin, an architect, and Asia, a teacher; both now live in the UK.

And there was the youngest son, Ismail, who's three years older than me. Ismail was very clever academically and came second in the final high school exams for the whole of Iraq— that's no small achievement. He studied to be a lawyer, but deliberately failed one subject each year so he had to stay on at university and couldn't be conscripted into the army. He managed to stretch a four-year course out to eight years before he finally qualified—and then promptly escaped Iraq and went to Germany. That's how smart he was . . .

But Ismail was always a worry for the family. He talked down to the rest of us and called himself German rather than Iraqi. When he eventually went to Germany, he found it really difficult to integrate and was badly beaten up by a group of neo-Nazis. After that, he became a committed Moslem. He married another cousin, which is common under Islam, but she doesn't cover her head, and this challenges his religious beliefs.

Ismail was always arguing with his older brother Saheel, another high-achiever. He was in the Republican Guard, but after being buried alive in a US bombing raid, he was left with massive emotional scars. As he recovered from his horrifying ordeal, he developed interests away from the military and went on to become an artist. He now lives in Holland.

While my family was establishing itself outside Baghdad, I was still in Basra, pondering my future, and becoming more convinced by the hour that, now the university exam was out of the way, my place was back with my family.

## Downtown Dreams to Bombing in Basra

So after spending the first day of the US-led attack doing as much as I could to treat the casualties at the hospital, I drove to a friend's house about seven o'clock in the evening. As well as my friend, there was an older guy I'd never met before. He was an engineer in his mid-forties, handsome and well-dressed— and I was to spend one of the most terrifying days of my life with him.

# 4

# DEFYING DEATH IN
# THE DESERT

The first day of the Gulf War had been exhausting and unnerving.

After arriving at my friend's house, we started talking about the chances of being stuck in Basra for the duration of the war and potentially what a dangerous location it would be. Plus, naturally, I wanted to be with my family. Should I stay, or should I go?

In Basra all phone communications had been cut and, after our conversation a couple of days earlier, I couldn't talk to my parents. At this stage, I didn't know exactly where they were—and they didn't even know whether I was alive or dead.

# Defying Death in the Desert

I explained my predicament to my friend and the engineer. No sooner had I said I was thinking of heading back to Baghdad than the engineer was urging me to make the journey. And he made no bones about telling me he wanted to go as well, although he didn't explain why. He quickly latched onto the fact that I had a car and asked if I could take him.

If only the decision had been as simple as that. Sure, I had a car—a ten-year-old blue Toyota Corona. My family had bought it new and I'd looked after it, so I didn't doubt that the car itself was up to the task of making the journey to Baghdad. The tyres, though, were a different matter. They were Iraqi made, which wasn't the best quality to start with, and they were quite badly worn. But there weren't any other tyres available and we'd have to take our chances with them. My other major concern was fuel. I had barely enough to get us halfway to Baghdad, roughly 550 kilometres away. Petrol, of course, was a rare commodity because the Americans had bombed the oil refineries and any available petrol was being reserved for the Iraqi armed forces.

'Don't worry about that,' the engineer said. 'I have some connections in Samawah. We can get petrol there.'

There are two highways between Basra and Baghdad—the old one to the east and the new one to the west. The eastern highway essentially goes from city to city. Samawah is about halfway to Baghdad on the western highway. Unfortunately, the western highway was by far the more dangerous of the two roads. Even in peace time, it's a tricky, potentially dangerous drive—where it crosses large tracts of desert, it is extremely isolated.

Now, at the start of the war, there was another troubling factor. The western highway runs directly past the Imam Ali Air Base—the biggest military air base in Iraq and an obvious target for American bombers. There was no secret, even at such an early point in the conflict, that it was being bombed constantly. Driving on the highway amid those air raids, we could be hit by a bomb, rocket or machine-gun bullets and it would be very easy to be caught by the shrapnel fragments which, inevitably, would be flying around in the maelstrom. There was a genuine possibility that along the way we would become what is euphemistically called 'collateral damage'.

So, I had to face the fact that this was not going to be a routine and relaxing drive from Basra to Baghdad. First, we had to cross a remote desert region, then we had to beg, steal or borrow enough fuel to get us all the way to the capital. Because of the extent of the bombing, we couldn't be certain the road remained intact and open the whole way. The tyres may or may not last.

And, of course, the biggest danger was driving past an air base that was under relentless attack by the most powerful military force in the world.

Even while I was still considering the options, the engineer was pressuring me to drive back to Baghdad. Obviously he was anxious to return to the capital, and he saw me and my car as his main chance. His logic was that within a few days, the air raids would be replaced by a ground invasion and Basra would be taken by the coalition. He believed once that happened, Basra and the south would be set up as an autonomous region and we would be stuck there. He didn't want to take that chance.

After some thought, I agreed to do it and as soon as I'd made the decision, the engineer took charge, saying, 'We must leave early in the morning; any later and the bridges will all be bombed and we'll lose our chance of getting through.'

The wisdom of his words was underlined by the events of the evening and night. The bombing of Basra continued, targeted at military and logistical objectives, but still inflicting extensive damage on the city. And it was clear an invasion was to follow.

Despite the air raids, I had ventured out during the evening to look for my university friends from Baghdad. I wanted to offer a place in the car to anyone who wanted to head back to the capital. But they were nowhere to be found. My guess is that most had already sought safety somewhere else.

So, by default, it was me and the engineer.

The atmosphere was tense and sleep was hard to come by that night. We had no idea what fate held in store for us.

We started making preparations early the next morning, as the engineer had suggested. I removed my belongings and packed them into the car. The engineer brought a few things with him. Finally we left Basra about seven o'clock.

I was thinking of smearing mud over the car so it would be camouflaged, if only a little. But the engineer said, 'Don't bother. The Americans will know what's a military vehicle and what's civilian.' To this day, I'm not sure I share his confidence!

The early stages of the drive were tense, but relatively straightforward. Out of the bomb-ravaged city of Basra, through the suburbs and into the surrounding areas, everything went to plan.

As soon as we got out of Basra province, we had to cross the Euphrates River and a series of other waterways. The bridges were the only crossings, but they'd been mercilessly bombed. So had the suspended stretches of road over the marshes. Apart from the dangers of actually being bombed en route, the damage inflicted by the US-led aerial assault meant sections of the road were likely to be impassable. But we were in luck that day. Knowing the military and strategic significance of these crossings, Iraqi engineering teams were replacing the bridges and suspended roads almost as quickly as the Americans were bombing them.

In that part of the country, the Euphrates is about 750 metres wide from bank to bank and covers a vast floodplain. Aware the river crossings would be an obvious target, Iraqi engineers were prepared. After the bridges were bombed, they quickly laid hundreds of sections of massive water or oil pipes side by side to create the foundation of a new bridge across the river where the coalition bombardment had struck. The pipes allowed the water to maintain its usual flow while sand packed tightly on top of the pipes created a makeshift roadway. The new road was usually in place within a day or two of a bombing attack—an enormous task to be carried out so swiftly.

The pipe-based replacement roadways were very ingenious and effective—at least until the next bombing raid, although at some crossings where the engineers were still making repairs there was a floating military bridge as a temporary crossing.

While I was very grateful that all the bridges we encountered were in working order, driving across them was still a frightening experience because they were rough and a constant target for the coalition bombers. These huge aircraft were rumbling around in the skies above us all the time—we could hear them constantly—and at any moment a plane could plunge down and bomb the bridge we were approaching.

But, as fortune would have it, again that day they obviously had more important targets than my old Toyota Corona or the bridges we traversed.

Driving over the bridges was nerve-wracking enough. But, just as we had anticipated, the most terrifying part of the journey was alongside the Imam Ali Air Base a couple of hours out of Basra.

I was at the wheel—and driving through the danger area as fast as I could. I guess we were going about 100 kilometres an hour at that stage. Which may not sound particularly fast, but you have to remember the road was rough and peppered with bomb craters. Then there were the Toyota's seriously worn and unsteady tyres. Adding to the tension, parts of the road were shrouded in the smoke and dust haze caused by the constant pounding of the air assault, bombs and rockets. And as we rumbled relentlessly along, we had to not only keep our eyes on the road but also keep watch on the skies so we knew where the next attack was coming from.

We approached the air base about nine o'clock in the morning. To the right of the road, we could see what we were getting ourselves into. The air base is in the middle of the flat, open desert and there's nothing else around. No settlements, no trees, nothing. Even from a distance we could see the smoke and the coalition planes sweeping across the skies. Then, as we neared the base, we could hear the dull thud of bombs dropping all around us.

While I was panicking, throughout the ordeal the engineer seemed calm and composed in the passenger seat. He was clearly much braver than me. It was almost as if this was a familiar experience for him. It certainly wasn't for me. Realising how terrified I was, he kept up a stream of advice, telling me not to look at anything other than the road. He said the Americans would be bombing the air base, not the road.

'You need to drive as fast as you can,' he instructed urgently but calmly.

Which, believe me, I did.

From the time we arrived in the general vicinity of the air base until it was well behind us, we were bombarded with the non-stop wail of American aircraft above us and the thunderous noise of the explosions. I could hear and feel the thudding as the Americans hit their target time and again. The impact of the explosions was so powerful they seemed to be only a few metres from the car and they were shaking us as well as the vehicle itself.

I was convinced we would be hit by a bomb or debris from the constant blasts. I thought I was going to die.

There was smoke everywhere—I could hardly see in front of the car. I just kept my hands gripped on the steering wheel and my right foot on the accelerator, pressing it as hard to the floor as I could. We had our heads ducked down as low as we could to make our bodies as small a target as possible.

All the time, the engineer was talking to me, trying to keep me calm.

That drive felt like it dragged on for hours. In reality, it probably took no more than fifteen minutes. But they were fifteen minutes of sheer, utter terror.

It was an enormous relief to leave the Imam Ali Air Base and the bombing behind; the journey was much safer from there on. We could still see the American planes, but their targets that day didn't include anything else on the western road to Baghdad. Our troubles weren't over, though. The car would soon run out of fuel. We had to get to Samawah, where the engineer had contacts. In the meantime, if the car stopped, there would be no one to help us.

The images we passed along the way told a story of destruction and death—Iraqi military vehicles that had been hit by the coalition attack lying abandoned on the side of the road. The only times we saw any other operational vehicles were at the river crossings, where a handful of cars might be queuing to drive over the makeshift bridges. To be among the only cars on what was normally a busy six-lane highway was surreal and unsettling, but not surprising—no one without an extremely good reason was foolhardy enough to expose themselves to the air attack, particularly near the air base.

As we reached Samawah, we saw that the bridges there had also been bombed and replaced by the pipe-based roadways. All the nearby power plants had been comprehensively attacked as well. Unlike the bridges, they remained rubble; there was no way they could be swiftly repaired.

The engineer, who was obviously very familiar with the town, directed me to an official building of some sort. I have no idea exactly what function it served and there were no signs on the exterior to indicate its purpose. He went inside and a little while later came out with a letter. Again, I have no knowledge of what the letter said; I didn't read it and he didn't brief me on its contents. But clearly it was some form of authority to get petrol.

We drove to a checkpoint a couple of kilometres away, where the engineer showed the letter to the military officials at the barricade. I sat in the driver's seat, terrified, but trying to look like I'd done this many times before. Surely, we'd be refused entry—or worse. I could hardly believe it when the officials sent three soldiers to take us to a petrol station. The gates across the front of the petrol station were locked, but the soldiers opened them and we filled the car with fuel.

As we were leaving I quietly asked the engineer whether I needed to pay someone. He just shook his head and said, 'Don't worry. Keep driving.'

And so I did—non-stop through Hillah, near the old city of Babylon, and from there to Suwayrah where I would hopefully find my parents and the rest of my family. I had a rough idea of the location of the house they had rented. In our last phone conversation, they'd told me it was just down the road from the soccer stadium.

We reached Suwayrah around sunset and, after driving around for a while, we found the house. When I walked in, alive and unharmed, my mother collapsed with relief.

My parents had gone to Suwayrah because they thought it would be safe. But from day one of the war, the town had been heavily bombed. They only found out later that there was an undercover Iraqi helicopter base about 5 kilometres down the road, and 15 kilometres to the south, a rocket launch base which was firing missiles. Between Suwayrah and Baghdad was a major nuclear reactor.

My family had walked right into the thick of the war.

Driving into the town, I'd noticed wide stands of palm trees and citrus. Beneath them, on both sides of the road, parked like cars, were helicopters. The coalition had bombed the original helicopter base until the bunkers were destroyed. The Iraqis had then moved the remaining choppers under the cover of the trees.

Worse signs of war were to come. From a distance, the soccer stadium looked fairly normal—we could see the empty seats in the stands and the terraces—but the playing surface itself was packed with tanks covered with camouflage netting. One division of the Republican Guard was based there to protect the approaches to Baghdad. It was another obvious target for the coalition bombs—although, strangely, it never was attacked.

My family said the town and surrounding area had been bombed every day. Almost every official building had been flattened. It wasn't surprising considering the concentration of Iraqi military hardware nearby.

I decided to stay with my family in Suwayrah but the engineer still needed to get to Baghdad. Two of my uncles who were at the house were going back to the capital that evening to pick up some belongings, so the engineer went in the car with them. That was the last time I saw him. And to this day, I can't remember his name.

Under normal circumstances, Suwayrah is a relatively sleepy rural town of about 45,000 people. The Tigris River runs through it and provides the water for the farms that dominate the surrounding region. Most of the people are poor, but there are wealthier families, mainly living close to the river.

# Defying Death in the Desert

The house my family had rented was large and comfortable, in a residential area close to the commercial centre. It was a smarter part of town. But its location didn't provide any respite from the war. When we went to bed that night, we were kept awake by the noise of planes overhead and the sound of explosions not far away. We could see the blasts and flying shrapnel from the bombs, but we couldn't identify the specific targets.

The next morning, we heard knocking at the door. The visitor's face was familiar—it was the husband of one of my mother's cousins—but unusually he was wearing his helicopter pilot's uniform. He never visited our family in uniform, so this immediately rang alarm bells. He explained that he was stationed at the nearby base and had heard from other relatives that we were in the area.

'What the hell are you doing here?' he said as soon as the front door closed behind him. 'This is not a good place to stay.'

My mother sat him down to eat something while he quickly explained that the helicopter base was close by and had been constantly bombed. He stayed only briefly, repeatedly warning us of the dangers, then returned to the base and his duties.

Life in towns like Suwayrah went on regardless of the bombing, because the housing in the town itself wasn't being targeted. I was told that for the first couple of days of the war, air-raid sirens had been sounded to warn everyone to take cover in the shelters. But the bombing raids were constant so the whole exercise quickly became futile. People stopped hiding because they realised that the bombs weren't hitting the residential area of the town.

From time to time, I went to the top floor of the house to watch the American planes coming in on their bombing raids and hitting the military targets, especially the rocket launchers. They were obviously avoiding non-military targets.

Fortunately, within a couple of days the immediate danger of bombing raids close to our house diminished when the Iraqi Army mobilised the tanks from the nearby soccer stadium. The order brought a flurry of military movement all around the town and it was a relief to see them disappear from our neck of the woods.

For me, one of the saving graces was that the library in the town was still open. It meant that every day I could go there and continue my studies. The library was a legacy of the days of Qasim's presidency. In four years, he'd done a lot for the town. As well as the library, he'd ordered the building of the soccer stadium. The people of the area loved him and hated Saddam.

There was also one bright side to the military damage for the people of the town—ice cream and milk were being given away free!

I remember on one visit to the downtown market I watched a large refrigerated truck from a nearby dairy factory pull up at the edge of the stalls, then the doors were thrown open and containers of ice cream were given away. It was an odd sight— people were stopping to grab free ice cream while coalition planes were flying overhead on bombing missions. It transpired that the American raids had cut the electricity to the area and the factory had no way of keeping the ice cream cold. So the people running the factory decided to take the produce into town and give it to the local community.

The factory was also giving away free milk, but you had to be on your toes to make the most of that opportunity. The milk arrived in the town immediately after it was picked up from the farms each morning so you needed to be at the market with a container at about 7.30 a.m. to have any chance of beating the thirsty throngs.

The market itself was flooded with Iranian products—canned food, chocolate, cookies. We found out that as soon as the war started, border controls collapsed. The Iranian border is only about 100 kilometres from the town, so opportunistic traders simply brought in all their goods and sold them where they could.

With no work available we had plenty of time on our hands and my uncle, the sculptor, decided he wanted to create something to keep us occupied and provide a minor distraction for the town. He went into the countryside and found a dead eucalyptus tree he thought had a particularly attractive shape. I helped him dig the tree out of the ground and we cut off some branches until it was about 5 metres long, then dragged it back with my car.

My uncle planned to make the tree into a statue, so we took it to a residential area and placed it on the corner of a street. It transpired that a bank manager lived on that corner and at first he came out of his house shouting, alarmed because he thought the Americans would think it was a rocket! Then he saw my uncle—who was very famous in Iraq—and decided it was okay for the tree to stay. So we dug a hole and cemented in the foundations.

There was another, smaller dead tree on the other side of the road; this one was about 1.5 metres tall and my uncle decided that it would also feature as a statue. My uncle painted the two trees very artistically. We spent about three or four days working on them and by the end they looked fabulous.

About a week later, we read a front-page story about this work of art in a national newspaper. The story said that this was an example of the Iraqi people showing defiance—which, frankly, was considerably overstating the case. We largely did it to keep ourselves occupied; there wasn't much else to pass the time. Still, it made a good headline.

On another occasion we were lucky not to become a headline ourselves. In such a sensitive military area, it wasn't difficult to fall foul of the authorities and a group of us was very nearly captured and questioned on suspicion of being American paratroopers. My cousin Ismail and his sisters Ava Jasmin and Asia, who were staying with our family in Suwayrah, were good musicians and one day we decided, amid the military mayhem, to head out into the calm of some remote fields and play guitars. My cousins, being half German, had very fair skin and, for no particular reason I can remember, the two young women were wearing khaki tops. We were walking along in a lightly wooded area, carrying the guitars in cases, when suddenly we were intercepted by heavily armed paramilitary guards. We didn't know it, but we'd wandered into a high security area. The guards saw we didn't look like normal Iraqis, so they assumed we were American soldiers on a specific mission, carrying guns in the guitar cases!

Being the naïve young people we were, we initially couldn't work out if they were serious. It soon became clear that they were, indeed, deadly serious. They refused to let us go until we explained, several times, what we were doing. Then we added that my uncle, the sculptor, was a very close friend of a high-ranking official in the town and we gave them all his details. We found out later that emergency floating bridges were being stored in the area and we were suspiciously close to them.

I stayed in Suwayrah for the rest of the war, although I did make a couple of fleeting visits to Baghdad.

On one occasion in February I ventured to the capital to check on the family house. I drove up during the day, which meant getting past various strategic installations that had been severely bombed. The nuclear reactor and the Dora refinery were both badly damaged. But I was surprised that the Diyalla River bridge hadn't been touched. Neither had the Nahawind region, which was the capital of the old Persian Empire.

# Walking Free

I stopped overnight in Baghdad and went downtown to see the damage for myself. At that stage, Baghdad at night was like a fireworks show. The anti-aircraft guns would fire haphazardly into the sky so the American planes couldn't penetrate the shield. The bridges were camouflaged by a smokescreen of burning tyres on both sides of the river. And to a degree it was successful.

Baghdad has fourteen bridges. The American bombers managed to destroy the suspension bridge, which was heartbreaking, because it was such a beautiful old structure. Al-Jumhiria Bridge had been hit as well and, while they had damaged the Sinik Bridge, cars could still use it. The other bridges were completely intact, although the areas surrounding them had taken a severe pounding. The lack of major damage was amazing considering the technology the Americans were using and the fact that the bridges are huge. You'd think they'd have managed to find the target on all of them, not just a few.

That visit was an emotional experience. I felt my city, my home had been violated. I felt sadness, fear and insecurity. We simply didn't know what would befall us. At the same time, I felt anger—why was all this happening? What was the point?

My anger and resentment wasn't so much against the Americans, it was more against Saddam—especially because, at that time, my cousin Saheel was missing and we had no idea what had happened to him.

# Defying Death in the Desert

Saheel was the son of my uncle who was with his German-born wife and our family in Suwayrah. Saheel, who was ten years older than me, was in the Republican Guard—the elite force that had been held back on the outskirts of Baghdad to defend the city and Saddam himself. He had been stationed at Al Taji, an Iraqi Army airfield, tank maintenance centre, chemical weapons production facility and the main Republican Guard base to the north of Baghdad. It was a huge base and, naturally, it was a major target for the Americans. It had been bombed extensively and constantly.

Saheel was in a bunker at Al Taji when it was hit in an air raid about seven o'clock one evening. The bunker collapsed under the onslaught and Saheel was buried alive in the rubble. He wasn't dug out until two o'clock the next morning—and the entire time he lay trapped amid the concrete and twisted metal, not knowing whether he was going to die or be rescued.

Those few days were traumatic for our family because we didn't know where Saheel was, or if he was still alive. Then one night when I was in our house in Baghdad I heard a knock at the door and answered it to find Saheel.

He was a pathetic figure. He was still wearing his tattered uniform, but he was covered in faeces and smelled of stale urine. His hearing had been damaged by the blast. But worse than his physical condition was his mental state. He was suffering dreadful post-traumatic stress. He had been dumped on our doorstep by the Republican Guards as soon as they had released him from the rubble.

Another cousin, Ammar—an electronics engineer who had worked on some of Saddam's most secret and sophisticated missile projects—was staying with me at the house. We quickly brought Saheel inside, removed his clothes and gave him a long warm bath. It was winter and Saheel was freezing. We had to heat as much water as we could on the stove, because there was no running hot water. That restored Saheel's physical dignity, but he didn't talk to anyone for days afterwards. All he would say was: 'I was buried alive!'

When we left Baghdad, we took Saheel with us to Suwayrah. Everyone was relived and happy just to see him alive. But he was in no fit mental state to adjust back into the family. We mostly left him alone because he was behaving very strangely. Every time a door banged shut in the house or a bomb exploded, he would become hysterical and we'd have to reassure him and calm him down.

It took months and months, but Saheel gradually improved. He never returned to the army. A relative in Suwayrah was a doctor and gave him medical certificates saying he wasn't fit for duty. And he wasn't. Even now, all these years later, he still has some residual trauma from being buried alive.

While we were in Suwayrah, my family was also devastated by the infamous Ameriya Bunker disaster, which occurred in the early hours of 13 February 1991. The bunker was about 8 kilometres from the centre of Baghdad and, at the time, the US said it was attacked because it was a well-known military telecommunications complex and Saddam might have been hiding there. If that genuinely was the intelligence they received, someone should have been called to account for abject incompetence. Or the claim was simply fabricated. Either way, it was completely wrong.

In reality, Ameriya Bunker was a public shelter, which had been designed to resist an atomic bomb attack. It was similar to the bunker at my old college and was built of heavily reinforced concrete with huge metal doors which automatically slammed shut in the event of an aerial assault.

That night the air-raid siren had sounded and the shelter was packed with civilians sleeping in air-conditioned comfort— when the US planes attacked. The first of the two laser-guided missiles went into the ventilation system to open up the bunker. The second slammed through the hole in the ventilation system and exploded inside.

My aunt Alham—who was married to one of my mother's brothers, Layth—was eight months pregnant with her fifth child and had come to live with us in Suwayrah to escape the bombings in Baghdad. Alham normally lived with Layth, their family and Alham's older sister, Ahlan, and her family in a house close to the bunker. Altogether, there were ten of them in the household.

We feared the worst the moment we heard that the bunker had been bombed. We knew Ahlan and her children sought safety in the bunker every day.

Alham hadn't heard the news and we specifically didn't tell her. We kept her away from the radio and the battery-operated

TV we had in the house so she didn't hear any news bulletins. Broadcasts of Iraqi TV were sporadic by that stage, but Iranian TV was readily available.

My uncle and I drove to Baghdad to find out what was happening and discovered a dreadful tale. The streets in the vicinity of the bunker were eerily quiet when we arrived. Very few people were around. We quickly worked out why. Almost everyone who'd lived nearby had been killed in the attack on the bunker. To add to the horror, there was an awful smell of burnt flesh permeating the area.

All but two members of Alham's family were in the bunker when it was attacked. Her husband and my mother's brother Layth, her sister Ahlan and six of the families' children were burnt alive—along with about 400 other innocent people. When the first American bomb penetrated the bunker's ventilation system, the heavy metal doors had snapped shut automatically, trapping everyone inside and delivering them a certain, tortuous death. It later emerged that those who hadn't been burned alive in the inferno were killed by boiling water which burst through parts of the shelter when the water tanks ruptured.

The only survivors from Ahlan's family were her youngest son, who was asleep at home, and another son Riadh, who was in his thirties and had stayed behind to guard the property.

My uncle and I went to the bunker again the next morning but the authorities wouldn't let us in. They were still carrying out bodies—all of them horrifically burnt, just charred skeletons, unrecognisable as human beings. The victims couldn't be identified, but we knew they were all locals from the surrounding homes.

We learned from speaking to other people who had come to look for relatives that when the recovery operation started, the would-be rescuers had to water the doors of the shelter for hours before they were cool enough to touch. They then cut the doors open to reveal the horrors inside. But before they could begin the grim task of bringing out the remains of the victims, they had to hose down the inside of the bunker because of the tremendous heat which had been generated.

I had never seen anything like it and I hope I never witness such an atrocity again.

By chance we later met Riadh in the street. Understandably, he was devastated and weeping profusely, in a state of deep shock. He'd just lost nearly all his family in one incident. That was the last time I saw him.

After the tragedy, my aunt Alham went back to Baghdad to see her nephews, but returned to Suwayrah to have the baby—a daughter she named Ahlan after her sister who died.

Months after the war finished, I went back to Ameriya Bunker. By then, Saddam had regained control of the country and the shelter had been turned into a museum with lights inside. Even then, you could still smell the burnt bodies. You could see the destruction inside the bunker—everything was still charred. On the walls were handprints in dried blood where the people trapped inside had desperately tried to claw their way out. But there was no escape. More than one in three of the victims were children.

It's hard to say that anything positive came out of the Ameriya disaster, but at least the US forces recognised the depth of the tragedy and, as a direct result, the coalition severely restricted the bombing of shelters in Baghdad.

My immediate family stayed in Suwayrah until the military conflict was over. Saddam ordered the withdrawal from Kuwait on 26 February 1991, two days after the coalition forces had launched a ground assault in Kuwait and Iraq, and accepted ceasefire terms on 3 March.

Once Saddam announced the retreat, it started raining heavily in Suwayrah. The downpour lasted for two days and was the most eerie rain I'd ever seen. It was black. If you opened your hand to catch the rain, you could see it was black against your palm. You could see the soot. One of our cars was white and when it rained the vehicle took on a grey appearance. I don't know whether the black rain was a result of soot from the burning oil wells in Kuwait or the American bombing nearby, but it was a strange, almost surreal experience.

By the time the rain finished, the dusty terrain around Suwayrah became a quagmire—another hazard for the defeated Iraqi soldiers, who by now were retreating in sham-bolic disarray back towards Baghdad. The initial part of the

Iraqi withdrawal was along Highway 80, which runs for around 100 kilometres between Kuwait City and Basra along with Highway 8 to the east. Collectively they became known as the Highway of Death.

With complete control of the skies, the US Air Force embarked on a series of sorties, dropping anti-tank mines, which blocked the road ahead of the retreating Iraqi Army. Effectively, this stopped the Iraqi troops in their tracks and created a massive bottleneck of tanks, military vehicles and soldiers stretched out along the highway. They were sitting ducks—and the US Air Force simply picked off their mostly defenceless targets.

Some of the Iraqi Army tanks had managed to divert off Highway 80 and Highway 8, but their escape was short-lived. They were targeted by US artillery and helicopter gunships and were destroyed over an 80-kilometre stretch of the roads and desert.

It was absolute carnage. The wreckage of the Iraqi Army was littered across the landscape in what became some of the signature images of the First Gulf War.

Amid the death and destruction, there was a backlash by disillusioned Iraqi soldiers who felt they'd paid an inordinately high price for Saddam's adventurism. They were encouraged by a couple of radio broadcasts from President Bush, who even before the Iraqi retreat, told the world: 'There is another way for the bloodshed to stop—and that is for the Iraqi military and the Iraqi people to take matters into their own hands and force Saddam Hussein, the dictator, to step aside and then comply with the United Nations' resolutions and rejoin the family of peace-loving nations.'

The message was reinforced after Iraqi forces had withdrawn from Kuwait.

'In my own view,' President Bush said, 'the Iraqi people should put [Saddam] aside and that would facilitate the resolution of all these problems that exist.'

Even in the early stages of the Iraqi retreat, the internal unrest bubbled to the surface. In the south, the catalyst came on 1 March, when an Iraqi Army tank shelled a giant image of Saddam hanging in Basra's main Saad Saad Square. The action was applauded by other army officers, who then raided nearby military buildings.

Quickly, other disaffected soldiers and many locals joined the rebellion and, within a day, they had taken over police stations and prisons as well as the Ba'ath Party Headquarters and the Secret Service building in Basra. The rebels showed no mercy for the members of the Ba'ath Party.

The first areas that succumbed to the uprising were the poorest suburbs—places like Fire Mile, Khamsa, Al Hayania and Al Jumhiria. They were followed by the middle-class districts. The last areas to fall were Al Jzer and Al Junayna.

My cousin Mohammed lived in Al Junayna, a suburb that is divided by a major road. The eastern side was under the control of the rebel soldiers and the western side was held by the Iraqi Army. A hail of bullets was fired across the street as the battle rolled on.

# Defying Death in the Desert

Mohammed's house was on the corner of the major road. He and his family—his wife Sundus, their eight-year-old son Duraid and two daughters, three-year-old Doaa and six-month-old Haneen—had been staying with relatives who lived in a safer area. But they had run out of water, so Mohammed and his family went home to have a shower.

As they approached their house, they saw an army tank parked in front of it. Mohammed was carrying Doaa and his wife was carrying Haneen. They were walking into the house when, from the other side of the road, one of the rebels fired a rocket-propelled grenade, which hit the front gate and exploded. Mohammed and his family were all knocked to the ground by the blast. When the smoke and dust cleared, they pulled themselves to their feet—and Sundus looked down to see that Haneen had been hit by shrapnel from the grenade. Half her skull was missing and her brain was in Sundus's lap. The poor child had been killed instantly.

It must have been obvious to all the soldiers engaged in the battle that this was simply a family returning to their house. The person who fired at them was nothing short of a barbarian whose heartless actions tragically wasted such a young and innocent life.

Not unnaturally, Haneen's death shattered Mohammed's family and we didn't see them for months afterwards. When we did see them again, Sundus had changed completely. Before, she was bright, cheerful and bubbly. Afterwards, she was quiet and withdrawn.

While the largely uncoordinated uprising was going ahead in the south, in the north the two major Khurdish political parties saw the opportunity and enthusiastically launched an anti-government rebellion which won popular support. A rebel force of more than 50,000 took control of most of the region. As the combined rebellion gathered pace, fourteen of Iraq's eighteen provinces came under their control—and Saddam felt his position was so parlous he offered to share power with the Shi'ite and Khurdish leaders.

The offer was rejected. By now, the rebel leaders had set their sights on complete control and were planning to march on Baghdad. But the offensive stalled. The expected Shi'ite uprising in Baghdad didn't materialise. Neither did the assumed support from the United States.

Crucially, Saddam retained control of the elite Republican Guard and significant numbers of tanks that had been kept behind to defend the capital. And while the ceasefire agreement prohibited fixed-wing aircraft in coalition-enforced No Fly Zones, helicopter gunships were free to roam the skies.

Gradually, the tide began to turn as Saddam's regime exercised its massive advantage in firepower, using tanks and helicopters against the rifles and other lightweight weapons of the dissident forces. Retribution against the rebels was swift and vicious. Mass slaughter was launched across the major cities held by the rebels.

In Basra, there were reports of chemical weapons being unleashed on the anti-Saddam forces and the civilian population, although a subsequent United Nations investigation did not confirm the claims. In other cities, helicopter and tank attacks were followed by indiscriminate executions and torture. Even the resistance of the Khurds in the north crumbled under the overwhelming onslaught, although the fighting there continued for months. Tens of thousands of Iraqis died as Saddam's forces regained control of the country.

In Suwayrah, we saw the defeated Iraqi Army retreating from Kuwait. There were thousands of troops walking the 500-plus kilometres from Basra to Baghdad. They were in awful condition. Some of the soldiers were clad only in their underwear—their uniforms had been jettisoned so they couldn't be identified by the US Forces. Others were swapping their guns for a sandwich. It was a complete humiliation.

At the same time as the army was retreating, the rebels came to Suwayrah, ransacking official buildings and removing documents.

It was time for my family to go back to Baghdad, too.

We had seven cars and packed everyone, plus our belongings, into them for the return to the capital. For safety, we travelled in a convoy.

Along the way, we passed a constant line of dishevelled soldiers begging for food and trying to hitch a ride. Just past the Tammouz atomic reactor, we reached the Diyalla River to the south-east of Baghdad. By the side of the road was a soaring pile of discarded weapons. The soldiers had all been ordered to drop their firearms before entering the capital. And, just in case anyone still harboured thoughts of supporting an uprising in Baghdad, a line of what appeared to be brand new tanks was protecting the city. The pristine tanks, designated to defend Saddam's regime, were a stark contrast to the dispirited retreating soldiers.

On our return to Baghdad, we could hear gunfire coming from Sadr City and noticed people weren't crossing over the canal from there, which meant it had been blocked off by the army. Even in peaceful times, there was regular trouble in Sadr City, which used to be known as Saddam City. Although it was just 5 kilometres from where I lived in Al Mustansiria, I'd only been to Sadr City twice in my life—once, believe it or not, to buy a sheep, and the other time when my car was stolen and I went looking for it. Sadr City was the obvious place to find a stolen car, but that time I was out of luck.

Life in Baghdad had changed dramatically. It was no longer a city of plenty with a comfortable lifestyle. Added to that, my father's health had declined significantly while we were in Suwayrah and by now he was confined to a wheelchair. So while we had made it home, in the turmoil that followed the First Gulf War, my family's future had never looked more uncertain.

# 5

# A DEGREE OF MEDICINE

In Baghdad, life was a struggle and the standard infrastructure simply wasn't working anymore. There was no electricity, which meant no business, school or university, and no petrol for cars. Water was still available for drinking, but the separate supply for the gardens wasn't working.

To counter the lack of mains power, every household bought generators to create their own electricity supply. But the generators didn't produce enough electricity to operate the air-conditioning. It was winter and cold, so we used kerosene and gas heaters to keep the house warm and mainly cooked with gas.

Faced with the lack of petrol, the people of Baghdad came up with some ingenious alternatives. For example, they found a way to use gas from the domestic cylinders, which were in almost every house, to provide fuel for their cars. At the bottom of the cylinders, there's usually some heavy fluid which routinely goes to waste. The locals developed a way to install a new valve in the bottom of the cylinders and extract every last drop of the liquid, then used it in their cars instead of petrol.

I would go to the neighbours' houses, collect their gas cylinders and drain the last of the liquid to keep my car on the road. It worked really well in the short term, but over a period of time, caused severe damage to the engine of my trusty Toyota Corona, which had carried me back from Basra and through the stay in Suwayrah. And there were a few unfortunate incidents when the gas cylinders exploded as the new valves were being fitted, giving the improvising engineers severe burns. Happily, that didn't happen to me.

The roads remained largely deserted of cars for two or three months until fuel supplies started to become available again and the service stations re-opened. Whenever I had spare petrol, I drove around Baghdad looking at the damage and visiting my friends—making sure they were all still alive and catching up with what had happened. They all had war stories to tell.

There were military checkpoints dotted around the city, but I wasn't aware of any looting and there was no need for regular army patrols on the streets. The army regained control

LEFT: My father,
Abdul Razak Al Muderis,
in his middle years.

BELOW: My mother,
Kamila Al Muderis, from
her teacher identification
papers. She was in her
early forties when this
picture was taken.

My parents at their wedding.

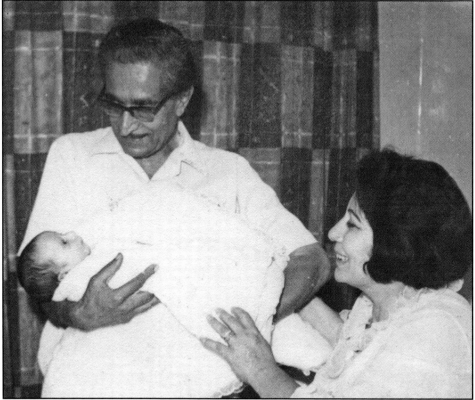

TOP: My mother (far left) with a group of her teaching colleagues and senior government officials before the revolution that overthrew the monarchy in 1958.

ABOVE: Baby Munjed, with my mother and father shortly after I was born.

Me, aged twelve months. I can even recall as a four-year-old, a bangle with bells on it had been placed loosely around my ankle. With a pair of pliers I removed it and refashioned it so I could attach it to my cat. My neighbours discovered this when the cat walked noisily into their house and immediately removed the adornment, which I had so carefully applied around its neck. This is my earliest memory of wanting to operate.

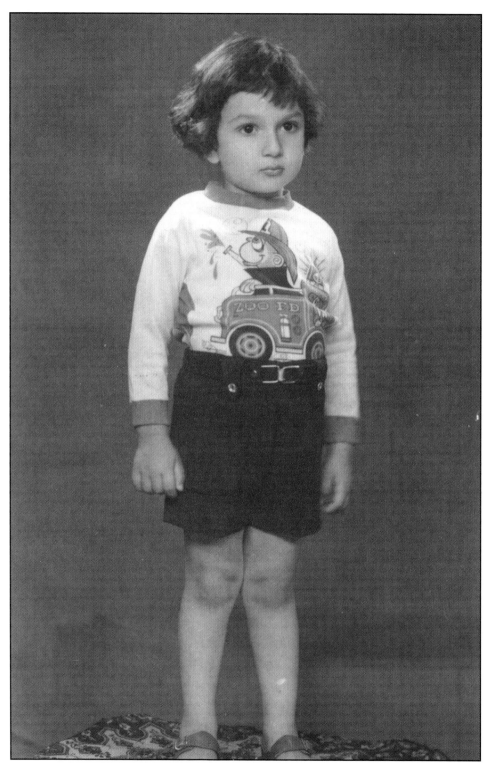

Me at the age of four or five.

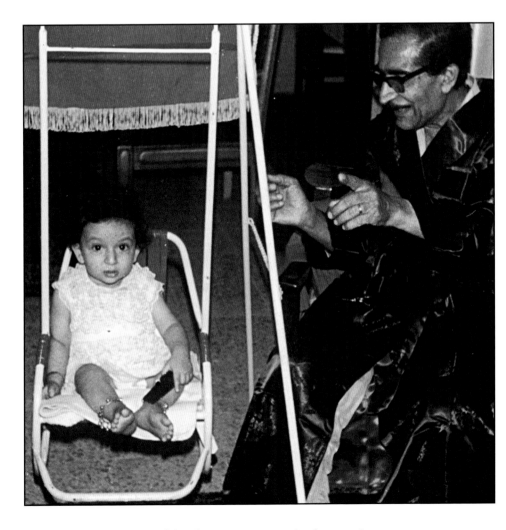

My father, keeping me entertained on a swing.

TOP: With my mother on a visit to see family in Cleveland, Ohio, in 1975.

ABOVE: My mother (left, in the dark glasses) at a school ceremony.

TOP: With my mother and cousins (left to right): Laheeb, now an electronics engineer in Perth; Asia, now an English teacher in London; me; my mother; Ava Jasmin, now an architect in London; Ismail, now an interpreter in Cologne; and Saheel, who was buried alive at the Al Taji base, now an artist in Utrecht.

ABOVE: Me with my cousin's dog Snoopy, Ava Jasmin, my uncle Ismail the sculptor and Reem, now a biomedical scientist in Auckland.

The Martyr's Memorial in Baghdad, which was designed by the Iraqi architect Saman Kamal and my uncle, the Iraqi sculptor and artist, Ismail Fattah al-Turck. © *DeAgostini/Getty Images*

TOP: In front of Baghdad College with a group of classmates in the mid-1980s.

ABOVE: From left to right: Ayser, me and Muhanad relaxing on a tree branch in the grounds of Baghdad College.

A high school trip to Habbaniyah—with skateboard and beat box.
On reflection, not a great look!

TOP: Me (fourth from right) with a group from Baghdad University outside the Prophet Jonah's shrine in Mosul. The shrine was blown up by ISIS rebels in July 2014.

ABOVE: On holiday with my family in Kurdistan in the late 1980s. Left to right: my aunt Alham (sitting), whose family was killed in the bunker tragedy in Baghdad; my uncle Layth (bending); Kawkab, now a dentist in Saudi Arabia and married to my uncle Ahmed; Ayser; Lahib; my uncle Ahmed—my father would never discuss religion with him; Fatah, now a dentist in the US; Ismail; Amir, now studying medicine in the US, plus two young cousins at the front.

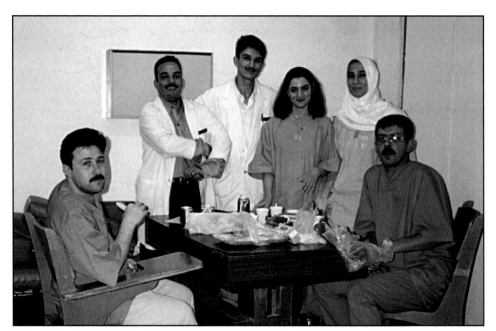

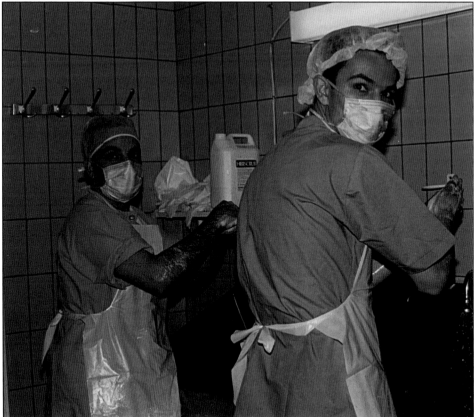

TOP: Me (third from left) having lunch with surgical training colleagues in Baghdad.

ABOVE: Scrubbing up with my senior registrar in Baghdad.

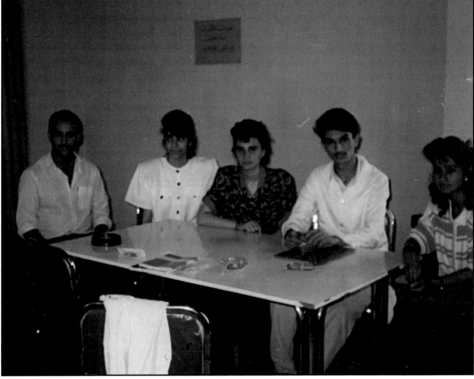

TOP: My mother in my house in the early 1990s.
She wore a head scarf in later life after suffering alopecia.

ABOVE: My colleagues at university in Ramadi—
Areeg is on the right and my flatmate Hayder is on the left.

My registration to practise medicine from the Medical Association of Iraq (left), plus my medical degree (below).

The Highway of Death, where retreating Iraqi soldiers were ambushed after the First Gulf War. © *Peter Turnley/Corbis*

of the city in a matter of weeks, but it was months before life in Baghdad began to return to some form of normality. As the day-to-day routine resumed a more standard pattern, shops gradually started to re-open.

But immediately we noticed the United Nations sanctions, imposed in the previous August, were cutting deep into the country's economy. It's hard to overestimate the hardship and suffering the embargo on oil sales brought to the homes and businesses of Iraq. At that stage, more than 60 per cent of the country's income was from oil exports.

The sanctions had been imposed to force Iraq into a parlous economic situation where it would agree to compensate Kuwait for the invasion. Subsequently, they were altered to specifically include the destruction of what were termed Iraq's 'weapons of mass destruction'. Some time later, when the magnitude of the human impact became obvious even to the harshest of Saddam's critics, further changes were made to ease the restrictions. The oil-for-food program was introduced, which allowed Iraq to sell more oil and use the money to buy supplies to help out the broader population.

Either way, the economic sanctions created a humanitarian crisis in Iraq. Over time, food was severely rationed and hundreds of thousands of people—a sizeable proportion of them children—died from malnutrition and disease. Clean water wasn't available across the country, because chlorine—which could be used in chemical weapons—was among the banned imports.

We had been back in Baghdad for about three months before reliable electricity supplies were restored. Only then did the authorities announce that the universities were re-opening.

As soon as petrol became available again, I spent a couple of days with my cousin Bassam—who was in army intelligence and had been one of the first officers to go to Kuwait—working on my car. The engine had been damaged by using the makeshift fuel and we had to replace the cylinders and pistons. That done, I drove back to university in Basra along the eastern highway.

When I got back to Basra, all Saddam's statues and portraits had been destroyed. The infrastructure around the city had been badly damaged, the telegraph poles had been removed and the cables cut. Eyewitnesses explained that the city had descended into anarchy during the uprising. A cousin told me about the horrific fate of his neighbour at the hands of the rebels. In front of the neighbour, the rebels shot his son, raped his daughter and his wife, then killed them. Finally, they doused the man in petrol and set fire to him, burning him alive.

Others relayed stories of how the rebels went to the Public Records Office, burnt all the paperwork they could find and looted the storage facilities for food. Anything that could be dismantled was taken apart and transported to Iran. Anything they couldn't dismantle was destroyed. By transporting so much to Iran, it became obvious that they had no intention of staging a long-term occupation. They were just there to rape and pillage the city and its people.

The rebels wore green or black headbands with religious slogans on them. They were fanatics who were taking their orders from the imams in the Shi'ite mosques with close links to Iran. They were also, essentially, thugs and hooligans who committed no end of atrocities.

When the Iraqi Army and the Air Force moved back into Basra, they faced some resistance, but the government forces quickly regained control of the city. Their tactics were equally as brutal and effective as the rebels. The Iraqi forces had their own informants, with photos and videos that helped identify the people who'd been involved in the uprising. One by one, they were hunted down by Saddam's troops and executed without trial. Street executions were an everyday part of life in Basra throughout that time.

As the city gradually recovered from the devastation of war, the government forces went about recovering all the weapons and stolen goods they could find. They would surround streets—mainly in the poorer areas—and drive in with trucks. Soldiers announced over loudspeakers that anyone who still had weapons or had looted goods from government buildings or palaces could deposit them in the trucks. After that, there would be a house-by-house search and anyone found with contraband would have their home destroyed. In this way, the regime disarmed the locals and regained control.

# Walking Free

The atmosphere was very different to the Basra I had left at the start of the war. Everyone seemed scared and I could see evidence of the uprising throughout the city. Shops were re-opening and the locals were repairing the damage, but it felt like the heart had been torn out of the city. And I immediately noticed that more of the women were covering their heads.

Saddam's palace in Basra had been looted. The Sheraton five-star hotel on the Shatt al-Arab waterway was badly burnt, although it was still standing. But the Gulf Hotel, another five-star establishment, was so damaged that the whole structure had collapsed. The Secret Service building in Basra was burnt as well.

The government started erecting new power poles, but the electricity worked for only about three or four hours a day and was constantly interrupted. There were no phone lines, either—and that was how it remained for the rest of my time in Basra. Petrol supplies were limited. We had to use coupons to buy fuel and, even then, there were restrictions. Petrol was available for owners of vehicles with even number plates on even-numbered days. Vehicles with odd-numbered plates could be filled on odd-numbered days. It meant we couldn't drive long distances and had to preserve what fuel we could get hold of. Most food was rationed, too. Everything except meat. But meat was expensive so it was a luxury a lot of people couldn't afford.

# A Degree of Medicine

Despite the surrounding chaos, I managed to plough on with my first-year university studies. This included going to the Al-Talemi hospital every day. The hospital had generators that maintained regular power supplies, but it was still constantly frustrating because some of the facilities we needed had disappeared. The anatomy laboratory, for example, had been hit and severely damaged by bombs.

There was a noticeboard in the foyer of the hospital where you could freely write your opinion about political events and developments. It was the first time in Iraq I had seen anyone openly expressing their views. One fifth-year medical student wrote about the atrocities. Saddam was saying he had won the war, but the medical student ridiculed that. He was very critical of the government and asked: 'What kind of victory was it?' He was talking about the massacres and the officers walking back to Baghdad with no shoes and in their underwear. He wrote about the number of casualties and the destruction in Basra. The student's attacks on Saddam and the government were savage.

I thought the author of these comments was either suicidal or a member of the Ba'ath Party who was communicating with sympathisers, though in fact I didn't know who he was and I never saw him. None of my friends knew who he was, either.

He put up these comments for more than a week. We were all eager to read what he had written, but we were also frightened to be seen reading his comments in case we were viewed as collaborating with him. No one else wrote comments—we were too scared of the consequences. I had been told that a few of the hospital's doctors were executed for helping the uprising, but I didn't know any of them.

The Ba'athists were facing a complete dilemma with the noticeboard. On the one hand, they regarded the messages as being little short of treason. On the other, they couldn't take down the board or prosecute the author because it was seen as sacred by the vast majority of people at the hospital.

Then, all of a sudden, the comments stopped. No one knew what happened to the author. Although of course we had our suspicions.

Gradually, Basra's resilience conquered the terrible traumas it had suffered and the city started to return to a routine. But the transition was much slower than in Baghdad, which hadn't experienced nearly as much turmoil and deprivation. Restaurants opened and one of the major advances was when ice cream became available once more. But, despite its collective strength of character, Basra was never quite the same as it had been.

Before the war, we used to fly from Basra to Baghdad for a weekend. But after the war the No Fly Zones meant going home by plane was no longer an option. I went back to Baghdad only once and that was by train—which, even then, was a dangerous journey.

The train line had been restored, but some of the soldiers who'd been involved in the uprising retreated into the marshes close to the railway tracks. The trains were especially vulnerable at that point because they had to go slowly through the marshes. From time to time, the rebels would break out of hiding and attack passing trains. When you got on and off the train, you could see the bullet marks on the carriages. You didn't need any further reminder that the outlaws were lying in wait.

I finished the year at university in Basra and, despite the disruptions, achieved satisfactorily high marks—which was why I managed to get a place at a university much nearer Baghdad the next year, along with most of my friends from the Iraqi capital.

And so, after completing my first year at university, I moved back to Baghdad to live with my mother and father. By that time, my father was bedridden. He was in his late eighties, and the war had exhausted him. My mother was more than twenty years younger than him, but I could see the change in her, too. Her eyesight had deteriorated and she couldn't drive a car anymore. So my life was changing dramatically at home as well.

For my second year at medical school, I went to university in Ramadi in Anbar Province, about 130 kilometres west of Baghdad. Anbar is Iraq's biggest province geographically and covers much of the west of the country. Large tracts of the province are desert and the climate reflects that—hot during the day and cold at night.

Around 95 per cent of the population of the province is Sunni and Ramadi is unquestionably a Sunni city. Most people were Bedouins originally and you could sense a strong tribal Arab influence everywhere you went. Ramadi is located on a fertile plain on the banks of the Euphrates, but the overriding impression is heat, desert, dust and desolation. It's not far from the infamous city of Fallujah, which suffered heavy civilian casualties during the initial Gulf War and also has a reputation for being a hotbed of Islamic fundamentalist insurgents.

The people of Ramadi were as rough and rugged as their surroundings. In the streets, the majority wore traditional Arab clothes. Certainly all the women who'd been born and brought up in Ramadi were covered. From my outsider's position, I found the locals were hostile—they weren't used to more worldly people from Baghdad or anyone wearing Western clothes.

The antagonism to Baghdad and the ways of the West was so obvious that we had to escort uncovered female students through the streets because they'd be subjected to all sorts of insults and unwanted suggestions from the local men. Even though they didn't believe in the act of covering up, some of the university women were so intimidated by the locals they put a shawl over their heads just to avoid harassment.

Another feature that immediately stood out was the number of people who carried guns. Everyone appeared to be heavily armed. There seemed to be a Kalashnikov automatic rifle in every car and when you went into a house, the weapons would be left lying casually around the rooms. I have an inherent dislike and distrust of firearms and had never experienced anything like it before.

I have to be honest, I didn't enjoy Ramadi one bit. I found the atmosphere in the city to be extremist Sunni, very hostile and insular. It's a strongly conservative city and there were no pubs or nightclubs, which are important when you're a student. There seemed to be little or no activity of interest—empty roads and the desert made the biggest impact on me.

It was a lifestyle I found completely foreign. For example, I remember being the guest of honour at a function held by one of the local tribal leaders. I was there simply because a friend had told them that I was descended from the Prophet Mohammed and royalty. Only men were allowed in the room, where we all sat on the floor because, by their custom, it was considered impolite to sit on furniture above the ground. With great fanfare, four men carried in a metal plate with a couple of roasted sheep, chicken, rice, almonds and sultanas. A remarkable feast.

Naïvely, I asked for a knife and fork—to the great horror of everyone else there! Apparently, it was an insult. I had no idea. In the end, like everyone else, I had to eat the whole meal with my left hand. Once the men had finished the vast meal, the remaining food was taken out to the women, who were in another room and were given the pickings of what the men didn't want. I was appalled.

I also went to a wedding that summed up why I was uneasy with the traditions of the Anbar region. It was exactly what I've always detested—sexism, elitism and the random firing of guns!

As at the earlier feast, men and women were segregated. The bride and groom sat with the women, but that was the only sign of the genders being mixed. As I sat with the men, I didn't see any of the women through the whole ceremony. Most of the men were wearing traditional clothes—a long white robe with a colourful, usually red, scarf on their heads. Some were clad in Western clothing—suits, collared shirts and ties.

Whether they were in traditional or Western clothing, many of the men had brought their guns with them. The bride's arrival was greeted by a prolonged volley of automatic rifles and machine guns being fired into the air. Gunfire, believe it or not, is an integral part of an Iraqi wedding!

The tribes of Ramadi are very proud people and hugely protective of their women and children. They have no fear—you can sense they're hard people who'll fight to the last drop of their blood if they perceive that anyone has insulted them. While it's a fundamental part of their traditions, to an outsider like me, there's no rationale to their thinking.

The university in Ramadi was established in 1987. In the time since I studied there, it's become known as the most dangerous university in Iraq—at times, US troops were based in the university grounds. Murders, beatings, kidnappings, ransom payments and general intimidation became common as law and order broke down.

For my year at the university, I lived in a small, simple, two-bedroom flat on the second floor of a newish building in the centre of Ramadi which I shared with Hazar, another student from Baghdad. He was very reserved, an extremely articulate and quiet man, whose father was a professor of literature in Baghdad. Hazar was a bit of a dreamer, but entirely pleasant company.

Most of our time was spent in the flat studying, but when we did go out, it would be to coffee shops or restaurants in the city, where we would play chess or backgammon. There was so little to entertain us in Ramadi that we would drive back to Baghdad on many weekends.

Now and then we would also visit Habbiniyah, 20 or so kilometres from Ramadi. It had been a large British air base and played a key role in the overthrow of the 1941 pro-Nazi coup in Iraq. But what attracted us was the fact that it was a resort town on a large artificial lake. So it provided a distraction from the dull day-to-day existence of university.

While I was in Ramadi, I also met someone who was to play an extremely important role in my life—Nissan, an administrator at Anbar University. He was in his thirties and, over the course of the year, we formed a solid friendship.

Nissan came from tribal traditions and his father was a tribal leader, so they were very well connected. The family lived in a large, two-storey house on a property on the edge of Ramadi where they grew oranges, date palms and grapes. Their traditions were very different from mine. When we went to his house, we would sit on the floor. And when you looked around the room, there were Kalashnikovs leaning casually against the wall and the furniture.

I also met my first wife, Areeg Al Wahab, at university in Ramadi—she was from Baghdad and in the first year of studying medicine. Her father, Kadhum, had a PhD in agricultural engineering from the old Soviet Union, but he had retired by that stage. He had been a member of the Communist Party, even though he came from a very religious Shi'ite family from Karbala. He was politically active and vehemently opposed to Saddam's regime. For his beliefs, he had spent a few years in jail and was tortured several times in the 1970s. Her mother, Farida, was a high school maths teacher, a formidable character who was slightly more religious than Areeg's father. Areeg herself was Moslem, but not devout.

It was a common practice in Iraq for the government to give different areas to certain groups of people. For example, in Baghdad there was a teachers' sector and a doctors' suburb. The government would take farmland and give it to these groups so they could build houses. The land cost them nothing, but people had to pay for the homes they built. Areeg was the oldest of four daughters and her family lived in the Green Area, which had been given to Iraqis, like Areeg's father, who had a PhD. It was on the outskirts of Baghdad in the north-west of the city, on the way to Fallujah.

After completing the second year of my university studies in Ramadi, I managed to win a place at Baghdad University's medical school and moved back to my parents' property.

The day I left Ramadi and returned to live in Baghdad has to be one of the best of my life. The relief at leaving Anbar was palpable. At last, my life was returning to some form of normality in familiar surroundings and I could resume a full university life—studying and socialising.

Baghdad University was a complete contrast after Anbar. Its medical faculty had been established in 1927 and the first dean was Sir Henry Sinderson, a physician to the British royal family. The surgeons training us were the elite of the elite. So the standard of teaching was as good as it got in Iraq.

It was a huge facility—491 students in my year alone, compared with about fifty in Anbar—with the 1200-bed Medical Centre built on the banks of the Tigris River. It included a ten-storey general hospital, children's hospital, dental hospital, special services section and forensic medical unit. It was extremely well equipped, with extensive auditoriums for student lectures. Ironically, this advanced medical facility was located next to a large cemetery!

# Walking Free

The legacy of the war had already started to have an impact at the university. Because of the UN embargo, the dress code had been eased and students no longer had to wear the blue jacket, white shirt and grey pants that had been the uniform for decades. And, gradually, other restrictions became more relaxed as well, although women still weren't allowed to cover their faces or wear pants. Iraq was a secular country at the time and hardly any women in Baghdad wore the burqa. And the female students were expected to wear skirts because at that time pants were regarded as male attire.

Like most students, we spent plenty of our time socialising in the university gardens and coffee shops.

I was living in my own house, next door to my parents and in the same grounds as their home. They had a big block of land in the Al Mustansiria district, so we subdivided it and built two homes—one for them and one for me.

By this stage, my father was quite ill. He talked a lot slower, which was a shame because I couldn't learn as much as I wanted to from him. He had been a great teacher for me—he was like an encyclopaedia. He spoke seven languages and had travelled extensively, and he could tell me stories from every country he'd been to. He was a man ahead of his time. For example, they talk today about music therapy to help relieve stress and induce a feeling of calm. Way before that was being widely spoken about, my father had used music therapy on my mother during difficult times in her pregnancy.

# A Degree of Medicine

We were in Baghdad throughout the embargo and that made things pretty difficult financially. But, for all that, we were fortunate enough to have an independent income from some commercial property—and we were still regarded as wealthy. The financial situation eased once we'd refitted the shops and offices we owned. With the extra money we made from the new shops, I renovated my house. Essentially, I gutted it and completely rebuilt the interior.

I used tradesmen from the local area—which was a bit of an eye-opener. They were a mixed group racially. Except for one, they all had a university degree but they were working as labourers because it paid much better.

The chief builder was Karim, a teacher by profession with a Masters degree in education. He left that job because, after the rapid inflation that was brought on by the embargo, his monthly salary as a teacher was barely enough to pay for a meal. (By this stage, the Iraqi currency was worth very little— about 1500 dinar to the American dollar. When I graduated it was even worse; I think it had slipped to about 3200 dinar to the US dollar then. In 1980, before the war with Iran, one dinar had been worth US\$3.39.) The labourers were all Iraqis and used to make fun of Karim because of his degree—they called him The Graduate.

In fact, the only labourer who didn't have a degree was Ahmed. He just had a high school education. Ahmed was Khurdish and lived next door to my uncle in a higher middle-class area. He was the funniest—he used to heckle everyone and give them nicknames. My uncle took him to Qatar in about 2000 as a handyman to help him with his sculptures. Ahmed lives in Europe now.

Adel came from a Shi'ite background. He was a classical Samarian—big nose, long, slim face. He came from the south, had a degree in English literature and was qualified to be an interpreter for diplomats. I met him in Amman in Jordan some years later. He now lives in the US with his family and I keep in touch with him through emails. He was the lazy one—he was always taking breaks and rests. Quite often, he'd sneak out for a coffee while everyone else was working and we'd eventually find him watching TV!

Asad was a mechanical engineer. He was a more serious guy, but a very hard worker. He came with his brother Nabil, who was an electrical engineer.

They were all working as labourers because they made about 3000 dinar a day. I paid the chief builder 5000 dinar per day. So in one day they were earning more than the government would pay them in a month!

The engineer who did the designs and looked after the project was Abolia. He had a Masters degree in civil engineering from what was then Czechoslovakia. When we started the contract, I paid him a lump sum. But because of the rampant inflation, by the time we were halfway through, he'd lost all his money. He came from a very good family. His brother, Ebthag, was a famous colonel in the Iraqi police force who ran a regular weekly TV show called *Public*

*Safety*, which went to the scenes of horrific car accidents and explored everything about them—how and why the accident had happened and how it could have been avoided. It was the forerunner of some of the shows we see on TV today and was way ahead of its time.

I spent a lot of time with these builders because I got deeply involved in the whole renovation process. Along the way, we became good friends. We'd socialise quite often as well. The guys would bring clean clothes at the start of the day and change into them after work. We'd spend the evening together, watching a movie or playing chess.

In my spare time, I would go and work as a labourer. I enjoyed knocking down walls and hammering in nails—much to the amusement of the professional builders, who would laugh at me! They would say I was weak and I didn't have rough hands like them—every time I hammered in a nail, I'd get a blister!

They got to know Areeg as well because she'd come over while I was working on the house with them. When she was around, they'd always say things like: 'The Big Boss has arrived!' So that sort of humour is just the same in Iraq as it is in Australia.

The renovations took about eight months and after the house was finished, I kept in touch with the guys.

But my closest friends were at university and we spent most of our spare time together. They were, indeed, a mixed bunch.

Mohammed Faiz was born in Syria and came to Iraq when he was a baby. His father was a leader of the Ba'ath Party in Syria, but he came to Iraq after the party split. They were very well treated by the Ba'athists in Iraq and lived in a high-rise block on the banks of the Tigris River. Mohammed was the rough boy of the group—built like a rugby player and very blokey. He's now a general surgeon in Saudi Arabia.

Oras Al Rawi was a Sunni from Anbar Province. His father was dean at Anbar University, and his mother was my Arabic teacher at high school. His uncle was the dean of Baghdad College, where I had studied. During my time at the college, the dean was well known for being strict and old-fashioned; unfortunately for us, he also believed in corporal punishment. But he was a very good teacher. Saddam's sons Udai and Qusay didn't think so, though, and eventually organised his sacking; he'd also been beaten up by the bodyguards of Saddam's nephews during his tenure.

Masoun Al Kubasie was another Sunni from Anbar. Her family were very wealthy merchants. Because of her background in Anbar, she was very conservative and was the only covered person in our group. She was living in the Green Area very close to Areeg and today is still in Iraq.

Broadening the racial and political spectrum, Media Bahaa was the daughter of the chief of the Khurdish pro-government group which was in charge of the northern area of Iraq. She's gone back to live in that region and is now a radiologist.

# A Degree of Medicine

Lubna Biden was a Shi'ite. Her father had been the head of the Workers Union and was one of the Ba'ath Party officials whose name was called out by Saddam Hussein during a famous televised party meeting in 1979, which led to the execution of a number of leading political figures. Saddam was in tears as he called the names of those who'd been chosen for the ultimate sanction. None of Lubna's family ever saw her father again. It was more than a decade later when I knew her—she never talked about her father or what had happened to him. I don't know where she ended up.

Another Shi'ite was Sabah, who lived about a kilometre from me. He came from a very rich family of tradesmen who also owned shops and other businesses.

My close group of university friends also included Christians. Dina Adeeb's mother was French and her father was an Iraqi doctor. Dina now lives in the UK. Nadia Hekari was the granddaughter of the first Iraqi doctor to qualify as an obstetrician. Her father was also an obstetrician and her mother was an English nurse. Nadia followed in the family footsteps and became an obstetrician. She lives in the UK, too.

And then, of course, with her strong Shi'ite background and ex-Communist father, there was Areeg, whom I became engaged to in my third year of university.

# 6

# A FUNERAL AND
# A WEDDING

My father died on 9 July 1995. He was eighty-nine.

He had been suffering from fluid on the lungs. The day before, Ali Ishmail—the brother of my old school friend Ayser and an intern who was two years older than me—brought over some intravenous fluids, a few needles for the IV drip and a couple of hydrocortisone injections. He put in the IV drip, but after a while it ruptured the vein—so I had to place another in my father's arm. I was a fourth-year medical student and that was the first time I'd carried out a cannulation on anyone.

The night before my father died, we were sitting around him. He could still talk, but only very slowly. Areeg and her mother were visiting and brought some cake. We gave my father a piece, which he ate. Weakly, he said: 'Thank you, that's very nice.'

During the night, he started gurgling and his younger sister—herself in her eighties—came over from the other side of the river because we knew he wouldn't last long.

Everything seemed to be going as smoothly as it could so, after spending the evening and much of the night with my father, I went back to my house on the other part of the property.

I was woken about seven in the morning by my uncle, the sculptor, knocking on my door. He'd never done that before, so I knew something must be seriously wrong. He told me my father had died during the night.

I hurried to my parents' house and asked my mother what had happened. Quietly, she explained that she and my aunt had been with my father when he died about 3 a.m.

Even at that stage, relatively early in the morning, she was wearing black clothes to demonstrate her grieving. In line with tradition, my mother had cleaned my father's face with rose water. But she hadn't been allowed to wash the rest of his body—according to the Moslem custom, that had to be carried out by someone from the mosque who specialised in the ceremonial process. After she had cleaned his face, my mother and my aunt had spent the time since my father died praying and reading The Koran.

I went in to see my father's body, kissed his head and covered him.

The Moslem tradition is to clean the body in the house, then transfer it to a coffin. But except for soldiers, the body isn't buried in a coffin.

We took my father to the Imam Abdul Qadir Al Kaylani cemetery. There's a family shrine in the cemetery: my grandfather is buried there and so is my father. There's even a place for me—although I think the chances of me using it are diminishing by the year.

Under Moslem tradition, bodies have to be buried as soon as possible, preferably by sunset on the day the person dies. So there's really not much time to get everything in order.

On the way to the cemetery, we had to get a death certificate. I went into the Emergency Department at the Al-Kindi Hospital and told the doctor I was a medical student. A couple of the other medical students recognised me and vouched for me with the registrar, who then confirmed that my father was dead and gave me the necessary papers.

As a civilian, my father's body was completely wrapped in a white shroud, tied at the ankles, the waist and the shoulder. He was laid to rest in classic Islamic style, with his head resting on a stone pillow and facing Mecca. My family threw the first handfuls of sand over his body. After we left, the cemetery workers shovelled the rest of the soil into the grave.

In Iraqi culture, as in many others, the size and style of the grave is a measure of the family's wealth. Some gravestones feature marble and gold, other families build mausoleums around their part of the cemetery—including air-conditioning and chairs. The more elaborate shrines tend to belong to Shi'ite families. Sunnis usually have simpler traditions, contending that they follow the teachings of Mohammed more closely and pointing out that the Prophet said the best graves are no higher than the knee.

My father's grave was very simple—one piece of marble, very low, with a headstone detailing his name, his date of birth and the date he died.

Moslem funerals are quite different from their Christian counterparts. While Christians normally follow a funeral with a wake that lasts a few hours, a Moslem funeral is extended over a whole year and many of the traditions may seem quite bizarre to outsiders.

To be honest, especially after the funeral of my cousin Ribal who had been killed in the final days of the war with Iran, I didn't want any form of official mourning after my father's burial. But my mother was adamant and, in due deference to her feelings, I complied. Although I insisted that, in line with my father's beliefs, we excluded the more extreme rituals often associated with Islamic funerals. In particular, there was no dervish—the self-mutilation ritual which often accompanies Islamic mourning.

The dervish is a bizarre custom. In the Sunni tradition, drums are rhythmically beaten as a group of men dance and feverishly nod their heads until they're in a trance. Then they launch into a frenzy of self-mutilation. One might put a dagger into his throat, another might put a sword into his chest or stomach. I've even heard of people shooting themselves in the head and chest. It's all completely barbaric.

How do they do it without serious injury? After studying their techniques, I noticed the men who were putting swords into their stomachs would place the weapon into existing scar tissue at an angle which ensured they weren't going to hit any vital organs. That's the only explanation I can come up with.

There are others, though, where there is obviously not even the merest hint of deception. I've seen videos on the internet where individuals are inflicting massive wounds on themselves with swords. Why they do it is entirely beyond me.

So, even though I'd given way on the funeral, I wouldn't have anything to do with the self-mutilation rituals. My father believed the people who took part in the dervish ceremonies were hooligans. I agreed.

Following my father's burial, we went back to our own houses. Then the relatives started arriving; traditionally, close family members usually stay with you for the first three days of the funeral. Because we were secular, there was some mixing of men and women outside the houses, but not inside. The women went to my mother's house while the men came to my home.

Normally, a funeral starts about 4 p.m. and the ceremonies last for the rest of the day. Beforehand, the family takes the furniture out of the house and the oldest son sits at the door to welcome people as they arrive. The other sons sit in order further away from the door.

# A Funeral and a Wedding

For the first three days, every night about eight o'clock you have to slaughter two or three sheep to feed the guests and visitors who are there as the funeral continues. The tradition is that the bereaved family buys live young male sheep and someone will come in, pray and slaughter them in halal fashion in the garden. The sheep carcass is hung in the trees before being skinned and cooked.

Because, almost inevitably, there's far too much food, neighbours come in and join the feasting. Then anything left over is taken to the nearest mosque and distributed to poorer people.

Once we'd clambered over the hurdle of those first three days, we started preparing for the seventh day. The seventh day was only for women. I think my mother commemorated the fortieth day and the first anniversary, too. I took part in only the first of the four stages. I was desperately sad at my father's passing—he had, after all, been my greatest mentor and the person who steered me in the direction of logic and learning. But, as I saw things, life had to go on.

To be honest, the whole ritual of the funeral ceremony was the last thing I wanted after my father had died. In many ways, I found it distracted me from the loss. And while some people might find that a welcome distraction, I wanted nothing more than to come to terms with my grief.

Instead, I was involved in what I saw as largely unnecessary pageantry when my preference would have been to reflect on my father's life and what he had taught me. I detested the ceremonial. The whole thing was so artificial.

≭

After the funeral, my fiancée Areeg started pushing me to get married. Her parents were particularly keen.

In contrast to their enthusiasm for us to be married, my mother opposed it. As she did with all my relationships. And, as with my other relationships, we argued about it. Regardless, I decided to get married three months after my father died. I was twenty-three and in my final year of medical school.

Like funerals, the Moslem wedding process is very different from the Western Christian expectations. Officially, Areeg and I were married two years before, when we were both studying at Baghdad University. But that initial wedding is more the equivalent of becoming engaged in the West. We just went to the court for a non-religious wedding and were pronounced man and wife.

That original ceremony involved us driving to the east bank of the Tigris River, crossing the river by boat to the west bank and the oldest courthouse in Baghdad. It was a very small ceremony—just myself, Areeg, my lawyer, my mother and her older sister, Areeg's parents and her next youngest sister. It lasted about fifteen minutes, then we went back to Areeg's house for lunch.

# A Funeral and a Wedding

In Iraq, this stage is called *Maher*—it means we're officially married, but we haven't started living together. It's very common there. In Iraq, it's still considered shameful for a woman to become pregnant at that stage of the relationship, before the full wedding.

For the second wedding, in the autumn of 1995, we decided to have another small ceremony—just forty or fifty friends from school and university. The only relative who was invited was Areeg's mother. We had dancing and singing at the reception, which was held at the Iraqi Airways Reception Centre, in what has more recently become known as the Green Zone of Baghdad.

The wedding didn't have all the standard trimmings you might expect. I simply drove to Areeg's house in the wedding car, ignored the expectation of kissing the bride's mother and father's head or hand and went on to the ceremony. That wasn't me being churlish. It simply reflected my deep dislike of what I consider unnecessarily elaborate ceremonies.

And you have to remember that, by this stage, I had already been through a series of religious traditions and ceremonials which I found seriously embarrassing, with my father's funeral and the lead-up to the wedding.

Before an Iraqi wedding, there's the equivalent of a hen's night. It's called *henna* and is staged during the day, usually in the afternoon. A group of women friends and relatives gather in the bride's house—along with the groom. The bride wears a nightdress covered by a gown and is fully made up. The guests use henna to make drawings on her hands and face. The bride's feet are put in rose water with rose petals and they drop rice and pearls on her head—depending on how rich the family is. Then the women start dancing.

As the groom, I felt completely ill at ease sitting there next to the bride while the women were carrying out the whole ritual.

As well, on the day, Areeg's mother insisted that we have a religious ceremony for the wedding. Shi'ites don't accept a civil ceremony—so I had to agree.

After the *henna*, they brought in an imam. Under the Shi'ite tradition, he sits with the groom, the bride's father and the male relatives in a different room from the bride. No one in that room can see the bride, who is still wearing the nightdress and the full gown.

The imam starts the ceremony and asks the bride 'Will you accept this man to be your husband?' fifteen times. She's not supposed to say anything until the imam asks the fifteenth time—because if she answers too early, it's supposed to indicate that she's cheap. But if she doesn't answer the fifteenth time, the imam can't go ahead with the marriage ceremony!

Also, because you can't see the bride, the imam doesn't have any idea who she is. She could be someone off the streets for all he knows!

Then the imam asks the father of the bride: 'Will you authorise your daughter to marry this man?' and the father complies.

Once those formalities have been completed, the father and the groom shake hands. The bride's brothers don't attend the ceremony, because—for some reason—it's considered shameful.

The Sunni tradition is different. The imam sits in the middle; there's no door separating the bride and the groom. The bride—or a representative of the bride—and groom hold hands and their hands are covered with a linen napkin while the vows are exchanged. But, believe it or not, the bride doesn't have to be there. Which is bizarre.

In more traditional areas the father and brothers of the bride will shave their heads and grow long beards for the wedding, then leave after the religious ceremony. The women, on the other hand, take part in a special ceremony exclusively for them. The whole thing goes on through the afternoon and into the evening.

Because my mother wasn't at the reception, we went to her house immediately after the ceremony. Everybody went—the whole wedding party. It was a motorcade fit for any head of government!

In line with tradition, a couple of my friends fired their Kalashnikov AK47s after the wedding ceremony. I asked them to stop, but they didn't.

Areeg and I couldn't take an overseas honeymoon because of the tensions between Iraq and the Western powers over the economic sanctions. Instead we spent three nights at The Rashid, a five-star hotel in Baghdad which was later bombed by American warplanes.

Traditionally, the morning after the wedding, the groom's mother brings breakfast—usually cream and date syrup and fresh bread. My mother did that and sat with us for a few minutes and then left.

After the three days at the hotel, we went back to my house and started living together. In the next few days, people came round and brought us presents. As in Western countries, the gifts will normally be something for the house.

In a cosmopolitan city like Baghdad, there's no great pressure for a couple to have kids as soon as they're married. But we did. It wasn't planned and it created considerable difficulties. I was in my final year of medical school and Areeg was a year behind me. So it was a critical time for our studies and our careers.

There was a lot of family support—which was of enormous assistance. But there was another side to the coin—there was a lot of family interference as well.

My mother was living next door. She would often try to impose her views. And, even though they were further away, Areeg's family kept interfering as well. Coupled with that, of course, I was pretty immature. So the whole thing was probably doomed from the start.

❦

The baby—a boy we named Ahmed—was born in the private wards of Baghdad University Hospital on 1 August 1996.

On the day Ahmed was born, I had a huge row with my mother. One of the key problems was the family assets. My mother was running our family business, centred on the shops and commercial office building in Baghdad, and controlling our money—and, at that time, we were quite wealthy. My father didn't leave a will. So, by law, when my dad died, I inherited seven-eighths of everything he owned. My mother inherited the rest. While my father was still alive, I asked him to register my house and his house in my mother's name. That arrangement remained in place after his death.

Areeg's parents didn't like the fact that my mother was running the family businesses and officially owned both our houses. They kept insisting I should take control of everything. When you boil things down, access to my family's assets was really at the very core of the problems.

Areeg and Ahmed stayed with her parents after he was born. But our relationship was deteriorating rapidly. It wasn't long before Areeg said she'd had enough and wasn't coming back to my house because of my mother's meddling.

On 7 August Ahmed's umbilical stump fell off—and there's a tradition in Iraq that the stump should be put in a place which indicates the baby's future. Areeg's family put it in a copy of The Koran. I was outraged—I suggested throwing it in the bin because the tradition was ridiculous, but if they really believed in the myth they should have thrown it at a school or in a hospital.

That caused a massive argument and, as happens in these situations, the dispute quickly expanded to uncover a wide variety of real and perceived slights which had occurred over the years. All sorts of things were brought up. The arguments became increasingly heated and irrational and ended with a decision that we were going to separate—which, on reflection, was all very stupid. We'd been married for less than a year.

Of course, when a marriage breaks up, the animosity doesn't end. Quickly, the inevitable legal issues started to emerge, complicated by the fact that in an Iraqi divorce, everything goes to the wife. Straight after we separated, Areeg and her family hired a lawyer and put a caveat on the entire contents of my house. But because the house was in my mother's name, they didn't have any claim on it. All this happened a month before my final exams—so I had no choice but to carry on studying. Which, I guess, took my mind off all the turmoil that was going on.

Areeg and I were divorced within a couple of months. The legal process was very similar to procedures in Western countries.

Areeg and her mother stayed in Baghdad after we were divorced and subsequently through the American invasion and its bloody aftermath. Their house was in one of the most hotly disputed areas of Baghdad, which was a battleground for the confrontation between Sunni and Shi'ite militia. It meant they were often caught in the cross-fire and the house was bombed several times as the fighting flared around them.

Areeg's father died after the war and at that point, Areeg, her mother and my son Ahmed escaped to the United States as refugees. I didn't see them again until February 2013, when I visited them in their new home in San Diego, California.

# 7

# THE JOURNEY BEGINS— ESCAPING IRAQ

Unless you've lived under a brutal dictatorship in a country whose economy has virtually collapsed, it would be hard to imagine what life was like in Iraq in the late 1990s. Without question, it was a terrible place to live in those years.

Saddam Hussein's excesses were becoming even greater and every Iraqi knew that you didn't challenge the regime—or even encourage the impression that you might question it. Blind obedience was required and the consequences of not following the Saddam line were awful. Many people were executed without trial for expressing alternative views or refusing to toe the line. It wasn't safe to speak up.

At the same time, the economy was in an appalling state. Hunger and begging were real prospects for many people who had previously held responsible, well-paid jobs. The war with Iran, the First Gulf War, the United Nations-led trade embargo and the consequent slump in the nation's oil revenue had all contributed.

The worst of the economic crisis started in about 1995 and continued for the next three years. As it went on, suicides became commonplace because families just couldn't see any way out of their financial spiral.

Plenty of educated, hardworking people were finding it difficult, if not impossible, to make ends meet. Inflation was at its peak and people were starving—especially many who had traditionally been part of the middle classes, which had been crushed.

After qualifying with my medical degree, I worked for a few months in a variety of hospitals around Baghdad as part of my one-year internship. I also helped an uncle, my mother's younger brother, who was based in Saudi Arabia with his humanitarian organisation, FARO—the First American Relief Organization—distributing food, clothes and money to families whose livelihoods had disappeared with the disintegrating economy. My uncle, Ahmed Al Turk, was an electronics engineer who'd been based in Saudi since 1982 after studying in Kansas City, Missouri.

Through FARO we helped people all over Baghdad, often Khurds and internal migrants from the south who had suffered particularly severely during the various conflicts of the previous two decades. Many of the people we helped were referred to us. I would ask friends and relatives if they knew any decent families who were doing it tough. My uncle would send me the money and I would distribute it.

It was dangerous work because Saddam wouldn't have approved—it would have been regarded as antagonising the government, even though it was purely humanitarian with absolutely no political or religious motivation.

I was working with between five and ten families to help prevent them drifting into begging on the streets. These were public servants, teachers, people with a background in the health sector, engineers; there were also a couple of university lecturers and some retired people. They all had families—we didn't support single people, not because they didn't need it, but we believed families were in the greatest danger. The people I helped were mainly middle-aged, so they couldn't follow the lead of many younger Iraqis and become labourers just to make a decent income.

These professionals were earning the equivalent of US$1 per month. Obviously, you can't feed a family on that. As an intern, that was also my salary, but I was fortunate enough to have independent assets which kept me going.

To survive financially in Iraq at the time, you either had to take a second job—such as driving a taxi, labouring or opening a shop—or sell your assets. Many in the middle classes were forced to sell their furniture, jewellery and other belongings.

All very short-term solutions. The money would run out pretty quickly and then they'd be forced to sell something else. Until everything was gone and they'd be left with no option but to resort to begging, stealing or taking bribes.

One of Areeg's neighbours was a university lecturer who couldn't get a second job and refused to resort to illicit means. When he'd sold the last piece of the family's furniture, he bought a chicken for a family feast, poisoned it, then fed it to his wife and four children. The whole family died together.

Bribery and corruption had become very obvious, especially in the justice system. Police officers would take bribes for anything and everything—from letting people off traffic offences, to purposely losing evidence or allowing criminals out of jail. It started with corrupt police, but it spread a lot further than that. Engineers, accountants, lawyers—they were all taking bribes.

It tainted the education system, too. School teachers would take bribes to pass students who wouldn't otherwise have achieved anything notable. The same happened at universities, although not so much in medicine as far as I was aware. We used to hear about students in Russia who got a degree for a bottle of vodka. The same level of bribery was happening in Iraq.

A lot of my friends came from families where their parents were prominent professionals. You could see they were all struggling financially. It was part of a massive social change in Iraq after the First Gulf War. That was the start of the rise of a new elite—people who quickly became very wealthy and influential but were generally lacking any education or legitimate basis for their wealth. They were carpetbaggers and profiteers. They made their money out of dangerous activities and crime.

For example, the government was offering large amounts of money to anyone prepared to collect the ordnance and metal remnants from the First Gulf War. And there was plenty of it—rockets, tanks, vehicles, other machinery that had been abandoned in the desert. People could earn heaps of fast dollars doing that and would form companies that specialised in recovering ordnance.

Then there was a class of farmers who were very disadvantaged before the war, but became extremely rich afterwards. The government would pay them swags of money to produce food because the embargo was limiting the amount of consumables that could be imported.

Food and petrol were rationed for most people. We were allowed a certain amount of wheat, flour, rice, cooking oil, sugar and, on occasions, legumes, such as kidney beans, chickpeas and the like. Sometimes we would be given chicken or eggs as a gift from Saddam. Doctors and paramedics were included in the rationing but, now and then, we would receive canned food in boxes as well.

Most people couldn't afford to go to the clubs and bars as they had done in previous years. Traditionally, these venues had been the gathering places for families and educated people to discuss ideas. Now, they were the gathering places for thugs—the new rich. And instead of taking their families to socialise or enjoy a game of chess, the new patrons were taking their mistresses and prostitutes to gamble and wheel and deal.

The rules of life in Iraq had changed. The old society was breaking down.

The crime rate rose, though it was still regarded as one of the safest places in the region because Saddam maintained a regime that ruled with an iron fist. Officially, if a thief was caught and convicted, they could face capital punishment. But because of the rampant bribery, they would often escape prison before the case reached court.

Tribal laws had started to appear again—Saddam actively encouraged it, as he did a number of the old-fashioned ways that had disappeared from Iraqi society. I remember a friend was driving his car and accidently ran over a man in the street. He took the pedestrian to hospital because there were no ambulances in service by this stage. (Sure, there was an ambulance at the University Hospital—but it was sitting up on blocks and had no tyres! That was the last ambulance I saw before I left Iraq.)

After that, the settlement was worked out between the leaders of the pedestrian's tribe and the leaders of my friend's tribe. They discussed the amount of blood that had been shed and how much compensation should be paid in return.

# The Journey Begins—Escaping Iraq

It was eventually agreed that my friend should pay for the pedestrian to be cared for in a private hospital and find him a job when the man had recovered from his injuries. If the pedestrian had died, my friend would have been forced to pay the victim's family a very large sum of money as well as lavish gifts upon them.

At the end of the year, I finished the internship, after spells in orthopaedics, gynaecology, paediatrics, general surgery, emergency and intensive care in the Saddam Medical Centre at the University Hospital, the Al-Karkh Hospital and the Al Numaan Hospital. Then I was accepted into the surgical training program. It was a dream come true. I'd wanted to be a surgeon—especially an orthopaedic surgeon—since I was twelve or thirteen and saw the first *Terminator* movie. The idea of half man, half machine really captured my imagination and made me think that in future surgeons would be able to replace damaged or amputated limbs with mechanical devices. My enthusiasm to become a surgeon was boundless, but resources were hard to come by. For urgent use, we were reduced to keeping drip lines, saline solution and such things in our lockers in the on-call room, because the supplies just weren't available.

There was always a lack of something. It was incredibly disorganised—and to some extent, I think it was deliberately disorganised. For months we would have none of the drugs we needed for anaesthetics. Then, all of a sudden, a truck would arrive full of drugs, all near their use-by date. Clearly, they had been stored somewhere nearby, but hadn't been released until the last minute.

We had to re-use all the suture material, which was supposed to be disposable. We'd put it in Dettol, pure alcohol or any antiseptic solution to re-sterilise it and re-use it until we simply couldn't eke any more life out of the thread.

We re-used the single-use sterile gloves. I think they were autoclaved between each outing. And we would re-use the plates and nails inserted in patients to help fractures heal. We'd take them out of one patient, autoclave them and put them back into another patient.

Many modifications had to be made to standard procedures. For example, the carbon fibre rods used to keep fractures firmly in place just weren't available. So one prominent orthopaedic surgeon injected bone cement into oxygen mask tubes to make replacement rods.

All our work was trauma. We didn't do much elective surgery because there were no prostheses. But there were plenty of traffic accidents and a lot of gunshot wounds, which were increasing at that stage—usually, they spiked when Iraq was playing a World Cup soccer match! When the national soccer team beat China, more than 1000 people were admitted to hospitals across Iraq in one day. And quite a few of them died. A neighbour of mine was shot in the chest that day—mind you, he was shooting as well. Most of the wounds were to the head—people were shooting in the air to celebrate the victory. But when a bullet goes up, it has to come down . . . and that's how a lot of the injuries happened.

Even though there were significant compromises, such as the shortage of equipment and drugs, as far as I know none of the patients suffered any serious problems as a result. The standard of my medical training was still good, too, because the professors were highly skilled and qualified.

※

In mid-1999, the events that forced me to escape from Iraq started to unfold.

Military service was compulsory in Iraq, and Saddam issued an order that army deserters should be punished by disfigurement. Among other things, he ordered they should have the top half of their ears surgically removed. On 22 April 1999, the Iraqi newspaper *Al-Iraq*, the official newspaper of the government, published a call-up notice for army reservists who were born in 1972. The notice stated that on 1 May all reservists would be obliged to report for thirty days' training, at the end of which they would be released. The notice said that the relevant legal provisions would be enforced against those who failed to report. According to a decree issued in September 1994, the Revolutionary Command Council ordered the amputation and branding of draft evaders and deserters, particularly the amputation of the ear (decree 115/1994). In November 1999 *Tark Al-Sha'b*, an Iraqi opposition newspaper, reported that Iraqi government agents were arresting Iraqi army deserters.

At the time, we didn't think it would have any impact on us—we assumed that only doctors in military hospitals would be required to carry out the operations. Little did we know . . .

One autumn morning, the surgeons and registrars met as usual to discuss the admissions from the day before. I started the ward rounds about seven o'clock, checking the patients who were recovering from surgery, before going to the operating theatres to start the day's list.

There were about ten operating theatres in the 1200-bed general hospital, which was the main area of the Saddam Hussein Medical Centre on the banks of the Tigris River in Central Baghdad. Before the trade embargo, it had been one of the best hospitals and medical systems in a developing nation.

Things had changed. The theatres were still in good condition, with the latest equipment available in Iraq at the time. But, along with a lack of basic supplies such as surgical materials and drugs, much of the support equipment was broken and couldn't be repaired because of the trade embargo. The CT scanner was broken, and so was the MRI scanner. This meant the waiting list for surgery was extensive.

The hygiene wasn't great, either, because there was a general feeling that many medical professionals had given up the fight and didn't really care anymore. Often, there would be a pool of blood on the floor of the operating theatre because no one had got around to cleaning it up. In the wards, there were no sheets on the beds, just bare mattresses. And the patients were never alone; cats roamed through the corridors and wards.

Around 8.30 a.m., before we could start operating, someone from the hospital administration came in and told us to abandon all the planned surgery. Three buses full of soldiers had arrived under control of the Military Intelligence Service officers and military police.

It was a complete shock to us, but a usual tactic for Saddam and his henchmen, who regularly relied on the element of surprise to force through their most extreme actions. Straightaway, the word spread that these were army deserters— and we were being ordered to disfigure them by surgically removing the tops of their ears, using either a general or local anaesthetic.

The situation was particularly terrifying for me because my mind flashed back to 1986 in Al Mustansiria, when one morning Ba'ath Party thugs had dragged our next-door neighbour, clad only in his underwear, out of his house. He was accused of desertion from the army, bundled into a 4WD vehicle and taken to the Ba'ath Party headquarters, where he was interrogated. Later that week he was executed by firing squad. His two brothers were forced to watch the horror of his execution. The family had to officially disown the victim, and even had to pay for the bullets that slaughtered him.

I could see the heavily armed soldiers from the elite Military Police bringing the deserters into the holding bays and ordering them to get on trolleys, ready to be wheeled into the operating theatres. The deserters were a ragged bunch—some were in uniform, some had no shoes, some were in civilian clothes, some in their pyjamas. I guessed that many of them were picked up on the road, while others may have been taken from their beds.

Perhaps surprisingly, they all seemed remarkably calm. Maybe they had just surrendered to their fate. Maybe they knew they weren't going to die—unless they protested or put up resistance. From their point of view, having their ears disfigured might not have been so terrible under the circumstances.

But in the operating theatre we were not so calm. Tension was rising rapidly and there was massive stress among the doctors, anaesthetists and surgical staff.

Then I saw three burly officers striding along the corridor towards the operating theatre. They were menacingly huge, heavily armed and dressed in full camouflage uniform with combat boots—the most finely honed instruments of Saddam's brutality. As they approached they were giving orders to staff to immediately begin the surgery. The most senior doctor in the operating theatre refused their instructions. He told the officers he had taken a solemn medical oath to do no harm to his patients. Straight away he was marched to the hospital car park, briefly interrogated and then shot in front of a number of medical staff. The military thugs then came back to the operating theatre and bluntly told us: 'If anyone shares his view, step forward. Otherwise carry on.'

I was confronted by the greatest dilemma of my life.

There were three options: carry out the operations as instructed, refuse to perform the operations and face the consequence—almost certain death—or hide. But, as happens in moments of crisis, there was no time for considered thought. This decision had to be made there and then without any careful assessment of the consequences.

I only seriously considered the last two options. I knew there was no way I was going to perform these operations—I just would not be able to live with the guilt I would have felt for the rest of my life.

But I also rapidly realised that I wasn't going to confront the might of the military.

The surgical staff didn't have a chance to discuss an overall strategy. We had been thrust into the middle of this crisis without notice or preparation. As I quickly glanced at the senior staff in the operating theatre—the consultant surgeon, the anaesthetists, the two senior theatre nurses—I could see the sheer terror on their faces. If they had looked in my direction, my trembling fear would have been obvious.

There wasn't a moment to waste. I only had one option—I had to escape. But how?

I couldn't run past the guards. And there was no other way out of the theatre complex. Quickly, I made the decision to sneak out, pretending to go to the toilet. Then I would have to find somewhere to hide.

No one saw me go—not even the surgeons.

Instead of heading into the men's toilets, though, I went straight to the women's change room, which was attached to the operating theatre. I was in luck. There were no women in the change room so I ducked in unnoticed, went straight into a cubicle, locked the door behind me and sat on the toilet.

I was terrified, breathless, my heart was pounding. This was it. There was no contingency plan. I would either escape . . . or face execution. Discovery was almost certain death. If the soldiers caught me, I would have been taken away for interrogation and quite likely tortured, probably culminating in a death sentence. As far as they were concerned, there was no justification for refusing to carry out Saddam's orders.

It was agonising to know that at any moment a ruthless brute could come into the change room, force his way into the cubicle and discover me. As I sat there, I listened attentively for every move and footstep that would indicate someone coming into the change room. I waited, for minutes, then hours. Three or four people did come in—every time sending my heart racing even faster. Luckily, they were all women. And no one twigged that one of the cubicles was permanently occupied.

The wait was interminable. The tension terrifying.

Five hours later, around two o'clock in the afternoon, a larger group of women came in and I could tell they were washing their hands and getting changed at the end of the day's sinister work. The frantic activity in the operating theatres had calmed down. Surgery normally finished around 2 p.m. in Iraq, so they'd kept very much to that schedule.

After the women left, I stayed in the cubicle for another fifteen minutes or so to make sure the coast was clear. When there was no further sign of movement, I cautiously opened the cubicle door, checked that the change room was empty, crept to the main door and, with my heart in my mouth, slowly opened it to see whether anyone was still in the theatre area.

I changed from my surgical outfit into my standard clothes and walked quickly through the corridors from the operating theatre area on the second floor of the hospital, making sure I didn't look agitated or in an undue rush. The last thing I wanted was to be conspicuous and attract attention, which might betray me to the Military Police or other government operatives.

Down the fire stairs and through the lobby at the back of the building, which served as the main reception area. Dozens of patients and their relatives were milling around in reception, so I could slip through without being noticed.

Out of the main entrance. I could have headed straight into the car park and attempted to drive away, but decided against it. The car park was almost deserted by that stage and I didn't know whether anyone would be monitoring my vehicle. I knew if I was to survive, I couldn't take even the slightest risk. Instead, I turned right into the slip road in the hospital complex, then left onto the highway leading to the nearby bus terminal.

A few hundred metres of brisk walking, head down trying to avoid eye contact, all the time my heart pumping with terror.

Before I reached the bus station, I stopped a cab and asked to go to the upmarket suburb of Harthia. It's to the west of the river—in the opposite direction to my house. Ali, a close friend of mine who had been a fellow student at Baghdad College, lived in Harthia. He was also a doctor and a couple of years older than me. His family had been long-standing friends of my parents. Because I trusted him and he understood the medical world, Ali immediately sprang to mind as someone who could offer the assistance I needed.

In the whirlwind of the morning and early afternoon, I had thrashed around various escape plans and routes. Eventually, I had decided to go to Ramadi, where I'd studied at Anbar University. Ramadi seemed ideal. I knew the city and plenty of people there and it was remote from Baghdad, culturally as well as geographically. The people of Ramadi lived life by different standards and protected their own. Much as I disagreed with their traditions, their culture would work in my favour at this traumatic time. It was a place where I could virtually disappear in the short term and know that my friends would not disclose my presence.

The only other options I had considered were Sawayrah, where I had stayed with my family during the First Gulf War, and Basra. I didn't know anyone who could help me in Sawayrah, while Basra was more than 500 kilometres away and I couldn't escape through the nearest border, with Kuwait—not surprisingly, after recent events, Iraqis were not welcomed into Kuwait at the time.

Ramadi was my only chance.

The cab drove over the Bab Al Muadam Bridge and about twenty-five minutes further to Ali's house. All the time, I was obsessed with how I could possibly get out of Baghdad—and eventually Iraq.

It was mid-afternoon when the cab came to a halt outside Ali's house. I paid off the driver and rushed to the front door. I banged on the door and, to my relief, Ali answered. He was dressed very casually in a tracksuit.

'Get changed. I need you to help me,' I barked at him.

He realised something major was wrong. Quickly he put on a jacket and pants.

'Let's get something to eat and I'll tell you all about it,' I instructed.

Ali drove us to the nearby Chilli House takeaway, which was familiar territory, in his dark-coloured Mercedes. During the short drive, I told him: 'Something horrible has happened and I need to get out of Baghdad.'

We bought sandwiches and ate them leaning against the car as I told him my plan.

'I need to go to Ramadi straight away. And I need you to drive me there,' I told him.

Ali agreed without hesitation and we set off. As we began our dramatic drive, I explained the horrors which had engulfed me that day. He wasn't surprised, but he was appalled. Ali's family were practising Shi'ite Moslems. His mother was covered, even at a time when many women wore Western clothes. The family had always strongly opposed Saddam.

I explained the scant details of my escape plan and that my friend Nissan, the administrator at Anbar University and my main contact in Ramadi, was the person I had decided to trust my life to.

It took around ninety minutes to drive there. We had to go through two major checkpoints at Al-Khdraa about 20 kilometres away from the hospital at the start of the highway and then at Abu Ghraib, another 15 kilometres away. The checkpoints were staffed by military police and militia. Mainly, they were checking for army deserters, but you never felt safe going through these roadblocks because the men on duty were fundamentally ignorant and you simply couldn't take anything for granted.

At these checkpoints we had to show a range of documents—my university identification, my medical papers and my army papers, which indicated that I had been exempted from military service because I was training as a doctor. The officials would always question me because of a technical discrepancy with my papers. On my military documents, my name was on the front, which was straightforward. But on my university papers, my name was on the back; printed on the front was the name of the dean of the college, which I always had to explain. This time, though, the questioning over my papers felt much more menacing and tense.

# The Journey Begins—Escaping Iraq

We sat in the car while they checked my documents and my blood pressure rose. In my favour was the fact that they hadn't installed computers at these checkpoints. So the chances of the officials being alerted to look out for me so quickly weren't great. Still, I couldn't be certain.

It was a huge relief when they let me through the first checkpoint, but not surprisingly the same problem with my papers happened at the second checkpoint. Which meant a few more terrifying minutes of explaining before they also let me through.

From there, we drove straight to Ramadi as fast as we could without breaking speed limits or bringing ourselves to the notice of the authorities. Fortunately, I knew the area well.

We arrived about six o'clock in the evening, just as it was getting dark. Straightaway we drove to Nissan's house and told him I needed to stay for a few days. He invited me in immediately, but didn't ask what was going on.

Once he was sure I was safe at Nissan's house, Ali headed back to Baghdad with instructions to contact my mother and explain what had happened.

Because of their tribal traditions, each member of the family was quite segregated within the house. I stayed in the guest area in Nissan's part of the house, which had a bedroom and its own bathroom. He just told his family he had a guest staying but he didn't say who it was and I didn't have to see any other members of the family while I was there. Which was exactly the way I wanted it—I didn't want too many people knowing where I was in case the word spread and I was discovered by Saddam's spies.

I rested for a while and then we had dinner. The normal Iraqi way is that you don't talk about anything substantial when you're eating. Nissan just asked how I was and we made small talk.

Then, around eight, we sat down, drank tea and started to talk. Now the meal was over, Nissan was quite blunt with his questions. Immediately he asked, 'What's going on?'

I told him what had happened at the hospital and he was very supportive. 'I think you've done the right thing,' he reassured me.

I was grateful for his support. But the problem was not so much what I'd already done—it was what I was going to do next. I didn't know how I could keep one step ahead of the Iraqi authorities, but I did know that if they caught me, I would face intense—and potentially brutal—interrogation before the ultimate sanction of death.

'What should I do now?' I asked Nissan.

He confirmed that obviously I couldn't go back to Baghdad. Nissan announced that he would go straight to Baghdad the next morning and check on my mother. But he said the most urgent thing was to start arranging to smuggle me out of Iraq. It simply wasn't safe for me to stay in the country one moment longer than I had to.

I guess I knew that was coming. What other option did I really have? It was impossible for me to stay in Iraq, or leave by conventional means—but never before in my life had I imagined that I would become a fugitive.

'Don't worry, you get some sleep,' Nissan said. 'We'll think of something tomorrow.'

In theory getting a good night's rest was easy. But, of course, I didn't sleep a wink that night.

The next morning, Nissan left for Baghdad. I had to stay indoors so I didn't raise anyone's suspicions. When he got to the capital, Nissan went straight to see my mother. She was terrified and frantically worried about me.

By that time, three officials—one a security operative, one from the Ba'ath Party and one a local councillor—had been to my mother's house to question her, wanting to know where I was. At that stage, she could quite truthfully say she had no idea and hadn't seen me since the morning.

It was awful not to be able to speak to my mother but it just wasn't possible. There were no mobile phones or internet in those days and it was too dangerous to call her on the landline phone. I was lucky I had Nissan to relay the news; so many others would never know the fate of their loved ones who suddenly and suspiciously disappeared. At least my mother knew I was safe. For the time being, anyway.

Of course, the situation was enormously dangerous. If Nissan had been seen visiting my mother, he may well have been followed and the authorities could have discovered where I was hiding.

He drove back to Ramadi the next day and arrived early in the evening. My mother had given Nissan about US$12,000 in cash to help get me out of the country.

The next evening, after dark, we went to a coffee shop in Ramadi and met two men. They were very scary looking— extremely tall and powerfully built, with huge moustaches. One was wearing a police uniform, the other was wearing civilian clothes. I learned later they were both senior Passport Office police who were based in Baghdad and had come out to Ramadi to do a deal.

They were completely clinical about the transaction: 'We need photos and we need money.'

I gave them the US$5000 they demanded as a first instalment and agreed to pay another $5000 on delivery of the false passport.

That's where my cousin Bassam, the army intelligence officer who was and still is living in Baghdad, took control. I told Nissan that Bassam would be the best contact in Baghdad. Nissan acted as the intermediary, issuing and receiving the instructions and updates on developments. I never knew the precise details of what went on, but I believe Bassam got some photos from my mother and gave them to the Passport Office police in Baghdad who were preparing the fake documents.

While the passport was being prepared, I made two surreptitious and hurried trips to Baghdad to see my mother and grab some clothes. Naturally, she was thrilled to see me and assured me nothing bad had happened to her. The authorities hadn't been menacing her. She gave me another US$10,000 in cash. I have no idea where she got the money, because we weren't allowed to keep US dollars in bank accounts. Maybe some relatives had stashed it away. She never told me how she came by it.

I returned to Ramadi and, within a couple of days, we were visited by Bassam and the two burly figures from the Passport Office. They had the passport, but gruffly demanded: 'Give us the rest of the money and you'll get the passport.' I handed over the final $5000 payment.

The new passport was virtually the same as the old one. But crucially, they'd changed my occupation—from doctor to handyman. Doctors weren't allowed out of the country—so, regardless of the incident at the Saddam Medical Centre, under normal circumstances I still wouldn't have been able to leave Iraq.

There were just two finishing touches to add. I had to sign the passport and add my thumb print. The two officers had brought the ink pad with them, so we completed the process and then they put the official seal on it.

That was the easy part.

The hard part was taking my name off the computer list of people who were forbidden from leaving the country. The officers couldn't completely wipe my name off the list, but had managed to remove it from the data at one particular border crossing into Jordan for a couple of hours. I was instructed to go back to Baghdad the next morning and get on a bus to Jordan. They told me I had to be at the crossing at Trebil in mid-afternoon, when my name would temporarily disappear from the list. There was no leeway, they said, no room for error.

Returning to Baghdad was a serious concern. I didn't want to be there any longer than I could possibly help.

Nissan drove me back to the capital with me sitting nervously in the passenger seat. He took me straight to the Al-Alawi bus station and dropped me there. We arrived some time after six o'clock in the morning and I was met by my cousin Bassam and my mother.

Waiting for the bus was excruciating. Armed security guards swarmed around the bus station and, at any moment, could have demanded my papers. If they'd checked my identity, they'd have found out I was a doctor, on a list of wanted people and certainly not allowed to get on a bus to Jordan. I was terrified. My mother was in tears most of the thirty minutes or so that we stood in the bus station and there was little genuine conversation.

I was lucky, though. The bus station was a chaotic series of sheds with thousands of people milling around. Despite my fears, I didn't stand out in the crowd.

The minutes dragged by as the 7 a.m. departure time approached. But finally, with a massive sense of relief that I hadn't been stopped by the security guards, I climbed on the bus. Saying goodbye to my mother and not knowing whether

I would ever see her again was difficult. But I had to make sure we controlled our emotions, because I didn't want to attract attention. I'd cleared one hurdle—although now I was on my own. The bus was pleasantly comfortable, new and air-conditioned. It was quite full and a young woman in her early thirties sat next to me. She was dressed in Western clothes and wasn't wearing a head scarf. She was taking her two children and her father to Jordan to meet up with her husband. Then the family was migrating to the UK.

We got talking and at one stage, she said, half-joking, 'You're a doctor, aren't you?'

I nearly panicked, but managed to maintain a calm demeanour and told her: 'No, I'm just a handyman going to Jordan for some fun.'

She didn't believe me. 'You don't look like a handyman.'

I was almost at my wit's end anyway, but her comments made me feel there was a very real chance my assumed identity and occupation weren't fooling anyone. If that was the case, I'd quickly be discovered by the Iraqi authorities.

Then there was the narrow window of opportunity. The road from Baghdad to the border is a five-lane highway each way, so it was a reasonably straightforward drive and the normal bus schedule would have me at the border at the right time. But a traffic accident, a mechanical breakdown or even a puncture could throw things completely out of kilter.

Psychologically, I was going through an intense ordeal. In the more anxious moments, I resorted to some of the medical techniques I'd learned to remain calm. I was pulling my ear lobes, taking deep breaths and holding my nose to stimulate the vagus nerve which supplies the heart. If you stimulate the nerve, it gives a signal to the heart to slow down and eventually lowers your blood pressure.

I was running through these techniques to try to induce an element of calm when we got to the border crossing at Trebil. I felt I needed everything to go in my favour to get out of this situation alive. It was crucial now that the immigration officials did not see any nervous or suspicious behaviour. I didn't rate my chances of pulling it off very highly. But this was my one and only chance. So I had to take it.

As we reached the border, I kept glancing at my watch—and we were on the correct schedule. Now, I was only a short distance from the relative safety of Jordan. Providing, of course, the Passport Office police had carried out their part of the bargain.

But as we walked into the immigration building, I had an unexpected and terrible realisation—I recognised one of the passport officers. He was a patient I had treated six weeks earlier when he had come to the Baghdad Medical Centre's accident and emergency department late one night with a badly slashed wrist after a bar-room fight. He was incredibly drunk, but I managed to stitch his wrist and stop the flow of blood. His life hadn't exactly been in my hands. But now mine certainly was in his.

The passport officers were sitting in a row at a counter behind security glass, like bank tellers. Just as you do in an immigration queue at an airport, we were lined up, and when we reached the front of the queue, we were allocated to individual passport officers.

At that moment, I knew my life was at a cross-road. I consciously thought: 'Shall I keep going and risk my life? Or shall I turn back?'

I made a snap decision that I would go through with this. The main hope was that I would be ushered off to be dealt with by one of the other passport officers.

Fate is a harsh mistress, though. Lo and behold, I got to the front of the line and there was one vacant passport officer. My former patient!

It was one of those moments in your life when you realise you have absolutely no control over what is about to happen. I was completely detached from reality. As I walked up to the counter, I was in a different world. All I could think was: 'I'm going to be caught and I'm going to die.' And there was a strange sense of acceptance of my fate.

I stood in front of my former patient and handed over my passport. He briefly looked at me—and to my eternal gratitude, there was not even a flicker of recognition in his eyes. He must have been so drunk that night six weeks earlier that he had absolutely no idea what the treating doctor looked like. As far as he knew, I was a complete stranger.

As he glanced at me, he asked, 'What do you do?'

'I'm a handyman.'

'And what are you doing in Jordan?'

'We have air-conditioning people in Jordan and I'm going to get some parts for an air-conditioner.'

It was an explanation I had prepared when I was trying to rehearse all the possible events that could unfold at the border crossing.

'How long are you planning to stay in Jordan?'

'Maybe a month.'

'How much money do you have with you?'

'One thousand US.'

'That's a lot of money to be carrying with you if you're only staying one month,' he said.

Once he asked that, I felt relieved, because it indicated that he was comfortable with my identity as a handyman and the fact that I was going to Jordan to collect some parts for an air-conditioner.

'Maybe I'll stay longer,' I responded.

'And what jewellery do you have?'

I was wearing a gold chain around my neck. I pointed to it and said, 'Just this.'

He paused, unmoved. Then came the wonderful moment when he stamped my passport and dispassionately said: 'Have a nice trip.'

But the ordeal wasn't quite over. I had to go through the luggage check and then the body search. I had my money strapped to my stomach, but no one found it or raised any more questions about the amount of money I was taking into Jordan.

# The Journey Begins—Escaping Iraq

We spent about an hour at the border crossing, while the bus was thoroughly searched and put on a ramp so the authorities could check underneath it. Meanwhile, I had to stay quiet and unobtrusive. After my close call at the passport desk, I realised that all it would take would be for someone to say: 'Hello, doctor,' and I'd be arrested immediately. My main distraction was watching people selling whisky and cigarettes because alcohol and tobacco were much more expensive in Jordan.

At long last, we were allowed back onto the bus. It took another three or four hours to cross No Man's Land from Iraq and get through the border into Jordan. It seemed to me the Jordanian officials were being deliberately obstructive and delaying things as much as possible. But maybe that was more about my circumstances and frustrations than the reality. Still, as we officially left Iraq and entered Jordan, I couldn't remember ever feeling so relieved.

Once we were through the border, the journey became much more tedious. While the road from Baghdad to the border was a brand, spanking-new highway, when we crossed into Jordan, it deteriorated to one lane each way. And the track through the desert was full of pot holes. To make matters worse, we had to share it with massive oil trucks. In Iraq, the oil trucks travelled on a parallel highway.

After another four or five hours, we arrived in Amman. The Jordanian capital was gloomy and miserable. There were no trees and the houses looked very poor. There were plenty of satellite dishes, but not much else to indicate that this was a thriving city.

We arrived just as the sun was rising on a new day. It was symbolic, because, at the same time, the sun was rising on a completely new phase of my life.

# 8

# WHERE IN THE WORLD?

My first impressions of Amman were depressing. In the hours after the bus dropped us at the Roman colosseum, I was struck by the number of Iraqi men, hundreds of them, standing round talking and smoking. They would have been living and working in Amman as low-paid labourers, waiting for their refugee applications to be accepted by the United Nations High Commission for Refugees or for people-smugglers to take them to Europe. I had heard there was a lot of people-smuggling activity going on in Amman.

My accommodation had been arranged. I would stay in a flat owned by my aunt, Alia Schurman, my mother's sister. Alia was the fifth oldest and four years younger than my mother. She had gone to the US to complete her Masters degree at Kalamazoo University in Michigan and afterwards Alia, an artistic person, stayed on at the university to teach folk-dancing. She married and settled in the US but she also bought a unit in the Gardens area of Amman, a wealthy part of the city. Her brother was living there.

I arrived at the flat and my uncle welcomed me in. I was feeling an enormous sense of relief at getting out of Iraq in one piece and when the evening came, I slept soundly.

But by morning, I realised I had absolutely no idea what I was going to do next. At that stage, the plan hadn't extended any further than getting out of Iraq.

My uncle told me I had to go to the nearest police station at Shmaisani and register so I could get a three-month visa. Under the system of the day, Iraqis could get an initial visa to visit Jordan and then another three-month visa. After that ran out, you either had to return to Iraq and re-enter Jordan or take your chances and stay illegally. That risked being deported back to Iraq and fined one Jordanian dinar for every day you'd overstayed.

Of course, returning to Iraq simply wasn't an option for me, but staying in Jordan also presented dilemmas.

I didn't feel safe there in the long-term because the country was teeming with Iraqi secret-service agents, who were extremely active. On top of my safety fears, Jordan really didn't have much of an economy or job prospects. The whole economy seemed to be based on the king and the royal family receiving financial support from the West to maintain the nation as a reliable buffer amid the troubles of the Middle East. Everything else just stemmed from the money the royal family spent on various projects.

Despite my concerns, I decided to explore the prospects of furthering my education and working in Jordan. I went to the University Hospital to check if there was any chance of a job. They were pretty blunt. The administration officials told me in no uncertain terms: 'We don't employ Iraqis. You might have a slim chance if you were a specialist as we have a shortage in that area. But you're not a specialist.'

I quickly realised that door was firmly closed.

My uncle told me there were some Iraqi doctors working in private hospitals, although they were earning less than half the salaries of the local doctors, worked the most shifts and were not given any training. Added to that, they were practising illegally, because they were not registered. This wasn't an attractive prospect for me, either.

I decided very quickly that I could not stay in Jordan—especially because I was paranoid about being chased by Iraqi secret-service agents. So I started exploring other options. Which were not many, because hardly any countries were willing to accept an Iraqi passport.

A friend of mine who was living in Amman told me it was possible to work as a doctor in the Malaysian capital, Kuala Lumpur. Malaysia was one of the few countries that did allow Iraqis to enter. My friend was a qualified engineer and had worked in Kuala Lumpur a few years earlier when the Asian economies were booming. But as soon as the Asian Tiger stopped roaring with quite the same ferocity, the migrant workers lost their jobs and he had returned to Jordan.

Apparently you could get a fourteen-day visa at Kuala Lumpur Airport and then extend it for three months by enrolling in a short educational course at one of the universities. In my case, I could enrol to study for a Master of Surgery degree, which would have included working in a hospital as an unpaid student intern. After that, the job prospects would be completely uncertain and an extension of the visa beyond the three months unlikely.

Even so, Malaysia seemed to offer much better prospects than staying in Jordan. I was becoming increasingly uneasy in Amman. I didn't feel welcome there.

Palestinians, in general, weren't terribly polite to Iraqis, and those with Jordanian citizenship were particularly hostile. They were strong supporters of Saddam, who was a hero to them for bombing Israel, so they viewed any Iraqi who left the country as a traitor; but they also resented the Iraqis offering cheap labour and competing for the same, scarce jobs as themselves.

I stayed in Amman for a week before deciding I would try my luck in Malaysia. At that stage, my life was completely up in the air. I realised I had lost my job, and potentially my career. I didn't know if I'd ever achieve my goal of becoming a surgeon—in fact I had no idea what my future would be.

I spent 400 Jordanian dinar on booking my flight to Kuala Lumpur on Gulf Air. This was a declaration of intent, but far from the end of my problems. It occurred to me that just getting out of Jordan could be complicated, because I was travelling on a forged passport. Even without the prospect of running into the immigration official who'd been my patient, my anxiety levels still rose as I approached Amman Airport, knowing my travel documents were false and would come under close scrutiny once more.

Again, I stood in the customs and immigration queues nervously waiting my turn, trying to hide any signs of anxiety. I went to the front of the line and, in due course, walked towards the immigration official. He scrutinised my passport, looked me up and down, hesitated, then applied the necessary stamp to the document. No one questioned the passport. The forgers had done a good job.

Once again, after we boarded the aircraft, I could relax for a few hours. The first leg of the journey took us to Abu Dhabi. The majority of the passengers were Iraqi citizens heading to Malaysia because of passport difficulties. The international attitude to Iraqis at the time was graphically illustrated when we got to Abu Dhabi and the immigration officials took away the passports of all the Iraqi nationals while we were in the transit area. Clearly, they didn't want Iraqis slipping out of the airport and into their country.

Hardly any of the immigration officers came from the United Arab Emirates; they were nearly all from the Indian subcontinent and didn't speak Arabic. The best way of communicating with them was in English, which ended up being the next crucial factor that would play a part in shaping my future.

We were in the transit lounge for about three hours. I sat next to a couple of young Iraqi men, who appeared rather restless and lost. As time passed they became more uncomfortable. They were chatting anxiously to each other and looking around nervously.

They were both dressed casually but reasonably smartly in shirts, jeans and running shoes. But I could tell the clothes were secondhand. It was very common for people to buy and wear secondhand clothes in Jordan. These guys were wearing Kickers shoes, which were quite expensive to buy new, but theirs had been repaired a few times. No one who could afford to buy Kickers would have them repaired; they'd just go out and buy new shoes. I looked at the men's hands and could see from the roughness of the skin that they were labourers of some sort.

One of them appeared to be in his mid-thirties. He was very slim, with sunken eyes as if he'd lived a very tough life. I later learned that his name was Ali and he was a carpenter.

# Where in the World?

He had lost the tops of a few fingers—not uncommon for carpenters in Iraq at the time. He looked classically southern Iraqi: dark skin, big hook nose, with a moustache. He was quiet and reserved, but when he did speak, it was with a clear southern accent.

The other man was a little younger, perhaps in his late twenties or early thirties. He had fairer skin and blue eyes and sported facial stubble, long before it became fashionable. He had a much stronger build than Ali and was a more outgoing character. I discovered that he was a plasterer and painter and his real name was Hassan but he called himself Hussein. He was Khurdish and a Sunni, but he pretended to be a Shi'ite named Hussein because he thought it would make things easier for him.

In the transit lounge, I sat close enough to them that I could hear what they were saying. They were asking each other: 'Will we ever get our passports back? Why don't we go and talk to the immigration officials?' But then they realised the immigration officials didn't speak Arabic. Their frustration was obvious.

I asked if there was anything I could do to help. They replied that all they really wanted to know was whether they were going to get their passports back.

I explained that the passports had been taken because the authorities were worried about letting Iraqis into the country and that they would give us back our documents when we were about to board the plane again. I tried to reassure them and said I could interpret for them if they had any problems. That seemed to calm them down.

We started a more expansive conversation and they asked me where I was from and what I did. I told them I was a doctor— because I figured I was safe from the Iraqi secret-service by then—and I was going to Malaysia to further my studies.

I asked where they were going. They didn't answer straightaway. Instead, they looked at each other in a slightly strange way and then Ali said, 'We're tourists.'

They were not very convincing, so I spontaneously responded, 'You don't look like tourists, what are you really doing?'

Hussein was rather more forthcoming than Ali and replied, 'Yes, we're tourists and we're going to travel around for a while.'

I worked out pretty quickly that they were refugees who had been living in Jordan for some time, and clearly they knew someone who had helped them get out. They didn't look rich, but they must have spent a lot of money to travel to Malaysia. They gave me the impression they had worked extremely hard to save up the money for this. And because they had so much invested in making this journey, they were constantly on edge, looking around at everything suspiciously. They couldn't speak Malay or English. So they must have had a plan to do something else.

I raised the issue with them. 'To be honest, you look like refugees,' I said.

They laughed. They were not the smartest of people but they had enough street wisdom not to give themselves away to anyone.

## Where in the World?

Then I added, rather cryptically, 'If you're going in this direction, there are only two islands where you want to end up. One is big, the other is small. Which one are you going to?'

They laughed again and Hussein said: 'If you stick with us long enough, we'll tell you.' He then changed the conversation.

At that point, an Indian immigration official came into the transit lounge and handed our passports and papers back. He pointed towards the gates and told us to board the plane. I walked on board with Ali and Hussein, but we were allocated seats in different areas, so I didn't see them again until Kuala Lumpur.

It was an uneventful flight, but there was still a massive sense of relief when the plane landed in Malaysia, where I was planning to explore the possibility of staying to work as well as further my education. Once all the passengers had disembarked into the immigration and customs area, Ali and Hussein approached me again because the immigration forms were in English. It was at that moment the two of them realised their plans weren't going to be plain sailing. They needed to speak English, and they couldn't—which suddenly made me a vital asset.

I filled out the forms for them and we went to the immigration checkpoint together. Then they encountered another obstacle. When Ali handed over his documents, the immigration officer told him his passport would expire within the next six months and said, 'I'm sorry, you can't come into Malaysia.'

Ali was confused and anxious. Obviously, the entire success

of his scheme, whatever that was, relied on him getting into the country.

So I intervened and promised the immigration officer that as soon as Ali got into Malaysia, he would go straight to the Iraqi Embassy and get a new passport. The immigration officer was a very polite and reasonable person. He was completely understanding when I explained that Ali couldn't speak English and wouldn't be able to afford to fly back to Iraq and return to Malaysia with a new passport. It took about fifteen minutes, but I persuaded the officer to let Ali in.

We got through the rest of the immigration process without further problems and as we approached the exit, Ali and Hussein said they had to look for a public telephone and call a number they'd been given. That was the first time they let on they had a contact in Malaysia. We found a phone and they tried to call the number. But the instructions on the phone were in English and they couldn't get through. These guys really were hopelessly ill prepared for what they'd taken on. So, in the end, I had to make the phone call for them.

When I got through, I handed the phone to Hussein, who spoke to their contact. It was only as they were talking that I realised the contact was Iraqi, then gradually I figured out he was involved in people-smuggling.

The contact must have said he was only expecting two people, because Hussein told him there was a third person with them who was a doctor and spoke English. So the contact asked him to put me back on the phone.

He was blunt. He told me he thought Ali and Hussein were risky because they had no idea what they were doing and therefore he would only give them instructions through me. It was then my responsibility to make sure they followed these instructions. So, suddenly, I was right in the middle of a people-smuggling operation, without having ever given the idea a thought.

A lot of my life has revolved around coincidences rather than planning. This was another example.

We emerged from the terminal into the heat and humidity of a Kuala Lumpur afternoon. We left the airport in a taxi. I sat in the front and gave the driver the instructions while Ali and Hussein sat in the back. The contact told me to go to a specific place in the Chow Kit district, where we were to wait for him. He would find us there.

Chow Kit is a bustling district with Chinese markets, traders selling all sorts of fake designer clothes, bags and watches and massage parlours. I later found out that it is the red-light area of Kuala Lumpur. I guess the contact chose the area because it was so busy and we would not stand out from the crowd.

The three of us stood at the designated spot, opposite McDonalds, for ten minutes or so before a 183-centimetre tall, very fair-skinned, Western-looking man approached us. He was wearing a khaki shirt and beige knee-length shorts. He looked very clean and smart and appeared much more northern European than Iraqi.

He approached me and asked, 'Are you the doctor?'

I told him I was and he introduced himself. 'Hi, I'm Mahdi.' Mahdi is the name of the Twelfth Imam so it's very common in Iraq. He led us about 50 metres along the road to a tiny hotel, which was like a backpacker hostel. Mahdi spoke Malaysian to the person at reception and booked two rooms—I insisted on having my own room, separate from Ali and Hussein.

We each changed some money at the hotel, but I was careful not to reveal how much money I had with me. On the plane, I'd separated US$200 from my wallet so they only ever saw I had a small amount.

Mahdi said he wanted to talk to me. So the four of us went upstairs to Ali and Hussein's room, where the first details of the operation were explained. Mahdi said, 'This is how it works. You give me your passports and US$450 each and I'll get you visas to Indonesia.'

I was terrified by the thought of handing over my passport—one of my most treasured and important possessions—to a people-smuggler. Clearly, he was a criminal and not to be trusted. I wasn't too worried about losing the money, but without a passport, I would be in serious trouble.

'I'm sorry, but how do I know I can trust you?' I asked. 'How do I know you won't just steal my passport and the money?'

Mahdi's response was very calm and polite. It surprised me—for someone who was deeply involved in the sordid business of people-smuggling.

'I have a reputation to protect,' he said. 'I've been in this business for a long time and that's the way it is. You don't really have any choice. You take it or you leave it. I won't need the passport for very long. I'll get it back to you today.'

The others gave him their passports and money straightaway.

I had to make a decision on the spot. Until then, I hadn't seriously considered putting my life and my future in the hands of people-smugglers. I had no idea how the process worked. So I asked Mahdi what would happen if I gave him the passport and the money.

'We'll get you into Indonesia,' he replied. 'From there, you'll meet someone named Omeed.'

I asked: 'Where I will I go from Indonesia—Australia?'

Mahdi was more evasive as he explained: 'We take it one step at a time. My job is to get you to Indonesia. After that you might go to Australia or you might go to Europe. I don't know. I don't get involved in that part.'

I considered seeking asylum in Kuala Lumpur; however, to date Malaysia has not signed the 1951 Refugee Convention or its 1967 Protocol, so it lacks the formal legislative and administrative framework for handling refugees. Seeking asylum in Malaysia is not only difficult but also dangerous, as you are treated as a migrant without paperwork and can be deported to your land of origin without any investigation into your situation. This is simply a risk that I could not take; a return to Iraq would have resulted in my death.

On the spur of the moment, and not really knowing what I was actually getting myself into—let alone the dramatic events that would unfold over the coming months—I gave him my passport and my money.

After Mahdi left with the documents and cash—we also had to give him extra money for the plane tickets to Jakarta—the three of us left the hotel. We changed money on the black market, because the unofficial exchange rate was about 30 per cent better than the rate at a bank, had something to eat and went to our rooms to rest.

Two or three hours later, Mahdi came back with our passports. He handed them over, along with tickets for a Garuda flight to Jakarta a few days later. I was surprised to find they were business-class tickets. Mahdi never told us why. They may have been the only seats available, or it could have been a ploy to make us appear less suspicious. He gave me detailed instructions about how to get through immigration at Jakarta Airport and also provided a phone number, saying, 'When you get to Jakarta, make sure you call this number from the airport.'

Everything was so overwhelming that I didn't even ask him any other questions. But I must say, for my first dealing with a people-smuggler, I was pleasantly surprised by his efficiency!

We had another day in Kuala Lumpur and I decided I wanted to see some of the city. While I was in Amman, by chance I'd bumped into my friend Nada, who was a medical student in Baghdad at the same time as me. She'd escaped from Iraq with her family. We got talking and I'd told her I was planning to go to Malaysia. She gave me the address and phone number of her sister and brother-in-law who were living and working in Kuala Lumpur. So I called them and took the train to see them at their house on the outskirts of the city.

It was comfortable to be around familiar people again, even if only for a few hours, and I told them I might be going to Indonesia the following day. They were very concerned about me getting involved with people-smugglers and warned me how dangerous it was. They also offered to help me find a job or continue my education in Kuala Lumpur if I decided to stay. But they confirmed what I already knew—I might find work, but it wouldn't be a paid job. It would be part of a university education that I would pay for. The prospects of finding work in the medical system afterwards weren't great. In reality, hardly any Iraqi doctors were working in paid positions in Malaysia.

Back in the city centre, I took Ali and Hussein to the Petronis Towers to get something to eat. They were absolutely blown away by the towers. They'd never seen anything like it. Of course, until then they hadn't travelled at all.

The next day passed very quickly. We went to the markets and hung around the Chow Kit area. Then we caught a cab to the airport, where we would find out whether our visas for Indonesia were legitimate—or at least whether they looked legitimate!

Naturally, we were all anxious when we were approaching immigration and customs officials at the airport. But there were no issues. The documents we were required to show were all accepted without question—until the final checkpoint, where we were unexpectedly stopped by the airline staff and asked what we were doing in Malaysia and why we were going to Indonesia.

I acted as the spokesperson and said we were tourists and wanted to see Jakarta while we were in the region. Which is absolutely ridiculous. Jakarta is a disastrous place. Half the population seems to live in tiny metal shelters. No one in their right mind would want to go there as a tourist.

Still, they accepted the explanation and we boarded the plane.

The flight was mercifully brief—only a couple of hours—and uneventful. Once we landed, we followed every detail of the instructions Mahdi had given me when he returned the passports. He'd told me very clearly: 'When you get to the immigration desk at Jakarta Airport, there will be four or five immigration officers. Don't go to the woman and don't go to the Chief Immigration Officer. Go to the guy who doesn't have any stars on the shoulders of his uniform.'

He described the scene in great detail and said: 'When you hand over your passport, leave a US$100 note in there and keep the passport closed.'

I had protested, saying, 'This is blatant bribery.'

Mahdi had responded, 'Just do what I say and you'll be fine. If you don't put the money in the passport, you'll be straight back on the next plane and I'll see you tomorrow!'

While we were still on board the aircraft, I'd put the money in my passport as he said.

When we disembarked and walked into the immigration area, the scene was exactly as Mahdi had described it. The woman was there, and the Chief Immigration Officer . . . so we went to the officer with no stars on the shoulders of his uniform.

I stood behind the other two so I could interpret for them if there was a problem. In turn, Hussein and Ali handed their passports to the immigration officer, who opened the passports, took out the money, put it in his drawer and stamped the documents. And he did just the same when it came to my turn.

To this day, I still don't know whether the visas were valid or whether Mahdi had just stamped the passports himself and the bribe got us through. Either way, it worked.

But I must admit the uncertainty was terrifying as we handed over the passports with the money inside them. Let's face it, bribing an immigration official is a serious crime. I still find it difficult to accept I did it. All I can say is that I had embarked on a certain course of action and was committed to following it through.

Everything went like clockwork. Except for one thing: as we walked out of the immigration area, Ali was laughing in a very cheeky way. When we asked him why, he told us proudly: 'I broke the rules. I only put US$50 in the passport!'

I couldn't believe it. He had put all of us at risk by being a stupid smartarse!

'Don't ever do that again!' I hissed at him. 'Just stick to the rules from now on.'

We collected our bags and found a phone at the airport. After the debacle at Kuala Lumpur, I insisted I make the call this time. I dialled the number and Omeed answered. I told him that Mahdi had given me his name and phone number. Omeed gave me the name of a hotel where he would meet us and instructed us to take a cab there. He sounded as though he was in a hurry and the conversation was very brief.

At this stage, I was thinking that we were getting so close. But when we arrived at the hotel, my hopes were very quickly dashed.

# 9

# PRELUDE IN JAKARTA

The hotel was a decaying, dilapidated six-storey building in a relatively undeveloped area on a bay north of Jakarta. It took us forty-five minutes to get there in a taxi from the airport and it was dark and steamy by the time we arrived at around eight o'clock. Even though the hotel was on a main road, I'd been told that access was through a door down a short alley.

The reception area was tidy enough, but it all went rapidly downhill from there. The rooms had a decidedly weary air. The furniture was intact, but was old and scratched. The whole place had seen better days—but, by then, it was little more than a final dormitory for escapees from the Middle East who were waiting for the call of people-smugglers.

I'd estimate more than a thousand people were packed into that old hotel. The majority of them were middle-aged men of Middle Eastern appearance—all talking loudly and smoking—and Moslem women wearing traditional clothes. In general, the men looked like thugs—they had long beards, were wearing dirty clothes, with thongs on their cracked feet. Most of the women wore the standard hijab over their hair, but others were in the full burqa with even their eyes hidden from view. But you didn't see them often. It seemed most of the women were largely confined to their rooms.

There was one group of women unaccompanied by any men—and they didn't seem to fit in at all. The leader was a woman who appeared to be in her early forties. With her were three younger females, aged from early teens to early twenties, and a boy. The younger people were all dressed in Western clothes and clearly came from a much wealthier background than most of our fellow travellers.

This group turned out to be pivotal to my life. The oldest of the young women was wearing carefully selected fashionable clothes and Western-style makeup. She was twenty-one, and her name was Doha. Doha was travelling with her sisters, nineteen-year-old Noor and thirteen-year-old Mary Anne, plus their brother Ali, who was ten, and their aunt Hoda. The children's mother, Hoda's sister, had died from cancer at the age of just thirty-nine. Their father was still in Iraq.

# Prelude in Jakarta

When I think about the people in that hotel, with the benefit of hindsight, I now believe that a high proportion of them were from Iran. Certainly some, it later emerged, were Iranians posing as Iraqis because they thought it would boost their chances of gaining permanent residence in Australia. Most of the people I encountered at the hotel spoke Arabic. I got the impression they were from the south-west of Iran, where the locals are of Arabic origin. I suspect many of them were from remote rural areas and had very little experience of life outside their own villages. That would explain their intolerance to other ways to life—their lifestyle was the only way they knew and, through the traditions of hundreds of years, they followed an extreme religious interpretation of the world simply because they weren't aware of alternative viewpoints.

Ali, Hussein and myself sat in the reception area while we were waiting to be allocated our rooms. There were four or five men sitting beside us. They all looked in their early thirties. Two introduced themselves as Raad and Raheem. They were very well built with massive, rough hands, like mechanics or labourers.

Raad and Raheem started talking about Doha and her family, as they walked through the reception area.

Raad was clearly disturbed by their appearance: 'How can they walk around uncovered like that? I'd like to put my hands in some grease and cover their hair and faces in it,' he thundered.

Raheem responded: 'Don't worry, they're hookers.'

They carried on saying dreadful things about Doha and her family, speculating whether they were Iraqis or from the Emirates. Increasingly, I was thinking, 'What on earth have I got myself into?'

Then Raad and Raheem began talking with us. They explained that the refugees mostly spent their days sitting in the reception area. In the evening, they would go to nightclubs or would get the receptionist to arrange for some prostitutes to come to see them. They told us some of the refugees had been at the hotel for two months, others four months. All waiting to get on a boat.

My heart sank—for the first time, the magnitude of what I'd become embroiled in hit home and it occurred to me that, in my ignorance, I'd made a big mistake.

They asked us which people-smuggler we were with. I was so naive I didn't even realise there was more than one people-smuggler.

'Is it Abu Ali or is it Abu Mustapha?'

I replied that we were with Omeed, even though we hadn't met him at that stage.

When I mentioned the number of people in the hotel, Raad and Raheem said it had been even more crowded until the previous day when Abu Ali had taken about 300 people on a big boat. It turned out the boat in question was the largest vessel to arrive in Australia at that stage and, because of the huge number of refugees involved, had triggered the Australian government's introduction of Temporary Protection Visas.

# Prelude in Jakarta

The way Raad and Raheem looked and spoke was extremely depressing. I realised they had been waiting in the middle of nowhere for months. I asked if they had the visas they needed to stay in Jakarta. Raheem responded, 'No one asks any questions.'

The conversation soon turned to what sort of work I did. Which, because of my experience in escaping from Iraq to Jordan, was a very touchy subject. I was wary of telling anyone I was a doctor because I didn't know what the reaction would be. But there was no need for me to be so secretive—Hussein told them anyway!

He added sarcastically: 'This one's not like us. He's not working class. He comes from the Nestlé generation.' In Iraq, the 'Nestlé generation' referred to people from the higher classes—they were supposed to be like chocolate, and would melt in the heat as soon as they saw hard times.

Once we'd been registered at reception, we were given the keys to two rooms. For some reason, Ali threw a tantrum and said he didn't want to share a room with Hussein. So I shared with Hussein instead. Our room was on the top floor of the hotel and, although I didn't learn this until much later, was next door to Doha and her family.

Then we just hung around, marking time, and waited for Omeed the people-smuggler to come and see us—if, indeed, he ever did. Raad and Raheem had told us not to hold our breath. They said there was no way he'd come and see us that night.

175

But they were wrong. Obviously, someone had told Omeed there was a doctor at the hotel.

A couple of hours after settling into our room, there was a knock on the door. When we answered, three men were standing there. One was in his thirties, the others in their twenties. The older man introduced himself as Omeed, the younger man was his brother Najad. The identity of the third man remained a mystery.

Omeed was neatly presented with a trimmed beard and moustache. He was shorter than me and of slim build. He was wearing a black shirt and black trousers. The outfit is common and traditional attire for Shi'ite men to wear during Ashore, which literally means the tenth day and coincides with mourning for Hussein bin Ali, the Prophet Mohammed's grandson who was killed at the battle of Karbala in the year 680. The others were in grey shirts and black trousers.

Omeed broke the silence. 'Can I come in?'

I beckoned him into the room and he was followed by Najad and the third man. They sat down and straightaway Omeed declared, 'I think I am a very lucky man. I prayed to God and God answered my prayers.'

Of course, we didn't understand what he was talking about and I asked him to explain.

'I prayed to God to provide me with two people,' he said. 'A doctor and an imam or a mullah. Before I go any further, are you a medical doctor?'

I confirmed I was.

'That's great,' he said. 'And a mullah is flying in from Tehran tomorrow.'

In my mind I was thinking, 'What on earth is this guy talking about?'

Omeed, Najad and their companion were completely ignoring Hussein. Yet Omeed was very talkative towards me.

'Can I ask you a question?' he said. 'Are you Sunni or Shi'ite?'

It was a rather strange question under the circumstances and I told him so. Then I added more diplomatically: 'However, if you insist on knowing, my family is Sunni, but I don't regard myself as either.'

He responded with a backhanded compliment. 'Eating Sunni's flesh is halal!'

This comment can have two meanings. Obviously, one is that killing Sunnis and eating their flesh is allowed. The other is that eating what Sunnis eat as their food is okay. Initially, I didn't understand what he meant and I thought it was offensive.

But he quickly explained himself.

'I'm Khurdish from Suleimaniya,' he said. Suleimaniya is one of the Khurdish provinces that is nominally Sunni but noted for being secular. 'My family is Sunni, but then I saw the light and converted to the Shi'ite faith.'

Of course, because Saddam was Sunni, outside the country a lot of Iraqis pretended to be Shi'ite. Although I may be maligning him, I suspected that Omeed also became a Shi'ite to help forge closer links with the business community.

I interrupted Omeed's chattiness and politely but firmly asked, 'So what have you got for us?'

'We have a boat leaving in three days for Australia. Would you be interested?' he asked.

'But I thought the waiting period was about three months,' I said.

He snapped back, 'It's a lot longer than that. There are hundreds of people wanting to leave.'

'So why is it possible for me to leave in three days?'

'You can leave in three days if you agree to come on my boat because I need a doctor on board,' he said flatly.

'Well, of course, *we* would be interested,' I responded with deliberate emphasis.

Omeed quickly cut in. 'No, you are coming alone. The others have to wait.'

The way he said it made me feel awkward. He was quite aggressive. But I was insistent. 'No, I came with these guys and I can't leave without them.'

Initially, Omeed refused to budge, saying they couldn't come on this boat because other people had been waiting for months. Suddenly Najad and the other man also became involved in the conversation, so all three were arguing with me. Meanwhile, poor Hussein could do nothing but stand there, listening in silence as his and Ali's fate was being decided.

I stood my ground and eventually Omeed changed his mind. 'Okay, it's a deal. All three of you can get in the boat.'

Once the plan had been agreed, Omeed asked me what I needed for the trip.

'How big is the boat and how many people will be on it?' I asked.

'It's a decent boat,' Omeed said. 'I've just fitted it with a new six-cylinder engine. There'll be about fifty people on board. I'll provide some food, but you'll need to let me know what medical supplies you want.'

Then came the devil in the detail. 'There are three women in the late stages of pregnancy and one of them is in her last month,' he added.

I became immediately concerned about what else he hadn't told me, but explained what I would need, which included drugs and tablets to prevent seasickness and vomiting—as much as he could get me, I said—and 100 litres of saline fluid, as well as canulas, needles and syringes. Then I asked, 'How are you going to get them?' Most of these supplies were only available at hospitals.

But Omeed didn't seem disturbed and, to my surprise, he responded that it wasn't a problem. 'Don't worry. I can get them. I have connections.'

'Can I see the boat?' I asked next.

'I'll take you to see it tomorrow,' Omeed assured me. 'Now tell the other guys to get their money ready.'

Omeed left the room with Najad and their companion, saying, 'Enjoy Jakarta!' As events turned out, I didn't see Najad again until he made the journey on the boat with us—though his identity as the people-smuggler's brother was kept secret then. After our voyage, I didn't keep in touch with Najad but I heard he was accepted into Australia then died in a car crash some years later.

Omeed charged me US$2000 for the boat trip. I don't know how much he charged Ali and Hussein. The usual fee was between US$5000 and $10,000. Which meant, if they really were taking as few as fifty asylum seekers, the people-smugglers were making between US$250,000 and $500,000 for every boat. More people would, of course, mean even higher profits.

But it wasn't Omeed who was making the big money; he would have been on wages. It was the overall boss who created an absolute fortune for himself out of people-smuggling. I never formally met the big boss, an Indonesian, but I saw him when he was taking the money from the refugees as we got on board the boat.

All the same, Omeed was still making a good income out of other people's misery. I learned later that he had befriended Doha's aunt Hoda and, over the month they were at the hotel, came to trust her. To such an extent that he went to their room, handed over a cloth bag and asked if Hoda would look after it for him for a few days. She thought it was curious, but agreed. At that point he said he felt as though they were honest people . . . and told her it contained $US500,000!

He came back a week later to collect the package without blinking an eye.

Omeed was not a man of great sophistication. According to Doha this was adequately demonstrated by his choice of beverage. Omeed drank tea and coffee—mixed together!

To this day, I don't know the name of the hotel or exactly where it was in Jakarta, but I do remember there was a nightclub called The Three Horses which was only a tuk-tuk ride away. Jakarta was full of prostitutes and The Three Horses was where the men at the hotel went to find them.

The majority of the men at the hotel kept themselves busy by going out and having a great time—alcohol and prostitutes were forbidden under Moslem religious traditions, but in that hotel in Jakarta, anything seemed to be fair game.

For those who couldn't go wild on the town, house calls could be arranged. I heard a story that one of the men at the hotel was in his late eighties and was blind. He was with his two sons, who arranged for a prostitute to come and spend the night with the old man. Under Islamic beliefs, being with a prostitute isn't acceptable, so she had to marry him for the time she was there.

It's called *Zawaj al Muta*—marriage for fun. It's accepted in the Shi'ite faith and allows a man and a woman to be married for a contractual period. All it needs is for someone—usually but not necessarily a religious person—to be there to witness that the two people have agreed to be married for a set length of time and for a certain amount of money.

Ali, Hussein and I were much more moderate in our behaviour. Having started to reconcile themselves to the fact that they could be at the hotel for months, Ali and Hussein were thrilled by the prospect that we would soon be leaving. Safe in the knowledge that we would be gone in the next few days, we decided we would just go for a quiet walk through the streets near the hotel and look for something simple to eat.

That turned out to be a lot more difficult and dangerous than we thought. As we walked along, we spent the entire time dodging the stampede of motorcycles in the street. Then, even though there were hundreds of street stalls, I couldn't find anything appealing to eat. It was a very rundown area and most of the stalls sold only rice with a few unappetising additions— everything looked particularly questionable to me. Eventually, Ali and Hussein took a chance and ate something, but not very much. Even they were dubious about the food on offer.

In the morning, Omeed turned up with the medical supplies. To my great relief and astonishment, he'd managed to get everything I had ordered. Clearly, his connections were every bit as good as he'd suggested the previous day.

Then Ali, Hussein and I went to a supermarket in the shopping centre nearest to the hotel and bought boxes of Coke and tinned tuna and baguettes as supplies for the boat journey. It was all going smoothly and looked promising as Omeed took me to inspect the boat that afternoon.

# Prelude in Jakarta

From start to finish, the drive to the boat was very scary. Omeed was at the wheel of his Jeep and beside him was the unidentified man who had come with him and Najad to my room. I sat in the back with the mullah, who had arrived the previous night. It dawned on me that my whole future was in the hands of people I didn't know and, frankly, had no reason to trust. They were nothing more than shady, scheming criminals. All I could do was hope we wouldn't be caught; I had no more control than that. But if I wanted to get to Australia, I had no choice but to put my life in their greedy hands.

The tension was matched by the discomfort. There was no roof on the Jeep, the tropical heat was clingingly humid, the atmosphere was dusty. It was thoroughly unpleasant.

Throughout the drive, Omeed avoided main roads as much as possible and kept checking the rear-view mirror to make sure no one was following us. Whenever we were forced to travel on a main road, Omeed was noticeably anxious. I suspected that he was known to the police and could be chased by them if he was spotted.

As though that wasn't sufficiently unnerving, he also kept reassuring me that he was very well connected—clearly implying that things could go wrong at any instant, but that he may be able to talk his way out of a difficult situation.

At the end of the drive, we arrived in the Penjaringan waterfront in the north of Jakarta and parked the vehicle in a slum area around the dock. Omeed quickly located the wooden boat that was to take us to Australia, one of dozens of almost identical and nondescript Indonesian fishing boats moored at the jetty. It was about 15 metres long, its old flaking paint light blue-green and white in colour, with a single deck and a covered area that stretched for the aft third. The food would be stored on a shelf in the covered area, which would be reserved for the women and children. Near the back of that covered section was a toilet—a 60-centimetre-square hole in the deck with a bucket, with two flimsy walls and a door for privacy.

Below deck was the engine room and a storage area for fish when the boat was being used for its original purpose. On our voyage, this would be used to house some of the catch of the day—refugees.

The boat was obviously tiny and ill-equipped for the journey ahead and I instantly realised that all of us who stepped onto it would be taking our lives in our hands. And from my point of view as the only medical professional, the fewer people who were on board, the more manageable the journey would be. I again asked Omeed how many passengers we'd be taking.

'Oh, about fifty people,' he repeated, trying to sound reassuring.

Omeed clearly thought this was an entirely reasonable number. I was horrified! I pointed out that it would be heavily overcrowded with that many people on board. But Omeed was confident the boat would comfortably cope. Only later did I find out why he was confident it would handle fifty people so easily.

# Prelude in Jakarta

We walked around the outside of the boat and Omeed asked the mullah to bless the vessel. During the ceremony, I reflected that we would need all the blessings we could muster.

When we got back to the hotel, Omeed informed me the boat would be sailing that night to the south of Java, to a secret location where the passengers would be boarding the following day. We were to leave the hotel on a bus between six and seven in the morning. He said I should take one small bag of belongings, plus my passport, but definitely no other documents. I paid him the money for my place on the boat, then after Omeed left my room to collect money from the other passengers, I spent the night restlessly preparing myself—mentally as well as organisationally—for the journey of a lifetime.

※

I woke early and clearly remember thinking that I had better eat breakfast because I didn't know when the next meal would arrive. Two fried eggs and toast, with a cup of tea—and it was all cold! Which seriously worried me because the risk of food poisoning was very real. And that was the last thing I needed in the middle of the Indian Ocean on a cramped and rotting old boat.

Outside the hotel was an equally unreliable-looking, ageing, dark blue and yellow single-deck bus. Omeed directed the passengers, about fifty of us, onto the bus and once everyone was seated on board, he left and we set off.

There was a strange atmosphere on the bus as we headed south from the hotel—a natural excitement among some of the passengers, as their dream of a new life in Australia was becoming a reality, and at the same time, a deep anxiety about the voyage we were about to undertake. And, indeed, how, where and when that voyage might end. I don't know about the others, because few of them would ever have been in a boat before, but I was well aware of the dangers and the fact that our lives were in the lap of the gods. The tension was palpable. We were heading into the complete unknown.

Even though everyone had a seat to themselves, the bus was crowded. The drive south was tortuous. The bus journey from the hotel to the bay where we would meet the fishing boat took about three hours—but we were on the bus for the whole day. We reached our destination twice before we finally stopped there. I can only imagine that either the boat wasn't ready or it wasn't safe to stop on the first two occasions.

Third time lucky, we arrived and started to disembark.

By that stage, day had given way to evening and then night. It was pitch-black apart from the searchlight that the fishing boat in the bay had firmly trained on the bus.

Omeed was there in his Jeep when we arrived. He was accompanied by an Indonesian guy in a brand new Mercedes Benz, who I assumed was the leader of the people-smuggling operation. He certainly seemed to be far wealthier than anyone else associated with the network. Alongside the two organisers were two security guards—armed with automatic weapons.

They were wearing civilian clothes, but there was no doubt they meant business and wouldn't hesitate to open fire.

To my astonishment, before long we were joined by two more busloads of refugees from different locations. Another 100 or so people to be crammed onto the fishing boat which I believed would be overloaded with just fifty! Clearly, the medical supplies that I had intended for fifty would be completely inadequate for 150 or more people.

The depths of the ordeal we were about to face were becoming terrifyingly obvious.

The people-smuggler's henchmen started collecting money from the refugees who'd arrived in the last two buses. If the refugees didn't have enough money, they were stripped of jewellery, rings, watches. Anything of value that could be quickly sold. For anyone who didn't have enough cash or belongings with them, the people-smuggler's heavies started negotiating and finding out whether they had money coming to them. A deal would be haggled for the people-smuggler to be paid later. I'm not aware that anyone was prevented from getting on the boat—but probably that was because no one would have been allowed on the buses if they couldn't provide evidence of their ability to pay.

Once we were off the bus, we had a ten-minute walk through the scrub to the sandy bay. It was remote and isolated and there were few signs of habitation apart from two or three fishermen's huts. The night was still and quiet around us.

There was no jetty in the bay, so the boat was moored in shallow water. Everyone had to be shuttled from the beach to the boat in a small tinnie, a handful at a time. Once the tinnie reached the fishing boat, we had to climb up a small ladder on to the deck. As it turned out Doha was the first person on the fishing boat—completely inappropriately dressed in her stylish top, pencil skirt and soaring platform shoes!

Doha and her family had been so horrified by the conditions in the hotel that they'd decided to take matters into their own hands for the boat journey. They assembled the creature comforts they thought they would need—a portable gas cooker, bottles of water, teabags, hand wipes, toothbrushes and toothpaste, face towels and even a refresher spray for their faces. I don't know what sort of voyage she thought she was embarking on, but I think it had closer connections to a luxury liner than the shabby fishing boat that confronted us.

Women and children were ferried to the fishing boat first and they huddled under the covered area at the back. Almost all the women were dressed in black hijab, with just their faces and palms exposed, in the traditions of rural Iraq and Iran. The mullah's wife was the only one in full burqa. Doha and her sisters were the only females in Western clothes— throughout the journey, the traditional Moslem women kept warning the three young women to stay away from their men, adding to the tension.

After that the men boarded and it was every man for himself. Mostly wearing shirts and jeans but with some of the older among them in traditional long, black robes, they jostled for the best spot as more and more people arrived.

The operation took about four hours, but before we had all boarded the fishing boat, the drama started.

One of the Iranian refugees had been a member of the Badr Brigade, defeated Iraqi soldiers who changed their allegiance and fought as a vicious militia for Iran in the war of the 1980s. They were savages, notorious for torturing Iraqi prisoners-of-war. My cousin's husband has no teeth or fingernails after being tortured by the Badr Brigade. He tells the story of three times being buried up to his neck in sand while they pulled out his teeth. He feared he would be decapitated a number of times—but they always stopped just short of killing him.

While we were waiting to board the fishing boat, the ex-Badr Brigade soldier had a fit. He was suffering from a high fever, so I gave him an aspirin injection—a treatment that isn't available these days but, at the time, it was all I had. Happily, he recovered. But, as can happen, it all came back to haunt me later. The same man I'd helped save went on to cause me no end of problems in the coming months.

Doha's sister Mary Anne, who was just thirteen, was at the centre of the other major incident. She was dressed like the innocent kid she was—in a casual one-piece top-and-shorts outfit with the cartoon character Tweetie on the front, showing her legs and with no head covering. The mullah was outraged and said if she got on board dressed like that, the boat would sink. Which, of course, sparked a good deal of panic among a group of people who were already close to their wit's end with worry about what the future held for them. Doha's aunt and

I had to intervene and pressed the mullah by asking him how he could possibly consider splitting up a family. Eventually he agreed that Mary Anne could come on board.

With such small numbers being taken in the tinnie each time, it was a protracted process; it wasn't until the early hours of the morning that everyone was on board. At that point, the appalling conditions became all too obvious. We had about 160 people on a boat that would struggle to carry fifty—and we had to share the limited accommodation with old fishing nets.

The women and children under the shelter at the back were sitting cross-legged, crammed in shoulder to shoulder. Across the rest of the boat, there was literally no space for anyone to sit down and stretch out. At the beginning, everyone was standing up on the open deck and in the hold below. It was jam-packed with people as tight as sardines in a can.

Everyone seemed to be shouting, trying to find their travelling companions and wanting to know where the doctor was. The atmosphere was frantically busy and charged with anxiety.

I was one of a few people who decided the best place, with the most space, was on top of the canopy over the rear part of the deck. Because many people were scared to go up there, we had a little more room to ourselves.

Beyond the crush of the overcrowding, my main concern was how I would be able to deal with any medical emergencies on board. I had enough medical supplies for fifty people but I was facing the prospect of dealing with three times that number.

And on top of that, of course, there were the three women in the latter stages of pregnancy.

There and then, it dawned on me what sort of human and medical catastrophes I could be dealing with. It was a shocking realisation and I knew we were all in for a horror of a journey. You didn't need to be a medical expert to figure out this was a recipe for disaster. We didn't know what the future would hold—and, frankly, even if we had a future.

We had heard on the news when we were in Jakarta about a refugee boat that had left a few days before ours and had sunk. No survivors. So our tenuous grip on life was extremely high in our consciousness.

All we had was some basic food, scant medical supplies and scarce water; no life rafts, no emergency beacons if the boat succumbed to the ocean and no escape or evacuation plan. There were a few life jackets on board. Adequate for the standard small crew of fishermen perhaps, but nowhere near enough for a passenger list of 150-plus people. Although, in fairness, I guess a life jacket wasn't going to be much use during a violent storm in the middle of the ocean anyway. In the event we had to abandon ship, it was almost certain death for everyone on board. Few, if any, could even tread water to keep themselves afloat, let alone swim.

And it wasn't only the boat that was a concern. The crew amounted to a short and skinny Indonesian fisherman who was the captain, plus two young Indonesian kids, one of them probably fourteen, the other maybe twelve years old. To get us to

Australia, they were equipped with an extremely rudimentary navigation system which wasn't even as sophisticated as the average portable satellite navigation system many of us have in our cars these days.

It was almost dawn on 7 November 1999 when the captain finally started the engine and we gradually began to move. I felt a mixture of excitement and anticipation that, at last, we were on our way—coupled with sheer terror at the dangers, traumas and potential disasters we might face.

# 10

# THE BOAT JOURNEY
# FROM INDONESIA

The early stages of our voyage of a lifetime, as we motored through the tranquil bay, were uneventful. The sea was calm, with just a gentle breeze.

While our initiation to the boat journey was reassuringly easy, it didn't stay that way for long. As anyone who's experienced ocean sailing would know, conditions change dramatically the instant you leave the shelter of a harbour or bay.

Within minutes of reaching the open seas, the waters became choppy and people started vomiting. Not only that, because of the crowding they were vomiting over each other.

And, naturally enough, as soon as one person threw up, a chain reaction followed among the others.

That set the tone. But it got much worse.

Few of the asylum-seekers had seen the ocean before, let alone been on a boat. A large proportion of them were from the rural heartland of Iraq and Iran, where the whole notion of the sea is a completely unknown concept. So this was a hugely confronting introduction to the art of ocean sailing. Our little fishing boat was like a twig in Sydney Harbour. We were completely at the mercy of the elements. It felt like we'd been thrown into the middle of a shipwreck movie set with panicked shouting and jostling and cries of '*Allahu Akbar!* [God is great!]' from many of the refugees.

Not long after the vomiting spread, some passengers, probably those most incapacitated by seasickness, started losing bladder control. The awful blended stench of vomit and urine began wafting through the boat.

Refugees who had survived trauma, conflict and, in some cases, torture in their own countries were now suffering even more indignities. They were covered in their own and other people's urine and vomit. I had never seen anything like this. It was squalid, degrading and, as though the danger of the voyage wasn't enough, a serious health hazard.

And at the age of twenty-seven, and with only two years' paltry experience since I had qualified as a doctor, I felt solely responsible for the survival and wellbeing of them all. Including three women in the late stages of pregnancy. With basic medical supplies I had ordered to cater for fifty people, not 150. Clearly it would be a miracle if we all survived.

※

After a few hours, I assumed we had reached international waters. I noticed a large, grey ship—which looked, at least to my nautically uneducated eyes, like a naval patrol boat following us. A dinghy was launched from the larger ship and drew alongside the fishing boat. As we bobbed about the ocean, the captain of the fishing boat—the man who we believed was responsible for steering us to safety—simply stepped into the dinghy and headed off to the safety and security of the ship.

The captain's action was hardly a vote of confidence in our prospects, and left our tiny, overcrowded, creaking boat under the command of two teenagers, with no obvious qualifications or merit, let alone authority.

It was some consolation when an Iraqi stepped up and announced he had served in the navy and would do what he could. He was no master mariner—but at least he was an adult!

Now, we were on our own. The ill-fated boat was battling the elements, its little engine, built for nothing more boisterous than the waters directly off the Indonesian coast, chugging and complaining in a constant battle with the increasingly angry ocean waves crashing against the hull. The accompanying soundtrack was the chilling noise of people moaning and throwing up as the result of chronic seasickness and weakly calling out for medical assistance. The only sounds from the motley collection of passengers were of strain and suffering. On top of that was the tense and unpredictable atmosphere on board. One of my biggest fears was the passengers themselves. I was convinced some of them came from extremely dangerous backgrounds, where life was a cheap commodity. To my mind, at least a couple were potential, if not actual, murderers. They were intimidating and menacing. If a serious argument had broken out, as nearly happened a number of times, I felt sure they would not hesitate to throw someone overboard. Where we came from, human life is worth as much as the bullet that ends it.

The weather didn't help. It was the wet season in the tropics. Soon it started raining—a constant, heavy, steady rain. And it continued that way for hours. All through the night and into the morning. Very quickly, people on the top deck who weren't under cover were soaked. They were completely exposed to the elements and were lying haphazardly on top of each other. Around ten or fifteen were comatose, others were simply vomiting where they lay. Below deck, the refugees were gasping for air in the space normally reserved for storing fish. And there was the added complication of diesel fumes from the engine.

With the rain, came the wind. The sea was rough, like a roller-coaster. We could see the bow of the boat crashing down into the waves and then riding up high again.

On board, conditions were rapidly worsening, with the refugees becoming weaker and weaker from dehydration. I was doing a constant round of the boat, in a lot of places having to step over bodies lying in my way and incapable of moving. I used every one of my saline drips and lines within the first twelve hours of the voyage. And there was still no indication of how long we would be at sea. From then on, it was a question of doing everything I could to keep people alive with virtually no resources.

My travelling companions Hussein and Ali were helping me in every way possible. They had absolutely no medical background, but were contributing as best they could. Most of the people on board appeared to have given up caring.

The mullah had brought his family with him: his wife, two daughters and two sons. The elder of his daughters was one of the three heavily pregnant women on board. After a few hours of lurching up and down and side to side on the ocean, she became seriously sick and needed a saline drip to keep her hydrated. She was in the covered deck area at the back of the boat, which was in her favour, because it was probably the most protected spot.

When I told her I would be putting her on a saline drip, she pushed her forearm towards me, still covered in clothing. I asked her to pull up her sleeve so I could find a suitable vein in her forearm to insert the needle. She refused. This was obviously because of her religious beliefs and a desire to retain her modesty, but her life and the life of her unborn child were at stake and I thought it was ridiculous. I asked her what unholy things I could possibly be thinking about her forearm in those circumstances. But she persistently refused to pull up her sleeve.

It wasn't until the mullah, who had been trying to organise and comfort other people on board, acknowledged her parlous state and intervened that I was able to treat her. He reassured her that I was a doctor and it was all right for me to see her forearm. At that point, she pulled up her sleeve and I inserted the drip into a vein. But because of the rocking of the boat, I fell on top of her in an unintentionally provocative manner. It drew gasps of horror from everyone who saw it.

There was no stand to secure the bag of saline solution, even if it could be secured on the rollicking deck, so someone had to hold it up at all times to maintain the flow of life-preserving fluid. Once the mullah's daughter was on the drip, her condition stabilised. But it was an extremely close call. I don't dare to think what would have happened if any of the pregnant women had gone into labour on board the fishing boat. There were absolutely no facilities, not even adequate clean water. I fear it could have been a story with a tragic ending.

The other two pregnant women were also in a bad way and needed anti-emetic injections—drugs effective against vomiting and nausea—which I'd reserved especially for them. One of them was part of a family with three generations of women on board—the grandmother who was probably in her sixties, the mother who I guess was in her thirties and very pregnant, plus the daughter who was about fourteen. They were all nearly comatose from vomiting and dehydration.

I was one of only about ten people who weren't routinely vomiting. I think I was simply too busy to feel seasick.

There were two men in their forties who were particularly ill. One was in a coma, and I seriously thought either or both of them could die at sea. Fortunately, they both survived.

The mullah's answer to the unfolding human catastrophe was to order the people on board to start breaking down their *Turbahs*—small tablets made of soil or clay from Kerbala, which is reputed to have been mixed with the blood of Mohammed's grandson Hussein, who died in battle there. The *Turbahs* are normally used in prayer, but now the mullah was suggesting that the token gesture of throwing the soil into the sea would calm the waves. His followers did as he instructed. But, despite their actions, I don't recall the surge and swell of the ocean subsiding in the slightest!

Along the way, one of the passengers went around telling people: 'If you have a passport, now's the time to tear it up and throw it overboard. And do the same with any other identification documents.'

No one ever explained who gave the order or why, but as the rumour spread the majority of people, including me, followed the instruction. Our resistance was low and, by that stage, most of us simply followed orders. On reflection, it wasn't a smart move—a passport could have helped significantly in establishing our identity later on.

Because of the conditions, none of us had any idea how, when or where this nightmare was going to end. It may sound ridiculous, but my main fear was that we would completely miss our target destination, Christmas Island, and sail straight to the South Pole!

Before we sailed, we'd been told the aim was to reach Christmas Island in about thirty to forty hours. The back-up plan, however unlikely it now sounds, was that if we hadn't found the island within three days, we should turn the boat east and sooner or later, we'd run into the west coast of Australia. But God alone knows where!

At one point, someone shouted, 'Sharks!' And, believe it or not, amid the medical disaster on the fishing boat, everyone strained to get a look at the killers lurking not far from us. Frankly, I think they saw some high-finned creatures leaping out of the water—which were more likely to be dolphins than sharks—but it showed how few of the passengers knew anything about the sea or marine life.

By this stage, we were all at the point of exhaustion and despair. The atmosphere on board was only getting worse. As well as being sick, most people had been sitting in a cramped position for more than a day and tempers were becoming quite frayed. Arguments were breaking out—especially within family groups. We were tired and filthy, with no idea if or when we would set foot on land again. We had no expectations because we simply didn't know what was going to happen to us.

# The Boat Journey from Indonesia

The rain remained constant and it was pitch black. The crashing of the ocean was almost deafening and the backdrop was the moaning of the passengers vomiting on each other. It was like a cargo of dead and dying fish spread across the decks.

Before we started on this voyage, I thought that when it was dark, we would be able to navigate by the constellations and stars in the night sky. It wasn't like that at all. You couldn't see anything because of the rain and complete cloud cover. Instead of my illusion, it was like ink. No lights, not even the lights of passing ships.

Finally, dawn brought a new day—and with it, the rain cleared, the wind dropped and the ocean conditions calmed. And as the weather eased, it didn't seem quite so chaotic on board. The day drifted slowly by and then, around seven o'clock in the evening after something like thirty-six hours at sea, we saw lights.

The Iraqi sailor who'd become our captain-by-default was perched on top of the rear deck cover and was one of the first to spot the glow. Not many people were awake or alert enough to see the lights by this stage—and rather than raise false hopes, we checked and double-checked to make sure we weren't just seeing the lights from a ship.

Silently, those of us in the know focused our eyes on the lights to check for any signs that could tell us exactly what we were about to encounter.

The glows were few and far between but provided strong hope that we were close to land. None of us wanted to make assumptions, though. A false pronouncement that we had spotted land at this stage would have been utterly devastating for everyone on board.

It took about twenty minutes before we realised it couldn't be anything else but land. And, most likely, inhabited land. That in itself was quite remarkable, since the navigation equipment had been so rudimentary and had been left, for the majority of the voyage, in the hands of an ex-Iraqi sailor and a couple of Indonesian kids.

The realisation that we were near the end of our ocean ordeal brought an enormous sense of relief coupled with eager anticipation.

We weren't quite there, with more than an hour of sailing to go, but we could almost smell the safe harbour of where we were heading—which we were pretty sure was Christmas Island.

Navigation wasn't a problem now. We just headed straight for the lights. In fact, as we closed in on the lights, the navigation equipment was ditched overboard. I can only think it was a precaution so the authorities couldn't discover exactly where we'd come from.

We were probably about one nautical mile away from the island when our boat was intercepted by an Australian Federal Police vessel. It was like a small military landing craft, made of metal with a blunt, square front. There were three officers on board, along with a driver.

The police boat came alongside and someone shouted through a megaphone: 'Stop! Where are you from?'

One of the passengers on our boat bellowed back: 'We are asylum-seekers!'

And I thought to myself, 'We've made it!'

That first contact with the Federal Police meant that we'd reached our destination, and while I was jubilant, I also had to reflect on how fortunate we had been. Without a word of exaggeration, people could have died if we'd had to spend another day at sea. The medical supplies had long gone by that stage and food was rapidly running out. Passengers would very quickly have become critically ill through a combination of dehydration and a lack of nourishment.

The Federal Police officers, two men and a woman, were appalled at the conditions on the boat when they first clambered on deck. They were wearing gloves but had no masks. And the smell must have been putrid—they were holding their hands over their mouths and noses but, despite their best efforts, were still dry-retching.

I met them as they came on board and took them straight to Doha because she was the only other person who spoke good English.

The first thing the Federal Police asked was: 'Where's your navigation equipment?' Of course, by that stage, it was at the bottom of the ocean, never to be traced.

The navigation equipment wasn't the only casualty. I think

someone sabotaged the vessel by putting sea water in with the engine oil as soon as the Federal Police made contact—to guarantee we couldn't sail any further in that boat.

Quickly, the process of unloading the asylum-seekers began. The police gave us strict instructions: 'Come off the boat as you are. No belongings. We'll bring the belongings off the boat and sort them out later.'

I was fortunate—I was in the first group taken into the Federal Police barge and ferried to Christmas Island, where we stepped onto a wooden walkway, made our shaky way to the end and finally alighted onto solid ground. And, believe me, putting my feet on dry land for the first time in thirty-six hours was a feeling of sheer elation. Though it would take more than an hour for my body to settle; at first, I kept feeling the rocking motion of the ocean and I was noticeably unsteady on my feet as I ventured tentatively on to shore.

Still, I recall thinking, 'Everything's going to be rosy from now on.'

Our expectations were that we would go through the immigration processing and would then travel to Sydney or Perth. On reflection, we didn't know anything!

The transfer of refugees was all very efficient but, by its very nature, wasn't quick. The Federal Police instructed us to wait at an assembly point immediately at the end of the walkway. They erected a tripod and camera, told us to line up and took a photograph of each person in turn. Then we were tagged with a bracelet, like a hospital tag when you're going in for an operation; each one had a number on it.

There were buses on hand to take everyone to wherever our destination would be. One bus would fill up, then the police would take the barge out again to collect another load of passengers. They did this again and again; the whole process took about four hours.

Once we had landed, Doha and I stayed at the end of the walkway to translate the instructions from the Federal Police to the other passengers. Finally, everyone was off the boat and we were able to board the last bus. I remember making small talk on the journey and asking Doha about herself, but she was preoccupied with other things—after the squalor of our journey, she was keen to go to the toilet in slightly more pleasant surroundings!

# 11

# CHICKEN AND HAM ON CHRISTMAS ISLAND

Our destination that day was the Christmas Island indoor basketball stadium, about a ten-minute bus ride away, the only building on the island at the time that could take 160 people under one roof.

It was close to midnight by the time we arrived.

Absolute chaos reigned. Everyone wanted a shower, but there were only three showers for men and three for women. So, after their thirty-six-hour ordeal, the refugees were queuing for hours to sluice themselves down.

Naturally, there were more queues for the food. It was being brought in as quickly as the officials could manage—rice with honey chicken wings from the local takeaway shop. Even with the regular arrival of refugee boats, the shop must have found it difficult to cope with such large orders. Another problem was that the average Iraqi doesn't mix sweet and sour flavours, so while the meal sounds tasty, it was a completely foreign culinary experience. I ate it because I was ravenous, but a lot of people didn't. Many of them were simply too tired or too sick to eat.

Yoga-style mattresses were spread all over the floor, along with huge bags of clothes from the Salvation Army and other welfare organisations. As soon as we had arrived, the Federal Police started distributing clothes so the refugees could change out of the attire they'd worn all the way from Jakarta.

I was clad in a shirt, jeans and sneakers, which were all soaking wet. But I refused to take any of the charity items. I felt it was beneath me to accept charity. I'd never done it before and I wasn't about to now. I preferred to stay in my own drenched and dirty clothes. It was a completely stupid approach. Before long, it was graphically demonstrated to me that my family, my name and my prestigious background counted for absolutely nothing in these straitened circumstances. Pretty soon, my attitude changed.

Once everyone had been showered and fed, they milled around and gossiped. The stadium was as noisy as a busy indoor market.

I talked to the Federal Police chief on the island and told him I could speak English and was happy to act as an interpreter or provide any other assistance I could. Doha spoke fluent English as well and offered to act as an interpreter for the women and children in the group.

After that, it was a matter of the Federal Police counting the number of asylum-seekers and taking their names. They quickly discovered that some people had kept their passports and documentation, while others, like me, had thrown them overboard during the voyage.

Because I was interpreting during this whole process, I was among the last to be registered. We didn't finish until early in the morning.

Everyone was exhausted by that stage and, even though there was no separation between the men and women, it was simply a case of settling down on your mattress, closing your eyes and having the first decent sleep in days.

When we woke, we were shown to a barbecue area at the back of the basketball courts for a breakfast of cornflakes, toast, jam, tea, with milk and sugar. That didn't go down well at all with some of the refugees.

The mullah, representing the boat people, came up to me as the interpreter and said: 'Please thank them for breakfast, but we don't eat that sort of food. We want the food we're accustomed to.'

I couldn't believe it. We were asylum-seekers who'd been picked up after a traumatic voyage from Indonesia and here we were, making demands already. I didn't even bother passing on the message.

The Federal Police had gathered up all our bags from the boat and added tags with the appropriate numbers. Not everyone had a bag with them; some people had lost their belongings along the way. The dirty items of clothing were taken from us and given a damned good wash in industrial-strength machines.

During the morning, they allowed us back into the barbecue area behind the basketball stadium. It was in the open air, but bordered by fences. From there, we could see the coast and, further away, the boat that had carried us on the dangerous voyage from Indonesia bobbing on the water. The authorities refused to bring it closer to shore because they thought it was a biological hazard—which I'm sure it was.

In stark contrast to the constant rain, winds and storms we had experienced for much of the voyage, the weather was clear, the sky was blue and it was warm and welcoming. It felt just beautiful to be safe and secure on land and waiting to start a new life in Australia.

But the illusion wasn't to last and I soon experienced the first indication that all was not as straightforward and jolly as we had assumed.

In the barbecue area, a Federal Police officer came up to me and said words to the effect of: 'Enjoy it while you're here because you'll be going to the mainland and the place where they'll be holding you isn't the sort of location you'll want to stay for very long. But your detention will be indefinite.'

The alarm bells started to ring.

❦

In due course, the Federal Police, who were extremely kind and understanding, brought us lunch. This time, there was some cheese, which would suit the Iraqi and Iranian diet. And there were sandwiches.

Now, you'd think sandwiches would be a low-risk proposition. But these sandwiches very nearly caused a riot. As soon as I tasted them, I realised they were ham!

I'd always eaten pork, so it wasn't a problem for me. But the meat of the pig is one of three things that Moslems are forbidden to eat—along with blood-based products and meat from animals that have died of natural causes rather than being slaughtered. Being Moslems, many of the refugees would never have tasted ham or pork, so they didn't know what they were eating. I'm sure they thought they were eating chicken. And, since they were now recovering their appetites, everyone tucked into their sandwiches enthusiastically.

By mid-afternoon, the Federal Police realised they'd blundered.

One officer came over to me and said something like: 'We've made a rather unfortunate mistake.' He told me about the ham sandwiches, which of course wasn't news to me, and added, 'Come with me, I need to explain to them.'

I took a rather more pragmatic approach and tried to stop him, saying they wouldn't have a clue they'd eaten ham. 'You'll just be creating a problem if you tell them,' I warned. 'Look at them. No one suspects anything. Leave it as it is—but make sure it doesn't happen again.'

# Chicken and Ham on Christmas Island

I was concerned providing the asylum-seekers with the full details of their lunchtime repast could lead to a major insurrection. But, for all the noble reasons possible, the Federal Police officer insisted on confessing to what had happened.

He called everyone together in the basketball stadium, sat them down in the bleachers and asked me to interpret. Effectively what he said was: 'Look, we've made a mistake—we gave you ham in the sandwiches. And we're very sorry about it.'

He couldn't have created more havoc if he'd tried. Everyone immediately started shouting and wailing. Then the mullah stood up and gave an impassioned speech. From what I remember, he said: 'We left our countries escaping persecution and dictatorship to come here and face this complete humiliation.'

At that point proceedings became even more frayed when a Federal Police officer started yelling at the refugees: 'Stop that! Keep quiet!'

Of course, the refugees did anything but stop it and keep quiet. Eventually, the officer shouted, 'Shut up!'

Well, that was the last straw. Every one of the refugees seemed to believe this was the ultimate insult on top of the humiliation they were already feeling. It was absolute pandemonium. People were shouting and yelling insults, demanding action. Arms were flailing in the air. I thought the refugees were going to take over the stadium.

Clearly, at least one Federal Police officer thought the same—because he pulled his gun out of its holster and started brandishing it in the air.

I don't remember whether any shots were fired to try to calm the mayhem. I doubt it. But in that atmosphere, anything was possible. These were seriously disturbing moments. But, fortunately, once the refugees saw the gun, things slowly began to settle down.

Now, it's always easy to be wise after the event, but to this day, I think a lot of unnecessary angst could have been avoided simply by not telling the refugees they'd just been eating ham. And I made no effort to avoid informing the Federal Police officer that I'd told him so!

Soon after, a representative of the refugees approached me and said they didn't want to be served with meat any more. Instead, they wanted fish. That night we dined on fish and chips. Which I, for one, found a thoroughly satisfactory compromise.

After dinner on Day Two at Christmas Island, the processing began. This involved officials going through documents, checking the passports of those who still had them.

Again, I had to help out because there were a few people, from both Iraq and Iran, who couldn't read or write. That was an eye-opening experience for me. I'd never met anyone who couldn't read or write.

The processing officers required very basic information such as date of birth, age, family members, home town and nationality. But it's all a mystery if you're not literate. A significant proportion of the refugees were from remote rural areas where life had revolved around subsistence farming and survival. Some people even had to leave a thumb print on their statement because they couldn't sign their name.

It was also fascinating to discover that many of the refugees who were in their fifties and sixties had the same date of birth, 1 July. Apparently, based on Iraqi law, anyone who didn't know their date of birth was registered by the government as being born on 1 July, the middle day of the year. Literally millions of Iraqis from the older generations are registered as having this date as their birthday.

Processing took hour upon hour of tedious documentation. People were queuing for long periods, based on the number they'd been given when they first set foot on Christmas Island. Doha and I were the only interpreters.

On the third morning, the Federal Police organised a game of indoor soccer in the basketball stadium. Which was fun and was going well until one of the detainees injured his ankle. Pretty badly as it happens. I strapped it up, but it was serious enough to warrant an x-ray. Christmas Island's only resident doctor was summoned. He was a lovely guy, but a young doctor without a great deal of experience. He was of the same opinion that the injured detainee needed hospital treatment. So off we went to the base hospital, where the x-ray revealed a fractured ankle, which required full admission.

Once all the procedures had been completed, the patient was taken into the ward. The fracture literally turned out to be a lucky break for him. Because of the injury he was flown directly to Perth, where his brother lived, for surgery. And once he was there, his application for asylum was processed much faster than ours.

While we were there, the resident doctor showed me around the hospital. There were two operating theatres where he could carry out emergency procedures like caesareans and appendectomies.

The young doctor told me he was relishing his time on the island. To the extent that he tipped me off that if ever I managed to complete my medical qualifications in Australia, there were plenty of worse places to be. The money was good and he assured me the whole experience was a lot of fun. Enticing though his description was, my ambitions lay in other directions.

After the hospital tour, I was driven around the island. And, yes, it's absolutely true what they say about the crabs on Christmas Island. They're everywhere!

We were literally driving on crabs, crunching under the wheels. I understand there are somewhere between 50 and 120 million crabs on the island—and it's estimated around half a million are killed on the roads each migration season. In fact, the roads were red with crabs that had been crushed by the vehicles.

Back at the basketball stadium, I was given more advice about my future in what I hoped would become my new homeland. This time, it came from a Federal Police officer. He suggested I should go to Tasmania, then pointed to one of his colleagues who he said was Tasmanian, singled out a scar on his colleague's shoulder and claimed it showed where his second head had been removed! I knew very well it was actually the result of an operation on his clavicle. Even on Christmas Island, the people of the Apple Isle were copping it!

It was a momentous afternoon. As the shadows lengthened and sunset approached, we were once more ushered outside into the barbecue area. Looking through the wire fence and out into the bay, close to the horizon, we could see the Indonesian fishing boat that had carried us on the treacherous voyage from Indonesia.

The Federal Police said to us, 'Come and see this. With a bit of luck, it'll signal an end to your ordeal.'

We all watched as explosives were detonated on the fishing boat. While it had been solid enough to complete our journey, it was no match for the explosives. In an instant, the boat disintegrated, with wreckage flying high into the sky.

It was a formative moment, because it symbolised the fact that there was no turning back. Whatever fate brought us was largely out of our hands now. But I think most people felt a sense of excitement that a new chapter in our lives was about to start.

After the destruction of our boat, the Federal Police joined us in a game of volleyball, which was a wonderful, friendly and relaxed event. There were some good players and some not-so-good players, but everyone joined in happily. It was a prime example of how sport unites people from all sorts of backgrounds.

Those were comfortable and comforting days on Christmas Island. Had we known what the next chapter would involve, I'm not sure we would have been quite so eager to move on to the mainland.

The next morning, I was woken early with an urgent request from the Federal Police. Another boat of asylum-seekers had arrived off Christmas Island and they wanted me to act as interpreter.

We went in small boats to meet the refugees. I was in a boat with only one other guy, who appeared to be of Indonesian origin. While we were separated from the Federal Police officers in the other tinnies, he hurriedly asked me, 'Have you spoken to your family yet?'

'No, I haven't had a chance,' I replied. 'And, anyway, we're not allowed access to a phone on the island.'

He reached into his bag and pulled out a satellite phone.

'Here, call your mum,' he said as he thrust the phone into my hands. 'Tell your mum that you've arrived safely in Australia and that she may not hear from you again for a year or two. But that you'll be safe and she shouldn't be upset. But don't tell anyone else that I gave you the phone to call her.'

## Chicken and Ham on Christmas Island

The last time I'd spoken to my mother was the night before we left Jakarta, so I didn't need any persuasion to make the call.

Luckily, she was home and answered the phone.

She was in a highly distressed state and was convinced I was dead. She couldn't believe it when she heard my voice and found out I was alive. There had been reports in Iraq of a boat missing and believed sunk in the waters between Indonesia and Australia and she had convinced herself that I was on the stricken vessel.

I went on to explain that she might not hear from me for a while because I was going to be held in a detention centre and wouldn't be allowed to make phone calls. Of course, I gave her various assurances that I would be safe and well, though in the circumstances, whatever I said must have sounded hollow.

The entire phone call can't have lasted more than ninety seconds. But it was one of the most important calls I have ever made.

I have never been able to say an adequate thank you to the guy in the boat who let me use his phone. As well as giving me the opportunity to reassure my mother I was alive and safe, he took an enormous risk. He could have been severely punished if the authorities had discovered what he did. I never knew his name. I have no idea what became of him or where he is now. But I owe him an enormous debt of gratitude.

The latest boat to arrive was even smaller than ours but, to compensate, there were considerably fewer people on board.

No more than forty, many of them children. The irony was that they were all Vietnamese and I could do nothing to help with the interpreting.

It was obvious they had suffered over an extended voyage—their journey had been much longer than ours—and everyone on board was in pretty bad shape. They looked exhausted and malnourished, although I formed the impression they were much better prepared and had a far deeper understanding of the ocean than we did.

Once we'd done everything we could in the short term, we returned to the island and briefed the Federal Police before they took out the barge to collect the passengers.

As we'd already learned, facilities on the island were rudimentary. Now it was the turn of the Vietnamese. They came ashore much as we had and were shuttled to the same basketball court where we were sleeping. In a token gesture of segregation, the Federal Police put up a rope to divide the two groups and instructed us not to mix with them in case we contracted diseases from each other. But, to be honest, we were only a few metres apart and, while it may have eased their minds, the division was little or no protection from a wide range of life-threatening conditions.

The next day, the charter planes arrived on Christmas Island to take us on the next leg of our journey. Life was about to take a distinct downward spiral.

# 12

# THE CURTIN COMES DOWN

Climbing onto the aircraft on Christmas Island was a sad moment. I can't speak highly enough of the way the Federal Police had treated us—with respect, civility, generosity and good humour. They were absolutely outstanding ambassadors for Australia.

The aircraft that were to fly us away from the friendly existence on Christmas Island were small four-engine commercial jets capable of carrying about seventy people. Already on the plane were half a dozen or so staff from Australian Correctional Management (ACM), the organisation that ran the mainland detention centre. The guards on the plane were all Australian, mostly men, and a couple of women. They looked tough and hardened and had a distinctly military appearance, wearing sandy-brown uniforms—shirts, pants, wide-brimmed hats and prominent belts with handcuffs. And they were as harsh as they appeared; a completely different breed from the Federal Police. We noticed immediately that they didn't engage in conversation and were much rougher in their whole approach.

Doha was on the first flight out, but the Federal Police decided I should stay and act as interpreter until the last of the three flights left. Not that I realised it at the time, but the delay put me at a considerable disadvantage because it established me at the far end of the processing line.

Before I left, the Federal Police chief had a quick chat with me and said: 'I wish you all the best, but remember, it's not going to be easy. Don't be surprised if you're sent to the desert. Just bite your tongue and do your time.'

It was good advice, which, in time, faced with the absolute degradation and humiliation of the detention centre, I chose to ignore.

The officer's prediction that it wasn't going to be easy did indeed prove correct. My flight left Christmas Island late in the morning and was uncomfortable. At a little over two hours, it wasn't a particularly taxing journey, but we weren't offered even as much as a glass of water in that time. Then I remember looking out the window as we started to descend and seeing nothing but desert.

It was early afternoon when we landed at Curtin Air Base

near Derby in the north-west of Western Australia, which was to be our home for the indefinite future.

After the plane landed, we taxied across the tarmac to our disembarkation point. When the engines died, so did the air-conditioning on board. We were left sitting in the increasingly stifling aircraft in the blazing heat of the Australian desert awaiting instructions. Waiting . . . and waiting.

It seemed we were lodged there on the runway for the best part of an hour. We were absolutely sweltering. And the atmosphere among the detainees was increasingly unnerved, too, as we sat in silence wondering what was about to happen. A couple of people tried to stand up, but were immediately shouted at by the guards, in an aggressive and abusive manner, and ordered to sit down. Apart from issuing the occasional surly instruction, the guards didn't talk to us.

It soon dawned on me that this was a disastrous situation and we were in serious trouble.

Eventually, a bus drove across the tarmac and parked next to the aircraft, and we were ushered from one to the other for the short trip across the air base to the detention centre next door. We went through the checkpoint at the front gates of Curtin Detention Centre, past the signs warning unauthorised personnel not to enter, inside the wire fences, until we drew up alongside the plain demountable building which served as the administration block.

As we drove through the gates, we were greeted by detainees, mostly Middle Eastern, who'd arrived before us.

They lined up on both sides of the bus, shouting and pleading with us for information about their relatives who had also tried to make the dangerous journey from Indonesia by boat. There was an element of desperation about them.

Others were shouting warnings and asking: 'Why did you come here? It's awful.'

Climbing from the bus was like walking into an oven. The heat hit us immediately and, to make matters worse, seemed to be reflected from the desert earth.

Straightaway, a guard was there with a permanent marker pen, writing a number on our wrists and shoulders. It wouldn't wash off. And that was our new identity. From then until the day I left Curtin, I was known by the authorities only as 982. Never by my name. Just my number.

Later, we were given photo identity badges with our allocated number.

It was, as many things were in Curtin, completely dehumanising. And, I feel certain, it was purposely so. Our initial contact with the Curtin officers was equally as confronting and depressing.

'Go home,' they were telling us. 'If you think Australia's a land of milk and honey, think again.' And: 'Be careful, there are deadly spiders and snakes all over the camp and if they bite you, they can kill you in a few minutes. There's nothing you'll be able to do.'

Welcome to Australia.

❧

Curtin is around 35 kilometres south-east of Derby, six hours from Port Hedland and about thirty hours by road from Perth. Set firmly amid the red dirt of the north-western Australian desert.

It has subsequently been described by the Refugee Action Council (Victoria) as 'the worst of Australia's hellholes. It was the most secret, most isolated and the most brutal.' The immigration minister of the time, Philip Ruddock, was quoted in 2011 as describing Curtin as the 'most primitive' processing centre. He wasn't wrong.

From the outset, the commander of Curtin, Greg Wallis, didn't like me. And I didn't like him, one little bit.

And certainly it didn't help matters when I initiated actions to highlight the plight of the refugees being held under such inhuman conditions.

Wallis was middle-aged, about 175 centimetres tall and of an average build, with short blond hair. In appearance, there wasn't much to single him out from the crowd. But his attitude completely rubbed me up the wrong way. I found him to be almost unfailingly arrogant and dismissive.

Wallis worked for the Department of Immigration, over-seeing the day-to-day operations of Curtin, which were carried out by the ACM staff. He later ran Baxter Detention Centre.

It was no coincidence that plenty of people who spoke up against the way things were run in Curtin found themselves in solitary confinement, in a unit that became known as The Hotel, or in Derby Police Station. Perth barrister Laurie Levy, who later represented me, was quoted in the *Australian* in March 2001 as saying: 'Detainees were locked up in The Hotel at his [Wallis's] whim.'

ACM was a private correctional company. Most of the officers at Curtin appeared to come from a pretty rough background. Many were completely lacking an education—to the extent that some could barely read and write. Brutality was among their more common traits. The Australians were generally the most evolved and normally had higher positions. There were a lot of other nationalities, though—Americans and Pacific Islanders were the two main groups. They were like the worst hoodlum security guards and bouncers you'd find outside bars and clubs on a Saturday night. Physical intimidation was their greatest weapon. Let's face it, they had little else to offer. Threats of violence, even if they weren't carried out, were frequent. Verbal abuse was constant—name calling and derogatory remarks. We were treated like a sub-species, somewhere between the animal kingdom and human beings. There wasn't even the merest hint of respect.

The detention centre itself was not a pretty sight. It was simply an expanse of arid dirt surrounded by a high wire fence, covered with green shadecloth and topped with barbed wire. Inside, our accommodation was large, rectangular, metal-framed military-style tents which each contained about twenty stretcher-type beds. But the canvas of the tent roof and walls offered little protection from the torrential rain. And, believe me, it rained heavily and often in the tropical climate of Curtin.

# The Curtin Comes Down

The detention centre was divided into compounds with military-sounding names: Alpha, Bravo, Charlie, Delta, Echo, Foxtrot and The Hotel. I was in Delta Compound. Most people were in Alpha and Charlie. Foxtrot was the management area and The Hotel was the punishment unit. Over the months, I became very familiar with the hospitality on offer in The Hotel and spent the last forty days of my time in Curtin in its sparse facilities.

There were communal toilets and a tap in each compound, but we didn't have any containers to store water. Each time you wanted a drink, you had to go to the tap.

Every night, the compounds were locked down at seven o'clock. As I remember, the curfew continued until seven the next morning. Although you could occasionally get away with walking around your own compound, the majority of detainees just went to their tents and stayed there. We'd be woken around midnight by a guard shining a torch in our faces, checking our identity.

Our detention was also played out to the sometimes deafening noise from the adjoining Royal Australian Air Force base. Around twice a week, the RAAF jet fighters would take off and land, thundering over the detention centre. It was another reminder of our place as uninvited guests.

Shortly after we arrived, a woman of apparently high rank from the Department of Immigration came to talk to us. She addressed all the detainees gathered in the open air outside the Foxtrot administration building, using a loudspeaker to deliver her message. As I recall, it was explained that we were in Curtin Detention Centre and we were informed in no uncertain terms that life had changed dramatically. She used hateful words like: 'You are not welcome here. The Australian people do not want you here. You will be detained indefinitely. It could be a very long time and there is no guarantee that you will be allowed to stay in this country. However, if you choose to go back to your homeland, we can help facilitate your return.'

The hostility was palpable.

We were also sternly warned against attempting to escape: 'If you escape, the area is full of snakes and saltwater crocodiles, but it's more likely you'll die of thirst and starvation because the nearest town is 200 kilometres away and you'll get lost in the desert.'

She also assured us that any escapee would be quickly spotted because everyone would realise that an individual with an unusual complexion would have to come from the detention centre.

Our bags had been taken from us when they were loaded on the plane. And once we arrived at Curtin, they were placed in storage. All we were allowed were the clothes we stood in. We were provided with toothbrushes, toothpaste, thongs for our feet and towels. Which, it was made clear, we were not, under any circumstances, to lose.

Anyone who admitted to having money when they arrived had it confiscated and put in a safe—although some of the detainees did manage to hide their money and keep it with them.

The first formality was to have our photos taken for the identity tags. We were queued up for a while doing that. Then, once the task was completed, we were simply released to wander off among the other detainees. Just left to our own devices. As an absolute stranger in a foreign land, with no contacts and no one to care for you or offer support, that doesn't give you a feeling of welcome or belonging. Or even being worthwhile as a person.

Like everyone else in Curtin, I felt completely lost, isolated and helpless.

I went to look for Doha because I wanted to find out what had happened to her group. They were just being fed when I tracked them down. Her spirits were low. Her group had been through a similar experience to ours before being settled into Charlie compound, not far from where I was in Delta.

The first thing she showed me was the washing area. A bank of washing machines and a 4.5-litre container of washing fluid. I slipped a towel over me and threw my clothes into the machines. There were no driers—you didn't need them in that desert climate. We simply put the clothes outside or wore them wet. Either way, they dried in a matter of minutes.

Much worse, though, were the toilet and shower facilities. They were worse than anything I had ever seen before—or since, for that matter. Worse than the most rudimentary squat toilets in developing nations.

The problem wasn't the toilets and showers themselves. The problem was that the vast majority of the detainees— from remote rural areas of Iran and Iraq—had never seen anything like them and had no idea how to use them properly. Rather than sitting on the Western-style toilets, most of the detainees would stand on the seats and squat in their normal fashion. Of course, that created all sorts of appalling and insanitary conditions in the toilet cubicles. Added to that, the seats obviously weren't intended for standing on, and often broke. There were a series of injuries—in some cases, quite serious—to people who'd plunged to the ground when the toilet seat broke as they were squatting on it. I remember a man suffering a deep gash to his foot and being rushed to Derby Hospital for treatment, as the result of one mishap.

Worse still, some asylum-seekers wouldn't use the toilets at all. In an absolutely disgusting ritual, one detainee would routinely defecate in the shower. What wasn't washed away, he would scoop up in one of the plastic food containers and leave it on the window ledge above the shower head. We only discovered this was going on when a plastic container was dislodged from its perch and spilled over another detainee using the shower. Beyond anything else, it was a serious health hazard and made me shiver with horror.

It could have all been so easily avoided with some simple, friendly induction into our new facilities and way of life. Although the detainees would have found it different to their own, I'm sure they would have changed their behaviour over a relatively short time.

The first night at Curtin was utterly depressing. Just the sheer realisation of the awful circumstances. And the fact that Curtin would be our home for an indefinite period, with no guarantees about our fate. On Day One, already there was no end in sight.

Even before we'd settled in, the first flashpoint emerged. Cigarettes.

While smoking is generally frowned upon in Australia these days, the majority from our boat were smokers. And our boat was symptomatic of the rest of the detainees. These people were addicted to nicotine—so cigarettes were a crucial part of their daily routine.

In the early days, detainees were given three cigarettes a day. Non-smokers like myself would trade our handout with other detainees and some guards also would boost supplies. But soon, because of the growing number of detainees and the rapidly increasing demand and cost, there were no more cigarette handouts. There was no black market, either, because supplies had run dry.

It was only a short time before the first riot started. A large group of detainees gathered inside the detention centre gates demanding cigarettes.

I tried to act as an interpreter and intermediary between the protesters and the guards. But it was spectacularly unsuccessful. Because of my background from a nominally Sunni family, most of the protesters, who were predominantly Shi'ite, rejected me. 'We escaped from Saddam, we don't want another leader who's a Sunni!' they shouted at me.

These people were accusing me of being on the side of the detention centre guards and management. Which, clearly, I wasn't. Neither was I making any attempt to become their leader. In these confronting circumstances, I was busy enough attempting to look after myself.

The authorities at Curtin filmed the whole incident, identified the people they thought were the ringleaders and carted them off to the police station in Derby for a few days. It was a horrible explosive atmosphere to be living in. But at least things settled a little once the punishment had been meted out.

That was the last we saw of the free cigarettes. And the detainees seemed to realise there and then that the game was up and cigarettes were never an issue again.

The incident became known in the detention centre as The Cigarette Uprising and, on reflection, it was a dreadfully unfortunate start for me. It set the tone of things to come.

At the beginning, there was absolutely nothing to do during the day. Rather like an international flight that lasts for months, meal times became a highlight, because they were punctuation marks amid the boredom. Yet, at the same time, meals were a nightmare. We would stand in queues for a couple of hours every day for each of our three meals. Part of the waiting was simply the process of serving food to that many people, but largely it was because meal times were used as a roll call. As we stood in the queues, guards would check our ID numbers and tick us off the list.

The meals themselves were awful. For breakfast, we had cornflakes, a small container of milk, two slices of toast, a sachet of jam and a sachet of butter. We were given colourless and tasteless mincemeat and colourless and tasteless spaghetti for lunch and for dinner. With lunch we were given an apple, with dinner an orange. They were alternated each day.

For Easter, we were given a boiled egg as a treat.

It seemed to me we were the victims of the corporate system which was operating the detention centre. A lot of time and effort appeared to be spent on counting the cost of keeping the detainees and maximising the difference between that and the money the federal government was paying for the management services.

Shortly after we arrived, we noticed that some detainees were smuggling food into the tents. Mainly it was toast, jam and butter. Which was stupid, because the food attracted snakes, lizards, rodents, ants and all sorts of insects.

I saw quite a few snakes around the camp, mainly after dark. It was the middle of the desert, after all, and the animals obviously viewed the area as their domain. It wasn't long before one of the detainees found and killed a snake in his tent. That was traumatic enough. But the incident had plenty more ramifications. The snake had caused a major commotion among the detainees in that area and the guards rushed over to investigate. Very quickly, there were serious discussions and furrowed brows, and the guards advised the detainee the dead snake was a protected species. Mind you, illegally killing a snake was probably the least of the detainee's worries at that point. As I recall, there were no significant repercussions. But it was another unsettling occurrence—as if we needed any more—which emphasised how unwelcome we were.

Most people spent their time loitering, sitting around, doing remarkably little. Each day was tedious and stretched into the next equally tedious day. And all the time, we were wrestling with the heat, the native wildlife and the overbearing presence of the guards.

I studied my medical book, *Last's Anatomy*, for long spells. But, believe me, the fact I could follow such an innocent and academic path was an achievement. I'd left the book in my bag, which had been confiscated the moment we arrived at Curtin. Even though the book was obviously an academic tome, it had taken hours of persuasion to talk the guards into releasing it to me.

When I wasn't studying, through boredom I also started using any implements I could find to carve shapes in the concrete blocks that held up the tent poles. Sure, it was puerile, but there was no access to the outside world—no TV, radio, newspapers or magazines and no phones. There was absolutely nothing else to do.

Other people found their own ways of filling in their days.

Detainee Number 1 was known as The Walker. His name was Ahmed and he was a doctor from Baghdad. He didn't interact much with the other asylum-seekers. He would wake up each morning and embark on a daily walk along the perimeter fence. As far as he could go, then back. Then up to the limit of the perimeter fence and back again. For most of the day. Along the way, he would count the number of steps he'd taken. It was a routine he maintained throughout our detention. At the time, the more ignorant detainees regarded him as a joke and many thought he was mad. He wasn't. He's now a respected obstetrician in Sydney.

Another detainee was known as The Doctor. He was very religious and quickly gained the respect of fundamentalist Shi'ites. He spoke with a great deal of authority and was highly regarded by them. To the extent that he was trusted to carry out a number of routine examinations on the Shi'ite women in the detention centre. It was only later that we found out he wasn't a qualified doctor at all . . . he was a vet!

There was, in fact, no appointed doctor available to the detainees at Curtin. Instead, the only medical professional officially available in the detention centre clinic was a rostered nurse. The nurse was provided on rotation from the local health service, but only for limited hours. It simply wasn't possible for the nurse to keep up with the demand from the refugees, many with chronic illnesses and others with occasional complaints. Also, because the clinic shift was filled by different individuals, the lack of continuity undermined the effectiveness of the system. It felt like a token gesture rather than a genuine effort to look after us.

As an example of the inadequacy of the health facilities, there was one occasion later on when a detainee suffered a serious wound playing soccer. Blood was pumping from his head—he'd ruptured an artery and was in need of immediate treatment. He was taken to the medical centre, where a bandage was applied. But it was clearly inadequate and soon was soaked with blood.

In desperation, the authorities called me in and instructed: 'You're a doctor, do what you can!'

I told them I needed a needle and suture material. They rummaged around and found some. Happily, I managed to staunch the bleeding and sew up the injury. The patient made a full recovery.

We sensed the detention centre management was trying to deprive us of everything, including our names, in an effort to force us to go back to the countries we'd come from.

As often happens in such circumstances, the dynamic establishes an 'us and them' mentality. The approach of the management completely backfired—it merely made the detainees more determined, resourceful and creative in their resistance.

Just as we were given no resources, we were given no information, either. Partly, I suppose, because information is power and they wanted to retain as much power as possible over us.

TOP LEFT: A Curtin Detention Centre photo identity that belonged to Noor, Doha's sister. These kits were later replaced with plastic IDs. © *Ghassan Nakhoul*

TOP RIGHT: Early hours of the day in Curtin—the tents where we were forced to sleep on stretchers, keeping our meagre possessions in plastic bags. Life was tedious and tough in the Western Australian desert. © *Ghassan Nakhoul*

ABOVE: Because of the searing heat, it was often more comfortable to sleep outside, where there was at least a breath of air. © *Ghassan Nakhoul*

TOP: Children sitting around in Curtin Detention Centre. There was nothing to keep them occupied. © *Ghassan Nakhoul*

ABOVE: Army stretchers at Curtin, with even the luxury of a metal bed for one lucky asylum-seeker. Just more of the day-to-day degradation in the ill-equipped detention centre. © *Ghassan Nakhoul*

TOP: The different compounds at Curtin were separated by barbed wire fences, and the detainees were locked inside their compound after dark. © *Ghassan Nakhoul*

ABOVE: The queue for the head count before a meal. The lines stretched around the buildings and asylum-seekers huddled in the shade to avoid the heat of the desert. It was a ritual we had to repeat three times a day. © *Ghassan Nakhoul*

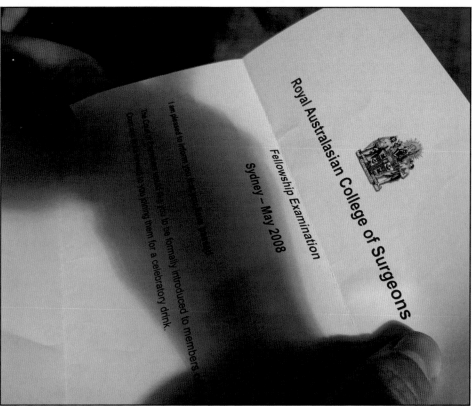

TOP: At the University of Sydney, nervously awaiting the Royal Australasian College of Surgeons Fellowship exam results, 2008.

ABOVE: The letter informing me I had been successful in the RACS Fellowship exams.

TOP: In front of the Brandenburg Gate in Berlin during my post-Fellowship studies, 2009.

ABOVE: My sons Adam and Dean in front of the Brandenburg Gate, 2013.

TOP: Swimming with Irina and Sophia in Sydney Harbour, 2011.

ABOVE: Pro bono activities in India—operating on complex orthopaedic cases with colleagues, including the organiser Sharan Patel (far right) from Bangalore and Professor Thorsten Gehrke (third from right), medical director of the HELIOS ENDO-Klinik in Hamburg.

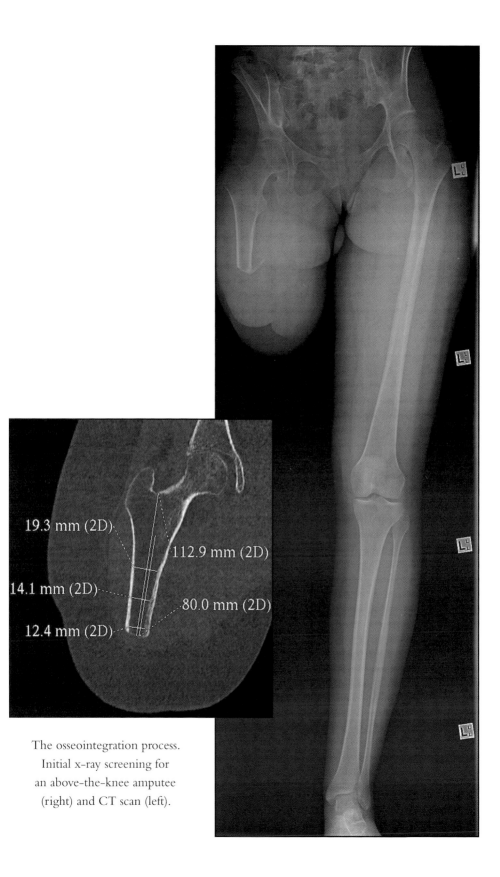

19.3 mm (2D)

112.9 mm (2D)

14.1 mm (2D)

80.0 mm (2D)

12.4 mm (2D)

The osseointegration process.
Initial x-ray screening for
an above-the-knee amputee
(right) and CT scan (left).

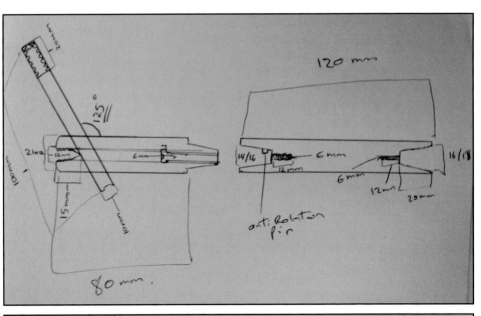

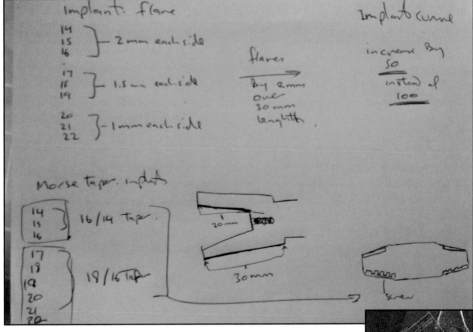

TOP: My hand drawings of a custom-made implant design.

ABOVE: Custom-made implant adaptors with different sizing options.

RIGHT: Engineering drawings based on my sketches applied to the CT scan model.

TOP: Home workshop, applying the design theory using recycled implants and plastic bone models.

ABOVE: With the local engineer, my fellow and the local implant company manager on a video conference with the prosthesis manufacturers in Europe.

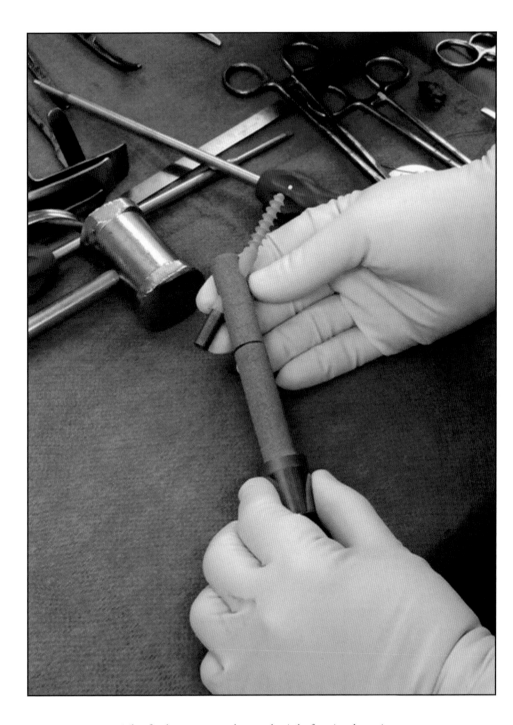

The final custom-made prosthesis before implantation.

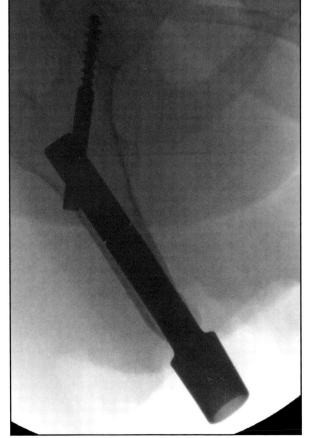

ABOVE: Nurse assistant Belinda Bosley and a surgical fellow in space suit theatre gowns, preparing for an operation.

LEFT: Image intensifier checking the implant position before completing surgery.

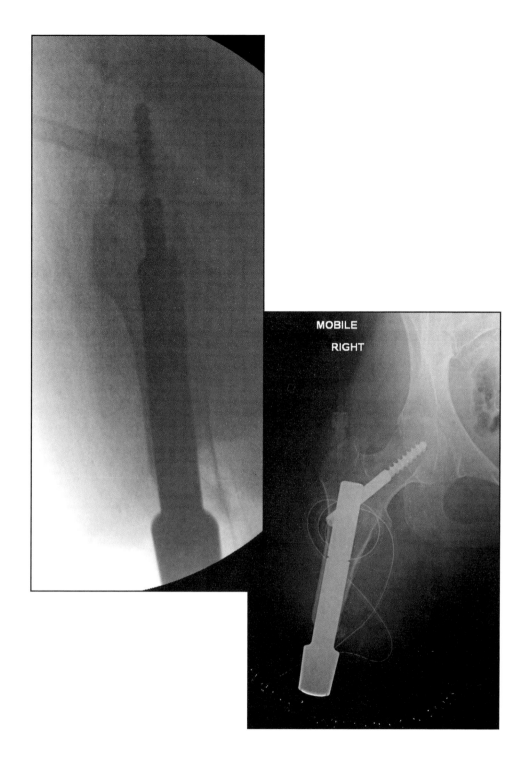

TOP LEFT: Image intensifier checking the implant position—one lateral.

RIGHT: A post-operative x-ray showing the implant in an ideal position.

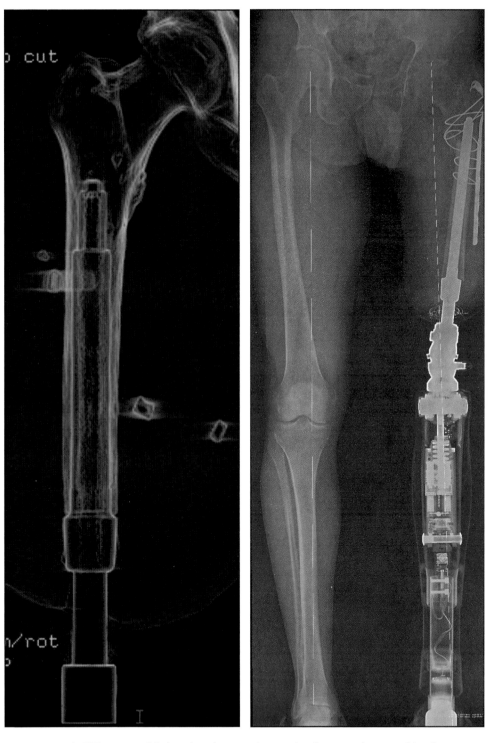

LEFT: A CT scan model showing the osseointegration between bone and implant.

RIGHT: My first case: a long-leg standing x-ray showing the complete
osseointegration system.

Mitchell Grant in his Good Vibes Fitness gym at Macquarie Park in Sydney,
three years after undergoing osseointegration surgery.

Michael Swain taking his first steps on his new robotic legs at
Macquarie University Hospital, Sydney, in early 2014.

Invitation (top) to witness Queen Elizabeth presenting an MBE to
Michael Swain at Windsor Castle in April 2014 (above).

# The Curtin Comes Down

At one stage, we counted about 1200 detainees, which, incidentally, was 100 more than the recommended maximum. The vast majority, while they may have been of Iraqi descent, had most recently come from Iran and their loyalities lay with the Shi'ite republic. Many thousands of Iraqis had fled to Iran because of persecution and during the war between the two nations. Some who had been based in Iran were simply pretending to be from Iraq, presumably because they thought it would give them a better chance of being accepted into Australia. I suspected large numbers of them were economic refugees. In contrast, the 117 from Iraq struck me as genuine refugees.

Many of the detainees quickly became quite depressed about their circumstances. Worst of all, of course, was the loss of identity, dignity and self-esteem which, I have to say, seemed a conscious approach by the people running Curtin.

And, for the record, these criticisms can't simply be dismissed as carping by queue jumpers. The observations and complaints were completely genuine and have been supported time and again by impartial observers. In 2001, an inquiry commissioned by the Howard federal government delivered scathing criticism of the two detention centres run by ACM. Among the major areas of condemnation were chronic over-crowding, inadequate training of staff, racial abuse, long delays in processing asylum applications resulting in self-mutilation and suicide attempts, a lack of follow up of incident reports and inadequate facilities for children.

A decade later, the Human Rights Commission produced another damning report on Curtin, indicating not much had changed in that time. This investigation particularly turned the spotlight on high rates of self-harm and suicide attempts, a lack of access to physical and mental health services, the psychological impact of indefinite detention, long delays in processing asylum applications, a lack of communication and perceptions of unfairness in decision making. The Commission concluded by urging the federal government not to detain people in remote locations such as Curtin.

❦

By late January 2000, the detainees simply couldn't put up with the appalling conditions any longer. The word went round that a hunger strike was being planned.

I don't know exactly who organised it, but it seemed very well orchestrated. I think it was probably some of the detainees who'd been living in Iran and belonged to one of the two Shi'ite religious–political groups, the Supreme Islamic Council and Al-Dawa. I got the impression they'd done this sort of thing before.

As soon as the instruction went around the compound that the hunger strike was on, large numbers of detainees simply stayed in their accommodation area, refusing to go to the food section. I estimate that about 300 people were demonstrably refusing food.

# The Curtin Comes Down

Subsequently, a handful of detainees sewed their lips together with needles and thread they'd managed to keep in their personal possessions. I was very much against the idea of sewing their lips together, because it was another form of the self-mutilation I so detested.

The atmosphere around Curtin became particularly tense during the hunger strike. Extra guards were brought in, all heavily armed with batons and handcuffs. An emergency medical room was set up to treat anyone suffering severe symptoms of malnutrition.

In fact, the hunger strike was part reality, part sham. Many, if not most, of the protesters who weren't going to the food hall were eating food others brought back for them. There was no chance of them actually starving.

However, by not attending the food area, we caused chaos in the administration of the compound. Remember, meal times were crucial to the guards checking our numbers and making sure no one had escaped. Without that mass access to the detainees, they had to go in search of everyone.

I joined the protest. But my contribution was mainly to use my medical knowledge to create a distraction. I stood outside the medical centre and hyperventilated to produce many of the symptoms of dehydration, which can result from a severe lack of food and water. A group of the other detainees saw what I was doing and joined in. To this day, I'm not sure the medical people at Curtin had a clue what was going on.

The protest I led completely overloaded the medical facilities. Extra nurses were brought in from Derby to look after the individual protesters. We were taken into emergency care and put on heart monitors for anything up to four hours at a time. The main thing was that it added to the disturbance of the whole camp.

The primary aim of the hunger strike was, of course, to unsettle the routine and draw attention to the awful conditions we were being forced to endure. It went on for more than a week before, at last, the detention centre management was forced to sit up and take notice. For the first time, they came to us and started talking to find out what we wanted.

Once the atmosphere eased, the management acknowledged that the detainees had some genuine gripes—and that I had a role to play in finding solutions.

As a result, they decided to form a committee that would represent the detainees. I think there were five of us on the committee, including myself and Doha. We had the privilege of being able to talk to the management. But the guidelines were confined to the day-to-day operations of the detention centre. They wouldn't answer any questions about the processing of asylum applications.

One of the main complaints the committee passed on was about the food. So, after the hunger strike, the management allowed Doha's aunt to become a kitchen hand and prepare something other than the dreadful, tasteless mincemeat and spaghetti we'd been subjected to, day in, day out. Immediately the standard of the food—and detainee moral—improved. I don't think Doha's aunt had ever worked in a kitchen before, but within a short time she was essentially running the operation. And very well, too.

Another major complaint was the sheer tedium the detainees faced each and every day. The committee suggested setting up a school. To their credit, the management agreed and we established the classroom straightaway, starting in the tents but eventually moving into one of the demountables that arrived later.

We had three main aims at the school—to teach detainees to speak English, to teach them appropriate toilet habits, and to teach them the manners that would be required in Australia. In the classroom, we started with very basic vocabulary and also emphasised the need to be polite. Things like asking 'Can I please?' rather than demanding 'I want'.

It was pretty unsophisticated and the equipment we were given to work with stretched only as far as a whiteboard, marker pens, an eraser, some watercolour paints and some basic materials to paint on. But given the limited resources and the massive variation in the abilities of the people in the camp, I think we achieved quite a lot.

A significant number of the asylum-seekers came to the school. Some genuinely to learn; others, I think, to pass the time of day and break the boredom. And, frankly, if all we did was keep people entertained, then it was still a step forward.

The management also set up a small room with about thirty plastic chairs where we could watch videos on a TV. Until now, there had been no entertainment or even minor distractions. It was only later when the atmosphere in the detention centre became completely toxic and tensions were at fever pitch that we were allowed to expand our activities to sport and play soccer and volleyball.

Around that time, we were informed we could write letters—which was a huge relief. But when we inquired why we hadn't been allowed to do this before, we were told: 'No one asked!'

Looking back, I think the hunger strike had three main aims.

The first was to cause enough disruption to bring about changes in the day-to-day conditions in Curtin. It certainly disrupted the management routine and brought about some noticeable reforms. Our existence in the detention centre remained awful, but slightly less awful. I'd give the hunger strike a pass mark on that one.

Second, it was aimed at raising the public profile of our plight, through the media and human rights campaigners. In reality, no one outside the detention centre and its management paid any attention whatsoever, so this aim wasn't achieved.

And third, it was an attempt to accelerate the processing of our asylum applications. From that point of view, it was an abject failure, I'm afraid.

Another result of the hunger strike was the introduction of an Iraqi interpreter from Brisbane. He was an extremely refined individual, in his mid-fifties, tall, clean shaven and slightly overweight. He was very calm, but in the furnace of the Western Australian desert, would sweat profusely. He had a PhD, although he appeared to be retired or semi-retired. He was a Shi'ite but came across as being very secular.

Initially, we were told he would simply be an interpreter, although, in the wake of the preceding unrest, he took on the role of intermediary between the detainees and the management. A lot of the asylum-seekers thought he was an informant, but I'm confident he wasn't.

From my understanding of his activities, he was trying to help the management understand the culture and traditions of the detainees, as well as talking to our committee, the asylum-seekers themselves and conveying their requests to the management. I'm convinced his heart was in the right place and he was trying to improve conditions. But throughout the time he was there, he remained stranded in the middle. He was an object of resentment by the more radical detainees and, to be honest, I'm not sure how highly he was thought of among the management.

Also, another Iraqi guy came to talk to the people in the detention centre. He also appeared to be in his fifties. I understood he was another PhD who seemed to be, in some capacity, advising the federal government and the immigration minister. In general, the asylum-seekers thought he was a horrible choice for the role. He was obviously religious and completely ignored Doha, because she was uncovered.

From the detainees' point of view, we felt he tried to manipulate the situation and a number of things changed after he'd been there. The structure of the committee, for example. A covered woman who was a devout Shi'ite and was rumoured to have family links with him was installed on the committee. It seemed to me she had been very active in the Al-Dawa political group in Iraq. She also was extremely aggressive. At one meeting with the detention centre management, she was constantly referring to them as 'you infidels', lecturing them and patronising them. Even the interpreter was advising her that he couldn't convey such inflammatory comments.

The government advisor quickly insisted on an election of committee members. As a result, the woman he had introduced to the committee was elected. So was Doha and so was I. Another representative, whose name completely escapes me now, was very highly respected with a religious background. It seemed he had held a position of some authority in Iran.

In Australian terms, he was a really good bloke. But the final member of the committee was someone I could not get along with in any way; he was known menacingly as Al Sayed, The Master.

Anyone named Al Sayed is descended from the Prophet Mohammed. The detainee was in his mid-forties, tall, with very dark olive skin, a narrow moustache and curly hair. He acted like someone who had authority. He was a practising Moslem, but he definitely wasn't someone who took a religious role.

Rumours about him were rife and conflicting. Some detainees were talking about him being one of Saddam's Secret Intelligence Service officers in the city of Omara, just north of Basra. Apparently, he told others he had defected and worked with the Iranians, infiltrating Iraq on assassination missions, and portraying himself as a mastermind who organised the murder of a Ba'athist leader in Omara.

Al Sayed appeared to me as not obviously violent, but quietly and darkly menacing. He spoke with a great deal of authority—the way Ba'athists used to speak when Saddam was running Iraq. There was plenty of opportunity in the detention centre for him to embark on a rule of terror. I was thoroughly intimidated and felt threatened by him. And certainly, I was always very suspicious of him.

Not long after, and completely out of the blue, one of the detention centre officials came to my door and told me: 'Be prepared, Philip Ruddock's coming to Curtin tomorrow. This is your chance to meet him.'

It was invaluable information because, officially, the minister's visit was secret and wouldn't be announced to the detainees. The plan appeared to be that Ruddock would come and go without any of us being aware he'd set foot in the place.

I asked my informant if we could request a meeting with the immigration minister.

'No,' I was told firmly. 'But use your imagination to create an opportunity to see him.'

I took the hint and quickly decided the best way to encourage a meeting with the minister was to organise a mass demonstration outside the administrative building in Foxtrot Compound.

So I sent out the message through some friends that everyone should prepare to gather outside Foxtrot the next afternoon and, in the meantime, should get working with sheets, permanent marker pens and watercolours to create banners protesting against the lack of progress with our asylum processing and the awful conditions in the detention centre.

The next afternoon, the same detention centre official came to see me and told me Ruddock had arrived.

I gave the signal and, within ten minutes, more than 1000 detainees had marched peacefully from one end of the camp to Foxtrot, shouting, waving placards and demanding a meeting with the minister.

# The Curtin Comes Down

An ACM manager came out of the demountable and asked who'd informed me Ruddock was there. I declined to answer the question, but told him we weren't going anywhere until we'd spoken to the minister. The manager went back inside for a few minutes, then came out and delivered the message that only the committee would be allowed in.

All five committee members trooped into the demountable. Inside, Ruddock was on one side of the table and we were on the other. He didn't shake our hands or make any greeting—he was as cold as an Antarctic winter and brusquely demanded to know what we wanted.

We asked how long we would be held in the detention centre and when our asylum applications would be processed.

His answer followed the lines that the process would take as long as it took and there weren't enough staff to go any faster. But he emphasised that if we wanted to go back to where we came from, the government could organise it.

Then I asked why they were spending around $160 per head per day to keep us in Curtin when they could tag us and allow us out to do something useful like working on a farm.

His reaction was simple and straightforward: that was never going to happen.

I also pointed out that there were many children in the detention centre and there had been stories of child abuse. We asked why they couldn't be released into the community with foster families—that way at least they could attend school and get an education.

Searching through my memory banks, my understanding of his response was: 'You broke the law to come here. If we release the children, it'll be rewarding them for breaking the law.'

I was shocked at this. To me it showed a much greater determination to push through a political agenda than demonstrate any understanding, concern or compassion for the plight of the refugees. Particularly the children.

Basically, his message was: 'Go back and we'll help you get there. Other than that, you're in detention indefinitely.'

The meeting lasted only about ten minutes. There simply wasn't any point in prolonging it. We realised there and then that we weren't going to get anywhere with the minister. He had no intention of releasing anyone quickly and we were going to be in detention for a very long time.

I think that was when I was marked down as a trouble-maker. No doubt the detention centre management figured out that I'd been a prime mover in orchestrating the confrontation. And they determined that I would pay a price for my activism.

❧

About three months after we arrived at Curtin, the management brought in demountable buildings, known as dongas, with air-conditioning. And while that was an immediate step forward and was regarded favourably by many of the detainees, I had a different view. More durable and substantial accommodation indicated to me that there were no plans for any of us to be transferred out of there in the short term. Clearly, our stay at Curtin was going to be a long one.

At least with the additional facilities, we could spend most of our time in greater comfort than before. The fear of snakes was largely eliminated and there were far fewer mosquitoes.

But there was a downside, too. Once we moved into the demountables, the midnight head counts became far more intrusive.

In the tents, you could leave your ID beside your head as you slept. The guards would come in, shine a torch at your head, quickly check the ID and be off without much disturbance at all. You became familiar with the routine and you would barely be woken.

The midnight checks in the dongas involved guards banging loudly on the door, shouting 'Head count' to announce their arrival, and barging straight in. There were women and children inside who weren't fully dressed and, because of their religious and cultural beliefs, were absolutely horrified and ashamed at being seen by the guards. But the guards intruded regardless—they didn't stop and they didn't apologise. There was no privacy.

And then there were the floors of the dongas. Moslems kneel on the floor to pray. Partly for religious reasons and partly for simple hygiene, the floors were kept scrupulously clean. Everyone took off their shoes and left them outside the demountables. But the guards completely ignored the custom and blundered into the dongas with their filthy boots, spreading mud and dirt across the floor, which had to be cleaned by the detainees. Absolutely no thought for the culture of the asylum-seekers.

The guards also constantly shuffled people around for no apparent reason. I guess they may have been trying to separate people they thought were potential trouble-makers, or just moving people around so they couldn't become too familiar with others and hatch plots. All the same it was another unsettling aspect of life at Curtin.

The majority of refugees thought that when they arrived in Australia, they'd reached the Promised Land. The reality proved completely different and in the detention centre, people lost all hope because they were being humiliated on a daily basis and had no idea when it would end.

# 13

# THE BREAKOUTS

It's hard for me to explain Curtin to anyone who hasn't been in that sort of situation. I'd describe the experience as being like your worst nightmare, where you shout as loud as you can but no one hears you. So you shout again—and the same thing happens. Absolutely no one is listening to your cry for assistance.

It's the ultimate dehumanisation. And, even worse, no one outside our detention centre appeared to care.

Imagine being one of the 1200 detainees who were there at the time. We didn't have even the most basic recognition as human beings—we weren't acknowledged as having a name. We were known only by a number. At the slightest provocation, detainees were routinely subjected to verbal humiliation, physical intimidation and even, occasionally, beatings. We had no personal privacy or rights. Our personal space was regularly, and enthusiastically, violated.

Worst of all, we felt bullied and demeaned on a daily basis. To us, it seemed all the might of the political and bureaucratic machine wanted only one outcome—to send us back where we'd come from, regardless of the fact that many of us were legitimate refugees, who faced torture and probably death if we did return to our homelands.

My life and the lives of the other detainees in Curtin were clearly regarded by some political operatives as being an extremely cheap price to pay for the achievement of their own ambitions and agendas. We were the external threat of the day that desperate politicians always seem to fall back on to demonstrate their strength and hero status to the gullible electorate. The easy-beats who could be flogged to present an image of protecting the nation's honour and security.

It's a trick that has been foisted on the public for centuries, but was particularly obvious with the George W. Bush administration's Second Gulf War campaign. And, in Australian terms, most blatantly, in the 'children overboard' deception of the Howard government. The problem, of course, is that it still works—so the politicians will continue to use it.

Regardless of that, gradually, during the early months in Curtin, through day-to-day contact, detainees began forming casual friendships with a small number of the guards and other officials at the detention centre. Some of the staff actually real-ised that we were human beings who were trying, like them, to forge reasonable, responsible lives. Mainly the friendly officials were Australians, by far the most rational and approachable of the authority figures.

As those friendly interactions started to unfold, from time to time we would discuss the appalling conditions we were living in, our mistreatment at the hands of some guards, and our feeling of humiliation and helplessness. While many of the guards were routinely bullying us—behaviour which, by the lack of sanction against the perpetrators, I can only assume was at least tolerated by the management—some of the staff were becoming more sympathetic to our plight.

In the first couple of months, largely through our shared interest in medicine, I got to know a male nurse, who would visit Curtin as part of the roster at the compound's health centre. During one of the conversations, the nurse suggested we should try to document what was happening. The nurse himself was writing down the more appalling events he had witnessed and urged me to do the same. I said it would be great if we could take some photographs to show people how depraved conditions were.

The idea struck a chord and the nurse offered to smuggle a camera into the compound. I could take photos, he could carry the camera out again in his personal belongings and send the images to the Australian media. All on the condition that he wouldn't be associated with the plot in any way.

A few days later, he came back and handed over a Kodak disposable camera. I kept the camera with me throughout the daylight hours and popped it in a plastic takeaway food container—they were readily available because that was how we received our meals each day—and buried it in the ground next to our sleeping quarters at night.

Hussein, who I'd befriended on the flight from Jordan to Kuala Lumpur and who'd got me involved in this whole mess in the first place, and another trusted friend walked around the camp with me, acting as lookouts while I surreptitiously took photographs. It was crucial we weren't caught by the guards or even seen by other detainees.

I took photos of the tent accommodation, the compounds, the food area, the detainees queuing for food, the water facilities, the toilets. Pretty much anything I could photograph without being spotted. The whole secretive process took two days.

When the nurse came back the following week, I gave him the camera. One week later, he returned with the photos and we sat together writing a description of the images and the awful living conditions.

The nurse took away the photos and descriptions and sent them to media outlets across Australia: newspapers, magazines, television and radio. By his account, not one journalist showed any interest. There was no coverage at all.

Whether it was by coincidence—the media may well have thought we didn't present a compelling case—or by design, we'll never know. However, you have to remember that, at the time, Australia was in the final stages of gearing up for the Sydney Olympic Games. It's not unlikely that many people in the general population, including the media, were feeling massive national pride and were extremely sensitive about revealing any negative images of the country.

Our hopes of the Australian public finding out about our plight were quickly and completely dashed.

The desperation of the detainees became increasingly obvious as time wore on.

After we'd been in Curtin for a few months, a couple of asylum-seekers—who I think were from the subcontinent—escaped by jumping the fence and heading south on the main road. Which wasn't terribly smart at all. And their bid for freedom went rapidly downhill.

The escapees clearly hadn't thought much further than getting onto the other side of the barbed wire fence. Outside Curtin, they went to the first petrol station on the highway and tried to buy some provisions with US dollars. It didn't take a genius to work out they weren't locals or bona fide travellers. Where else could they have come from than the detention centre?

The petrol station staff simply made a call and the escapees were whisked away to the local police station for a few days before they appeared in court and were sentenced. Quite what their fate was I never found out, but I don't recall seeing them again.

The whole breakout was really little more than a sign of complete desperation. It was never going to succeed and simply reflected the naïvety of the detainees.

As time went on, unsavoury incidents were becoming more common in the detention centre and, among some groups, normal standards were breaking down. For example, I had direct evidence of the claims of child abuse that were later mentioned in official reports.

A couple of young guys in their twenties had become very friendly with an asylum-seeker in his thirties who was there with his young daughter and son. The five of them used to spend a lot of time together. Without warning, the father made accusations that the two young men had shown his kids pornography and were interfering with them.

I acted as interpreter for the father as he was making his case to the detention centre authorities. It ended with the two younger men being taken away. We never saw them again.

There were other accusations of child abuse around the camp, but I purposely refused to become involved as an interpreter, because the whole area was so awful—so I wasn't aware of the details. As I'm sure anyone can imagine, these were hugely disturbing incidents in such a closely—and reluctantly—confined community.

People became extremely agitated the longer their captivity went on and, now and then, there were bashings. Familiar faces would simply disappear for days or weeks. It didn't take long to figure out they'd been banished to solitary confinement or the police lock-up in Derby.

Stealing became an increasing problem. The Salvation Army distributed clothes and sneakers because detainees were walking around with bare feet. There weren't enough shoes for everyone, so asylum-seekers were stealing from each other. I was fortunate—I never had anything stolen. But we were well aware of the potential of what was happening around the camp and doubled our efforts to protect our meagre possessions.

The levels of tension, unease and unhappiness were mounting—people were becoming depressed as time passed and nothing was happening to ease our plight.

❦

Early May 2000 was another turning point for me. When I thought things couldn't get worse, they did.

By that stage, serious divisions had developed among groups of the detainees. On one extreme end was a small collection of fundamentalist Moslems, led by my old combatant Al Sayed. At the other end were Doha's family and myself, who were all much more Western in our approach, although Doha and her family retained their Moslem faith and beliefs. In between were a variety of groups and factions. Tensions were constant.

Among the asylum-seekers was a Palestinian Sunni, who was constantly harassed by some of the Shi'ites. The outside of his donga was defaced with a Star of David and slogans accusing him of being an Israeli sympathiser.

At one point, Al Sayed approached me in the middle of the compound and advised me to tell Doha and her sisters to cover their heads. They weren't the only uncovered women in the detention centre but, clearly, they had been targeted. I refused to pass on the message and told Al Sayed it wasn't my place to act as his messenger.

That year, 9 May was an important day of mourning for the more fundamentalist Shi'ites, marking the death of Ja'far ibn Mohammed al-Sadiq, the sixth of what are known as the Twelve Imams, who was poisoned in the eighth century, apparently by the caliph. It's not an occasion that is widely commemorated in Iraq, but in the detention centre a group of hard-line Shi'ites with Iranian connections, led by Al Sayed, decided they wanted to recognise the event in their traditional fashion. That involved working themselves into a trance by shaking their heads vigorously over an extended period and then carrying out the self-mutilation rituals my father and I so detested. The group seemed to be mainly extremists who had followed these traditions since they were eight or nine years old.

On the morning of 9 May, I spoke to Al Sayed and told him: 'I don't think it's a good idea for you to go ahead with the ceremony. Do whatever you want once you're out of here, but if you do this, it will reflect badly on everyone inside.'

I explained that there were Christians and others who didn't share his beliefs, but going ahead with the ceremony would indicate that everyone in the detention centre supported their views.

One of the more violent supporters of Al Sayed started shouting the familiar line that the Shi'ites had been suppressed by Saddam for practising their religious beliefs. He bellowed that we had come to a country that called itself a democracy so they would practise their religious ceremony whether the Australians liked it or not.

By chance, and in complete contrast, 9 May also happens to be the birthday of Noor, Doha's middle sister. A couple of the friendly guards smuggled in a CD player, some candies and cordial so we could celebrate Noor's birthday. In the evening, we staged our own little party in the demountable. We were singing and dancing. Three or four of the guards were there with us. Nothing raucous at all.

Outside, the Shi'ite extremists were going ahead with their ceremony. To ensure the authenticity of the commemoration, they had ripped the metal from beds in the sleeping quarters, gathered in an empty yard and launched into their ritual of mourning and crying and beating themselves. That night, they started mutilating themselves with the metal weapons they'd created from the beds.

The management filmed them—and I was told the footage would be shown as a documentary to the Australian public. Clearly, if that was the case—and I don't know whether the film was ever shown—it was an attempt by the authorities to portray all the detainees as being mad and violent. Obviously, like the 'children overboard' deceit, it was material that could be used to manipulate and outrage public opinion.

Shortly after that incident and without any notice, about seven of us were called to report to the Foxtrot administration building. I'd been playing soccer and was having a shower when a detainee found me and passed on the news that the guards had been looking for me. I was the last to be called in. One of the guards just came up and told me: '982—you're wanted in the main office.'

I wondered what was going on, but went along to Foxtrot anyway to clear up the mystery. As soon as I entered through the gate to the administrative compound, I noticed an unusual number of guards with their handcuffs at the ready.

They told me to go into the nearest demountable and, once inside, I found others squatting on the floor. Al Sayed was one of them. Two of the people behind the Cigarette Uprising were there as well, along with another burly detainee in his fifties. They weren't people I spent any time with. In fact, from their reaction, they were equally as bemused to see me as I was to be in a room with them.

'Oh, you're here,' Al Sayed said. 'We thought you were the person behind all of this.'

'All of what?' was my immediate thought. I had no idea what was going on.

Events became stranger when we were herded up and stuffed into a van which took us to Derby Police Station.

# The Breakouts

I think the watch house had three cells in all, but we were forced to share two cells. Concrete cells that smelled of vomit. So many people in two small cells made conditions extremely cramped and we were forced to stay there for the night and the next day.

We slept on the concrete floor, lying on the towels we had been given when we arrived. But I didn't sleep much. Unlike the other prisoners, who seemed much more at home than I was. Regardless of the fact we were in a police station lock-up, we were still very much part of the detention centre regime. We were guarded by detention centre staff and the food was from the detention centre, not the police station.

I remember it was ferociously hot in the cell. There was no indoor shower facility—instead, we had to shower outside. And there was no privacy. Each cell had one steel toilet with no barrier around it. Everyone simply used it when they had to.

We were allowed outside into the exercise yard for about an hour the next lunchtime, but we didn't mix with anyone else. No one talked to us or told us anything. Except the various drunks they brought into the adjoining cells at night who shouted abuse at us.

I felt like the only alien in there. The two associated with the Cigarette Uprising had been in the lock-up before. They appeared to accept the situation and find it reasonably comfortable. But, apart from the detention centre, I had never experienced anything like this in my life.

The other detainees seemed to be divided about me. Half of them thought I was a victim like them—the others thought I was a mole for the authorities. I can assure you, I wasn't a mole. But those are the sort of conspiracy theories that happen when people feel powerless and haven't got very much to do with their time.

We were kept there for a few days. Without explanation. Then, with no notice, the deputy manager of the detention centre, a representative of the Department of Immigration, the mullah and Doha arrived to take us back to Curtin.

The official from the Department of Immigration addressed us and said words to the effect that: 'You were brought here to teach you a lesson and we want you to go back to the detention centre and behave. Will you promise to stop what you were doing?'

To this day, for the life of me, I have no idea what they thought I had been doing. But, like the others, I agreed. And so we were taken back to Curtin—and things simply returned to the miserable way they had been before.

※

Soon after, we were relocated to one side of the detention centre. All 1200 crammed into a single compound. We were locked in and, between us, gradually worked out that some sort of processing was beginning. Once we'd reached that conclusion, our spirits rose. At last, we knew there was an end in sight. The asylum-seekers started preparing their stories to present to the authorities.

We'd been in Curtin for six months by then and this was the first time we'd seen the immigration officers dealing directly with the detainees.

Because we were identified and addressed only by numbers, I knew it was going to be quite a while before my case would be scheduled for consideration. They started with number 1 . . . and I was 982.

The processing began with officers bringing pens and paper and giving the detainees a couple of hours to write their stories. Official interpreters were appointed for those people who couldn't read or write. Even that didn't go smoothly. The interpreters were largely Lebanese and quite often their understanding of what was being said was off the mark because of the differences in accents and vernacular.

I discovered afterwards that this first questionnaire, which was really very trivial, was the basis for deciding whether people would be processed. It was a very flimsy way to make any decision—let alone deciding the future direction of someone's life.

The Australian authorities didn't have a clue where anyone was actually from. In the end, the people who said they were from Iraq were granted visas—even though I'm confident at least some of them had been living perfectly safely in Iran and were simply economic refugees.

The people who had been interviewed by the immigration officials were sent to the main compound—presumably so they couldn't tell anyone what questions they'd been asked—while the others stayed in the processing area.

Because I could speak English, a number of the detainees came to me and shared their stories of why they had been forced to leave their homeland and how they ended up here. It could have been a very emotional experience for me but, after a short time, I realised around half of these people were telling me exactly the same story!

Apparently, they had been praying with Ayatollah Sadeq al-Sadr shortly before he and two of his sons were killed. A bomb, suspected of being planted by Saddam Hussein's henchmen, blew up their car after the ayatollah had given a sermon at the mosque in Kufa near Najaf in February 1999. The incident was particularly famous because the ayatollah wore his burial shroud to the mosque that day and informed his followers he was about to die.

By the detainees' accounts, all of them had to escape from Iraq to avoid persecution as a result of being in that congregation.

Now, it's a huge mosque and, by coincidence, all of these people could have been there. But, call me cynical if you will, there's also an even stronger chance that most of them were nowhere near Kufa on the day of the bombing, but had been carefully coached on what story to tell the immigration officials. Frankly, I doubt whether some of those detainees had ever been to Iraq. When I was talking to them, quite a number wanted to know what images were on Iraqi bank notes and others were even asking me to draw them a map of the country!

As time passed, Doha was called and went for her interview. So did her aunt and her siblings. As more and more people had been through the process, it came to what I thought was my time to be interviewed. But, mysteriously, my number wasn't called. I waited, assuming they hadn't progressed quite as fast as I thought.

The processing took somewhere between one and two weeks and, at the end, nearly everyone was moved into the main compound. Clearly, the processing had finished—and it was only then that I realised I had missed out completely. I hadn't just been held over until last—I had been deliberately left out of the process altogether.

That time was horrific for me. Among my worst in Curtin. While almost everyone else had some hope of being accepted into Australia, I was obviously going to be kept in the detention centre as a punishment. After that, the future was at best uncertain. But the writing was very much on the wall—and, in the view of the government and the officials at Curtin, it didn't include me staying in Australia for any extended period.

Which somehow didn't surprise me at all. Using nothing more than intuition, I had a strange hunch that the powers-that-be were saving up an unpleasant surprise for me.

Only a handful of us weren't interviewed. And no explanations were forthcoming. It was like watching sand trickling out of an hourglass and finally realising I was the last grain left and wouldn't be going anywhere. I felt there was no such thing as justice.

Naturally, I went to the officials and asked why I hadn't been interviewed. They didn't offer any clues and simply said they didn't know. That seemed a good enough answer for them.

The practical issue was that if I didn't get processed, I wouldn't be accepted or rejected as a genuine refugee. All would be well if I was accepted. On the other hand, if I didn't get rejected, I couldn't go through the legal processes and lodge an appeal.

By not having my papers processed, effectively, I didn't exist. I wasn't a person—I was still just number 982. That left the prospect I would simply remain in the detention centre, slowly declining until I rotted away or decided to go back to where I came from.

For everyone else who had been processed and transferred to the main compound, life had improved slightly and some restrictions were relaxed. Two fixed line telephones had been installed inside the administration centre and the detainees were now allowed to make phone calls.

A system had been introduced where the asylum-seekers were paid for carrying out certain jobs. For example, you could earn $5 by cleaning the toilets. It meant you could pay for phone calls, cigarettes and lollies—all advances that made life in the detention centre much more tolerable for many people.

At the same time, the authorities allowed the detainees to access the money they had brought with them. It seemed that now the refugees were processed and registered, they were slowly becoming recognised as having some rights as human beings.

But for myself, not much changed at all. I was still spending most of my time in the processing compound with a couple of other detainees who were in complete limbo. They were from an Iraqi background but had been born and brought up in Kuwait, where their parents had been living illegally. The families were kicked out of Kuwait when it was liberated and they became stateless. No one knew quite what to do with them.

Among other things, I still wasn't allowed to make phone calls because I hadn't been processed. And the officials from the Immigration Department had left—so there was no chance of that changing in the immediate future.

It was a bizarre situation. I was on the committee representing the detainees and was nominally in charge of the phones. But I was banned from making any phone calls myself. Of course, that didn't stop me. In fact, I was one of the first of the detainees to make use of the newly installed telephones.

The phone area was completely chaotic. Guards had been told to check the names of everyone who wanted to make calls. People were queuing all day to get to the two phones while the name checking went on. I got talking to one of the more affable guards and about 6.30 one evening, when he began his shift checking names, he smuggled me into the phone area through a security gate.

The first call I made was to my cousin Sam in Melbourne, who had come to Australia earlier that year from New Zealand, where he was a legal migrant working as a physicist for an oil and gas pipeline company. I asked him to find me an immigration agent in Australia. It was a very interesting and, to be honest, disappointing conversation. After listening to my story, he said: 'The news is really bad for you guys. I don't know whether there's any chance of you staying here—you might have to go back to Iraq. I'm not sure there's anything I can do for you.'

Not what I wanted to hear at all! I think he was upset that I was a boat person. He felt I had broken the law and that was the beginning and the end of the story as far as he was concerned. And I think he was also worried that I was going to ask him for money. Which wasn't the case at all.

Then I called my mother—it was the first time we had spoken since our brief and hurried conversation when I was on the Federal Police barge off Christmas Island more than six months earlier. I told her what had happened to me and that I urgently needed an immigration agent to put forward my case with the authorities.

She was very excited to hear my voice and was completely reassuring. My mother was always a very can-do person.

'Don't worry,' she told me. 'Leave it to me and I'll sort it out.'

I phoned her again the next day and she told me that my uncle Ahmed had made contact with an immigration agent named Dr Mohamed Al Jabiri who was based in Sydney. He had agreed to take up the case and she had organised a deposit payment for him to process my papers.

Dr Al Jabiri is a fascinating person in his own right. He was a close associate of Saddam's predecessor, President Ahmad Hassan al Bakr—a fact that had lifted him to high office in that regime. He had served as a senior Iraqi diplomat at the United Nations, as well as holding other high-level posts in Canada, Lebanon and North Korea, before becoming Iraq's ambassador in Spain. He was recalled shortly after Saddam assumed power and was promptly jailed without trial and tortured in the notorious Abu Ghraib prison. He was released after a couple of years and took exile in Australia, where he had become a leader of the Iraqi community and a human rights activist.

Naturally, I was delighted to have him on my side. But the only problem was that he couldn't do anything until he had talked to me.

To get the ball rolling, Dr Al Jabiri contacted the Department of Immigration and told them he was my immigration agent, then gave them my detainee number and told them he wanted to talk to me.

That caused all sorts of ructions at the detention centre. The guards took me aside and quizzed me about how I'd made contact with him. I didn't tell them much.

At last things were moving.

Dr Al Jabiri sent me a fax which I signed, confirming his appointment as my immigration agent. Then I sent him a handwritten account of my story. He arranged for it to be typed. I signed a faxed copy of it and my application was submitted to the Department of Immigration. Just like everyone else's had been some weeks earlier.

Now I was getting the same attention as the other detainees in Curtin. But it had been an enormous struggle.

About a week after I'd first made contact with my mother, the Immigration Department case officer came to the detention centre to interview me and hear my story. The interview lasted about an hour and covered the sort of ground you'd expect. Why I'd left Iraq, how I'd travelled to Australia. But he didn't ask me anything about Baghdad and didn't check whether I was in fact Iraqi. Which was weird.

The interview was carried out in Arabic through a Lebanese woman interpreter. It was recorded so it could be double-checked for accuracy. Of course, I could understand the questions perfectly in English and the interpreter knew that full well. It was funny, because she struggled with some of the translation into Arabic and she laughed when she realised she wasn't interpreting things precisely. I was having to correct her all the way through the interview.

As soon as the interview was completed, I was granted legitimate access to the phones for the first time.

# The Breakouts

One evening soon after, there was a lot of unrest in the detention centre. I think it developed as a direct result of the introduction of the two phone lines. This meant that, at long last, the detainees could communicate with people outside the camp—including relatives in Perth—and, through the grapevine, they found out that other boat people had been processed ahead of them in Woomera and Port Hedland. Clearly, things were on the move for detainees in those other centres. But events were developing much more slowly for us. The detainees didn't know what was going on and suspected they could be locked away in Curtin for another nine months or a year before they knew the outcome of their asylum applications.

I took a different view. I was actually relieved that the ponderous administrative process appeared to be progressing. I just wanted my application to be considered and a decision made.

I called Dr Al Jabiri on the night of 8 June—and, during that conversation, something was mentioned about the atmosphere at Curtin. That was all—just a mention of the unease people were feeling.

When I woke the next morning, I discovered that the wire of the perimeter fence had been cut and hundreds of people were gathered at the front gate demanding to be released. From talking to other detainees, I believe the breakout leaders had stolen some cutting implements from the kitchen and sliced through the fence.

It was a very tense situation and the government-appointed interpreter from Brisbane was talking to the detainees through a megaphone and trying to calm the situation. He was emphasising that they had been processed and the authorities were doing everything they could to expedite the situation. He was attempting to reassure the detainees that all they had to do was wait. 'It'll only be a matter of weeks before things get better,' he was saying.

Of course, that didn't reassure anyone. They had firsthand experience that they were being perceived as criminals. You only have to live through the humiliation of being known by a number for a very short time before you hear the message that you are regarded as the scum of the earth.

Not surprisingly, the crowd of detainees didn't listen to the words of the interpreter. In a situation like that, crowds begin to feed off themselves and build up a momentum of their own. Pretty soon, they took charge and surged out through the breach in the fence.

Obviously, the number of detainees was overwhelming—I think about 150 burst out of Curtin that day. So the guards demonstrated an unusual infusion of common sense and simply backed off. For once, they didn't even try to physically restrain the escaping asylum-seekers.

The first group ran out of the camp, thinking attempts would be made to stop them. But as soon as they saw the guards were taking no action at all, they slowed to a walk.

The interpreter was obviously frustrated that his urgings had been completely ignored and he started shouting things like: 'You're all idiots! You'll regret it!'

# The Breakouts

Because I knew there would be serious consequences, I made sure I stayed inside the compound and was noticed by the guards. That way, I felt there was no room for anyone to misunderstand my actions.

I was standing close to the toilets in the main compound, watching the detainees walking out. Keeping in a very safe place that was highly visible. But, strangely, I had a sense that something extremely wrong was about to happen—quite possibly, quashing all our visas or just delaying consideration of our applications indefinitely.

Curtin wasn't the only detention centre where tensions were running high. Although we didn't know it at the time, that day, something like 1300 people broke out of Woomera, Port Hedland and Curtin.

I don't know how it came about that the breakouts were so carefully orchestrated, but, for some reason, I have a suspicion it was organised in Perth.

To be honest, it was all rather futile. It certainly didn't do the asylum-seekers any good. Police blocked the road about 10 kilometres from the detention centre, intercepted the escapees, rounded them up and brought them back to Curtin later the same day. They were placed straight into isolation. A small group accused of violence and resisting arrest and the people suspected of being the ring leaders were taken to prison.

❦

Within a couple of days of the breakout, events took a distinct turn for the worse for me. One of the asylum-seekers knocked on my door and sternly warned me that I'd better be extremely careful because another detainee was spreading the word that I was the person who incited the whole breakout. The guy behind the rumour was dangerous and had an agenda against me. He had three wives in Iran and wanted to phone them all as soon as the landline phones had been installed. I stopped him because others wanted to make calls as well and had equally as much right to use the phones. He was furious and was looking for a way to get me back. I understand he conspired with another of the prominent Shi'ites, the ex-Badr Brigade soldier I'd treated for convulsions before we boarded the boat way back in Indonesia.

As happens with rumours among people who have far too little to keep them occupied, the word spread quickly around the camp.

Later, another of the detainees approached me during a meal and told me there were five people who were prepared to sign statements saying it was me who incited the breakout, hoping their actions would accelerate the granting of their visas.

I could see this whole scenario unfolding in front of me— but there was nothing I could do. It's almost impossible to prove a negative and I was completely powerless to stop the rumours.

A couple of days later, around 6.30 p.m., the inevitable happened. The guards came looking for me.

The moment I got out of the shower, a guard told me, 'We need you to come to the main office.'

# The Breakouts

I dressed and followed them to the administration area. I was taken to a room I hadn't seen before. There was a chair and a desk, with two strangers sitting on the other side. Ominously, they were in civilian clothes, which meant they'd been brought in from outside the detention centre. They had a tape recorder, writing pads and pens in front of them. They shook my hand and we sat down.

The first officer introduced himself as being from the Federal Police. The other was from the Australian Customs department. They said they wanted to ask me some questions about the breakout.

The Federal Police officer was doing most of the talking. He started recording and immediately asked, 'What do you know about Dr Al Jabiri?'

I explained that he was my immigration agent.

He continued, 'On the night before the breakout, you made a phone call to Dr Al Jabiri.'

I confirmed I had.

'What did you talk about? Did he incite you to break out?'

I responded with an emphatic 'No'.

The questions continued along that line and I repeatedly told them we hadn't discussed a breakout at all. Then the Customs officer turned the tape recorder off and said: 'C'mon, let's talk frankly. Did he or didn't he tell you to break out?'

I responded with two questions: 'What do you want from me? And what are my chances of sleeping in the donga tonight?'

The reaction was quite chilling: 'It depends on what you tell us.'

I told the officer emphatically: 'I had nothing to do with it. And we didn't discuss a breakout. Dr Al Jabiri is my immigration agent and we discussed my application for asylum. We did discuss the atmosphere in the detention centre, but that was as far as it went.'

The whole interview seemed to me to be an effort by the Federal Police officer and the Customs officer to extract a confession from me that Dr Al Jabiri was the mastermind behind the breakout and I was his puppet. The notion was complete nonsense and I repeatedly told them so.

Finally, the Federal Police officer ran out of patience and told me: 'Well, I have to arrest you. You are charged with inciting people to break out of the detention centre. Now you have to come with us.'

He asked whether I needed to take anything with me. I requested my medical book and said I would like to speak to Doha. I got one out of two—he allowed me to take the book, but insisted I couldn't speak to Doha or anyone else.

As soon as the book arrived, they marched me out. The Federal Police officer said: 'You seem smart enough not to escape. I don't need to handcuff you, do I?' I confirmed I didn't need to be handcuffed.

We walked to their four-wheel drive and set off for Derby Police Station. This time, I was given the full treatment. Fingerprints and a mug shot, before I spent the night in the cells.

# The Breakouts

Next morning, I was taken in a police ute with a cage on the back to Broome Court, around 220 kilometres away. Clearly, I was now being treated as a criminal rather than a detainee.

My first court appearance was a formality. I appeared with no one to defend me. The Federal Police were there and I was told that I was entitled to legal representation.

I was remanded in custody and, after the court hearing, was transported directly to jail. Broome Jail—Maximum Security, no less.

From that day, my whole journey changed.

# 14

# THE TURNING POINT

On the face of it, being charged with inciting a breakout from Curtin Detention Centre and being held in the Maximum Security section of Broome Jail should have been rock bottom and an extremely difficult position to recover from.

By the nature of my circumstances and my location—in a small cage with four beds and a steel toilet—I was keeping some pretty shady company, sharing my days with people charged over serious criminal matters. Stereotypically, one of my cell mates was Aboriginal and charged with murder; the other was from an Asian background and was facing drug charges.

# The Turning Point

And when it came to my court appearance, the company in the holding area wasn't any more select. The two people in there with me were accused of child molestation.

But, even taking all this into account, from the moment I stepped foot into Broome Jail nothing was ever quite the same—and certainly never as bad as it had been for me at Curtin.

For a start, I was now known by my name—Munjed Al Muderis. Even to this day, the sound of hearing my name provides a wonderful contrast with being known as detainee 982. Which had been my only identity for the previous seven months.

After the initial court appearance, which was merely a remand and adjournment, I went back to my prison cell. I had access to various additional facilities and was afforded a level of respect that had been denied me since my arrival all those months ago from Christmas Island. There was a television, a telephone and even a pool table. On top of that, I was paid something like $13 a day. And the food, after the rubbish we'd been served in Curtin, was nothing short of brilliant.

Don't get me wrong, there were still major challenges. While the court had told me I was entitled to legal representation, the people from Legal Aid didn't believe I was eligible because I wasn't an Australian citizen. As usual, I turned to my mother. It was marvellous to be able to make a phone call, unlike at Curtin, but it certainly wasn't easy when I had to begin the conversation by saying: 'Hi, Mum! Guess what, I'm in jail. And, not only that, in Maximum Security!'

Naturally enough, my mother was shocked at this latest turn of events—which she must have thought maintained my momentum of lurching from one complete disaster to the next. For the first time I could remember, she didn't know what to say or do. Fortunately, I was able to reassure her that my situation was a million times better than it had been in the detention centre. And, even though I was forced to wear the standard prison garb of green top and green pants, at least I could put them into the laundry and get a clean set.

Then I rang Dr Al Jabiri to let him know what had happened and discuss the latest developments. He was as supportive as he could be.

The prison guards were a big advance on the goons at the detention centre. At least these guys were professionals, had proper training and knew what they were and were not allowed to do. And you could talk to them.

At one point, I asked them why I was being held in Maximum Security. They explained that Broome Jail was essentially a Minimum Security facility and prisoners were allowed to come and go. But because I was a detainee, that couldn't happen. So they had no alternative to tucking me in Maximum Security.

In Broome, I had my first experience of being handcuffed. I had declined the opportunity to wear the cuffs when I was initially charged in Curtin. But this time there was no discussion. Every day when I went to lunch or dinner with my cell mates, we had to be transferred to the dining room in the main area of the jail. The stretch between Maximum Security and the rest of the jail was across a courtyard that wasn't secure so, routinely, the three of us were handcuffed together and led across the yard and back. That was the only thing I felt even remotely uneasy about in Maximum Security.

Sure, the company wasn't necessarily what I would choose, but it was interesting and, in plenty of cases, preferable to the detainees. One of my cell mates, the accused drug dealer, didn't talk much and that was fine with me. My other cell mate, the killer, I got to know quite well. He had handed himself into the police, admitted what he'd done and was awaiting trial for murder. I taught him to play chess and we played regularly and talked. Along the way, I learned that he had absolutely no remorse about what he'd done, because he believed the man he'd killed had raped his daughter. He also taught me about his Aboriginal culture. In return, he asked me about Islam and Arabic culture. They were quiet and often deep conversations and he seemed to me to be a peaceful person.

Not long after I arrived, another group of sixteen detainees was brought into the jail. They were the people who'd been charged with rioting and being the leading trouble-makers during the breakout. They came into Maximum Security as well, until pretty much the whole section was filled with detainees.

These were the most violent of the inhabitants of Curtin. Initially, I felt uneasy in their company, especially because of the surrounding rumours and conspiracy theories. Happily, though, things settled as the days passed. The others from Curtin were just as excited as I had been when they discovered conditions were so much better. And they made the most of it, many of them playing pool for large parts of their waking hours. So even these insurgent types seemed less aggressive in jail, which proves what an explosive environment Curtin had become.

We were in Broome for a few days before being transferred to Karratha Jail, 830 kilometres to the south, in a large prison truck. The inside of the truck was sparse. Small windows and a toilet in the middle. We were sitting on metal benches and if we needed to go to the toilet, we had to do it in front of everyone else. To make it worse, it was like an oven inside the truck. We were all sweating profusely. That many people sweating profusely in a confined space is never going to be a pleasant experience.

The journey was interminable. We left early in the morning and it must have taken twelve hours or more to reach Karratha. It was horrible.

The reason we were transferred from Broome to Karratha had nothing to do with our protection or comfort. Simply, they couldn't hold that many people for any length of time in Broome Jail. Certainly not long enough to prepare the case against me or the other detainees. Karratha, on the other hand, was a much bigger jail with far more Medium Security cells.

Not only was there more room, but we had individual cells—which was a luxury! The facilities were much more extensive, too. For example, there was a football field—so we could kick a ball around through the empty hours of the day. And we could have a shower whenever we wanted.

Importantly for me, there was a library where I could read books and study. Straightaway, I went into the library to check what was on offer, although most of the time I was reading my constant companion, *Last's Anatomy*. The only problem was that we weren't allowed access to the internet. But that didn't prove to be troublesome for long.

One of the Karratha prisoners had a computer and a TV in his room and was very knowledgeable about information technology. I think he was in jail for punching someone. No matter, he was very sympathetic to my story and helped me write material to send to Amnesty International.

He managed to contact leading Australian human rights activist Chris Sidoti, who, at the time, was the Australian Human Rights Commissioner. And although we weren't allowed to send emails from jail, we did phone him.

Following the discussions with Amnesty and Chris Sidoti and a phone call by Dr Al Jabiri, I was contacted by Perth solicitor, later barrister, Laurie Levy, who became my legal representative.

Meanwhile, the detainees in the jail had divided in two political groups. One was the Supreme Islamic Council faction. It was led by the ex-militant-now-physiotherapist I'd given an aspirin injection before we boarded the boat in Indonesia. As a member of the council's militia wing, the Badr Brigade, he had been a sniper for the Iranian forces in the north of Iraq. During our time at Curtin he kept singing the praises of Iran and telling everyone how it had been a generous host to him. But he was verbally hostile towards me and even accused me of being the person behind the breakout. I had challenged him to prove it, of course, to which he replied that he didn't need to because he'd heard other people talking about it. His group called themselves The Bears.

The second group was the Al-Dawa faction. Al-Dawa was the smaller political group in Iraq at the time, but its powerbase has risen in recent years and it's run Iraq since the US takeover. This group was dominated by Iraqis.

The situation boiled down to a simple turf war—the two rival Islamic groups playing out their internecine rivalries in an Australian jail. Bizarre by anyone's standard.

The time passed quickly in Karratha Jail. When I wasn't studying, a good proportion of the remaining hours were spent with the inmate who was the IT expert. He was more than happy to support me in my case, because it helped him fill his days behind bars.

I wrote letters to Amnesty International and to the media— *The Australian*, *The Age*, as many outlets as I could find—about the situation in the detention centre. And, for the first time that I saw, there was serious and active interest in our plight. If nothing else, the mass breakout had sparked attention—from Amnesty, if not the media.

# The Turning Point

The letters I wrote from jail also triggered a dramatic change in my fortunes, not only because, in some small way, they exposed the public to the awful conditions in Curtin, but also because they acted as the background for my legal representative.

So I spent my days incarcerated at Karratha studying, writing, playing football and occasionally watching TV. And there were times when I just watched the kangaroos. There was an enormous number of kangaroos around the jail.

All against a background of relative comfort! The food was terrific. There was halal food for the practising Moslems among the prisoners. The authorities were very aware of, and attentive to, our cultural requirements. The cell was clean and relatively comfortable, with a single bed and my own toilet. There was no chair or desk, but I could sit on the bed. And the sheets were clean.

But, of course, there was still enormous uncertainty. I had no idea how my saga would end. In fact, I had no idea if the legal representative would even turn up. Nor how I would pay him. I had to work on the possibility that I might have to represent myself.

I realised if I was found guilty of organising the breakout, that would be the end of my journey. There was no way I would be able to follow a career in medicine and, most likely, my future would be serving time in an Australian jail followed by deportation back to Iraq.

Needless to say, I knew I was innocent. I knew I hadn't committed any offence, beyond the initial entry into Australia without the necessary papers. But it didn't mean I would be cleared of the charge.

Another problem was that I had not been presented with the actual charges I was to face, nor the evidence against me. All I had heard was that four or five people had written statutory declarations saying it was me who incited them to force their way out of Curtin. The whole notion was ridiculous. Apart from anything else, I had never knowingly met two or three of my accusers, let alone incited them to do anything or persuaded them to cut the wire fences at Curtin.

The stay of around a week in Karratha Jail was enormously productive, but came to an end when we were transferred back to Broome. The journey north proved every bit as awful as the trip south had been.

✳

Back in Broome Jail, Chris Sidoti turned up.

When I met him, he emphasised that the federal government and the Department of Immigration were trying to prove a political point and we were just stuck in the middle. In itself, that message was reassuring. But only to a degree. In essence I think he was still on a fact-finding mission to clearly establish details of the conditions in the detention centres.

Chris's visit was followed by the arrival of Laurie Levy. I talked to him for an hour and handed him the background material I'd prepared in Karratha Jail. As you'd expect, he was more specific about the legal side of things, saying there wasn't a strong case against me, but it would depend on the witnesses.

So, regardless of my innocence, I was entirely at the mercy of the judicial system and whether the evidence presented would reflect the truth.

I didn't know it at the time, but the magistrate who was to hear my case was an interesting character. His name was Antoine Bloemen. He was born in Belgium in 1941, joined the merchant navy and sailed the world, before settling in the US where he enlisted in the army and became a paratrooper. The story goes that after he and his wife visited Western Australia she persuaded him to move there. Bloemen then studied law at the University of Western Australia, before working his way through the legal ranks and becoming a magistrate in the remote Kimberley and Pilbara region in the north of the state. He took an unconventional view of the legal system and introduced a number of initiatives to make it more accessible to Indigenous people, such as staging hearings in community buildings and inviting Aboriginal elders to sit with him. After his retirement in 2008, he became a member of the Advisory Board for the Kimberley Institute, a not-for-profit organisation that aims to improve conditions for the people of the region.

Bloemen's handling of my case was characteristically single-minded.

Laurie, who was representing me pro bono, arrived on a Thursday evening ready to head into court at nine o'clock the following morning and request an adjournment. His role was as instructing solicitor—preparing the way for the barrister who would be representing me when the case was finally heard. The barrister, Robert Richter from Melbourne, had phoned the authorities to request an adjournment, saying there was insufficient time to prepare the case for the defence. Laurie, meantime, was there to research the case and handle the preliminaries before I went before the magistrate. He had promised his wife he'd be back home in Perth for the weekend.

It didn't quite work out that way.

The magistrate completed the other cases on his schedule at four o'clock on the Friday afternoon. But rather than simply adjourn the case until Monday morning, he said he'd hear it at five o'clock that afternoon. Which sparked all sorts of furrowed brows as everyone desperately tried to prepare a cogent argument for an adjournment. Eventually, Bloemen agreed to delay the hearing—but only until Sunday!

Like everyone else involved, Laurie was caught unprepared—and, from starting out as instructing solicitor, he was instantly elevated to my lead, and only, defence lawyer.

My case was set down to last two days.

I was led into the court in handcuffs, charged with inciting a riot. In line with legal procedures, the prosecution presented its evidence first. And, to my delight and amazement, it wasn't long before the case against me started to unravel.

The first and second witnesses, who were supposed to be naming me as the ring leader of the breakout, denied any knowledge of my role in the incident. Essentially, they were saying they hadn't made the statements themselves—instead, the documents had been prepared by others for their signature. They admitted they hadn't spoken to me about the breakout, didn't know anything about my alleged involvement and didn't know why they were there in the first place.

I can't begin to explain what a relief it was to hear that testimony. Clearly, it was an enormous blow to the prosecution to see their case crumble before their eyes.

Very quickly it also became obvious the woman who was running the prosecution had never been to Curtin. At one point, she asked one of their witnesses whether he'd talked to me on the grass at the detention centre. He said he had. It was demonstrable nonsense because there was no grass at Curtin—it was all desert!

Later, one of my witnesses, an engineer friend named Rafid, underlined the point when he was posed the same question. 'What's grass?' he asked. Like everyone who'd been there, he hadn't seen any grass at Curtin. To give the observation even greater emphasis, those were the only words of English he spoke during the hearing. The rest of his evidence was in Arabic.

The magistrate adjourned for lunch and I was left in the courtroom with one of the prosecution witnesses. Naturally, we were given strict instructions not to talk to each other. But no one else was there and he came up to me and said, 'Please forgive me.' Which, in Iraqi culture, is a tradition when you don't want to die with something on your conscience.

He seemed to be under the impression he would be given favourable treatment if he provided evidence against me. He told me that on the way to the court, the ACM officials had taken him and their other witnesses to the beach and bought them a burger each. He added that, in return for their testimony against me, they'd been promised the immigration officials would look after them. I guess he may have been one of the asylum-seekers who'd broken out of Curtin but didn't want to be jailed or sent back to the Middle East.

As soon as the court resumed, I told Laurie what had happened and he raised the issue in court. The witness was then questioned about it.

When the court's attention turned back to the breakout itself, one witness claimed I had spoken to him in front of the gates at Curtin. Others claimed I had spoken to them at exactly the same time, but in completely different places. The prosecution's case was looking weaker all the time.

On the second day, we had a chance to present the case for my defence. We had four witnesses—Doha, her sister Noor, her aunt Hoda and Rafid the engineer. They were consistent in saying that I'd been with them at crucial times during the breakout and that I had nothing to do with it. Which was the truth.

Finally, I had to take the stand.

I was asked whether I had spoken to Dr Al Jabiri. I said I had but we had never talked about breaking out of the detention centre. A lot of questions seemed to focus on the role of Dr

Al Jabiri—to the point where it almost appeared it was him on trial rather than me.

The prosecution was attacking the credibility of Doha and her family, suggesting they would benefit by me becoming a doctor in Australia. Apparently, I would make their lives very comfortable. That was ridiculous, because Doha and I were nothing more than friends at that stage. And I had absolutely no guarantees about my future—whether I would be allowed to stay in Australia, let alone whether I would be able to work as a doctor.

The end came on Monday afternoon. Magistrate Bloemen—in his own idiosyncratic style—dismissed the case by saying he 'found the prosecution witnesses slimy'! And that was about all he said.

Not exactly the extensively argued judgment you'd expect in a court of law.

A couple of dozen people were watching the proceedings, including some of the police officers and prison guards who'd taken me to the court. As the verdict was announced, the courtroom erupted in cheers. Amazingly, the prison guards and police officers were among those applauding. It was an extraordinary show of support. Laurie Levy later said he'd never experienced anything quite like it.

It's hard to explain what a relief it was to hear the verdict. While others were cheering, I was crying. With relief.

But that wasn't the end of the matter. Once I'd been acquitted, the authorities had to decide what to do with me. On the one hand, I was free to go. On the other hand, I wasn't because I had to return to Curtin.

How would I get back there? My witnesses had travelled to Broome court by car. And when I saw Doha afterwards, she asked me to go back in their vehicle. As you can imagine, I was enthusiastic about that idea. Being in the midst of a friendly group for the first time in weeks would have boosted my spirits enormously. But when I spoke to the detention centre guards, they told me in no uncertain terms it wasn't going to happen. They insisted I would be travelling back to Curtin with them.

In the end, we took the journey back in two vehicles. Doha and her family in the first and me following behind with the guards. When we arrived at Curtin, Doha's family went into the main compound and I could hear detainees asking them what had happened in court.

My first night of my newfound freedom should have been a dream come true. Instead, it turned out to be a nightmare. I spent it in solitary confinement in a wooden box that was roughly 2 by 2 metres in size. No windows. It was the suicide monitoring cell.

In the tight confines of the cell I was trying to sleep on a slender mattress with a fluorescent light which was on twenty-four hours a day and with a camera recording my every move. A peephole the size of a 50-cent piece in the door was my only contact with the outside world. No natural light, no bed, no pillow. Back to the deplorable conditions in detention without any sort of interlude or opportunity to celebrate my acquittal. Back to man's inhumanity to man.

There was no explanation why I was in solitary. And at first I didn't ask any questions.

But if I was in any doubt that I was back in the detention centre, in the evening, I was delivered a takeaway plastic container of dreadful food. I ate it and slept. And, despite the surroundings, slept very well after the events of the day.

The next morning the detention centre guards brought me in more food in a plastic container. I wiled away the day wondering when this would all end. But when they brought me dinner in a standard plastic container that evening, I realised something was seriously amiss. At that point, I asked what was going on. But no one rushed to provide an explanation.

A day later, one of the officers suggested they were rehabilitating me after spending time with criminals in jail. The claim was utterly ridiculous and I responded pretty badly, saying: 'Oh yeah, rehabilitating me in a room where the light won't turn off!'

On the third day, I asked to speak to someone in authority who could explain what was going on. No one came. I was completely ignored.

When they brought me dinner, I told them: 'There's no point. I'm not going to eat. Until someone gives me an explanation, I'm on hunger strike. I'm locked in a tiny room in solitary confinement under twenty-four-hour watch. I'm not going to eat or drink until I get an explanation.'

Shortly after, Greg Wallis, the detention centre manager, came to see me and asked: 'What do you want?'

He went on to claim the authorities had genuine fears for my safety inside Curtin and that I might be harmed or harm myself. That was why they were keeping me in solitary confinement.

I wasn't about to swallow that. 'That's bullshit,' I said. 'Give me the real reasons. I've been to court and the court has found me innocent.'

Wallis corrected me: 'The court couldn't find you guilty.'

The discussion of the merits of the court's findings went on until I told him: 'I don't care what you think, I won't be eating or drinking until I know what's going on.'

That elicited a few more details. Wallis insisted I wouldn't be going back into the general compound and he made it clear that wasn't negotiable until a decision was made on whether I would be staying in Australia.

I repeated my decision not to eat or drink until he was completely honest with me.

He wasn't happy. 'God, you're a pain,' he said. 'What do you want?'

I told him I didn't have extensive demands. I was quite happy not to mix with most of the people in the detention centre, but I wanted Doha to be able to visit me in solitary confinement and I wanted access to a phone to call my immigration agent each day.

His response was unexpected. 'Is that all?' he said.

I already had my trusty medical book with me, so I confirmed those were my only requirements.

He agreed but asked again: 'And that's all you want? And then you'll end your hunger strike?'

I laughed. 'Don't be ridiculous,' I told him. 'It's all a stupid game. I'm just playing your game.'

Before he left, Wallis seemed to me to be making a point of letting me know that I may have won the battle, but the war was still going on.

His approach summed up the government policies of the day and the mentality of the detention centres. It was all a political and personal power struggle. There was little or no thought given to the people who were embroiled in this petty posturing. It was all about point-scoring. Showing that you were in charge and would not be challenged. All completely mindless. No one was demonstrating any moral values, compassion or judgment. They all appeared to think the prizes would go to the individuals who could show they were tougher than anyone else. All focused on themselves, rather than taking a common sense and reasonable approach to the people and the issues involved.

I still shudder when I think about those attitudes and run into people who demonstrate the same idiotic and disrespectful approach. Behaving like a thug is unacceptable under any circumstances—whether it's in a political, professional or social setting, or in detention centres.

The following day, Doha came to see me and I was transferred from suicide watch to the area known as The Hotel. There was a bed with a pillow and sheets. I had my own toilet and a small outside courtyard area. It was still basic and uncomfortable, but it was a considerable improvement. There were other rooms in The Hotel, but no one was in them at the time. The only minor disruption was when other detainees were brought in. Then I had to be locked in my room. That happened quite often, but was an inconvenience I could cope with.

I had two guards overseeing me at all times. Some of these guards were decent blokes. Over the forty days I was in The Hotel, I got to know about eight of them. They were supposed to keep me inside my room, but they didn't. I started playing Scrabble and chess with some of them.

Overall, it wasn't bad. I could study and relax largely undisturbed. And a major benefit was that I had access to clean toilets!

At one stage, they brought in a detainee named Abu Doaa. He was in his fifties, bald with glasses, and was apparently quite outspoken so the authorities said they feared he would be attacked because of his views. I found him to be a peaceful kind of person. In fact, he seemed naive to me, because when Saddam allowed other political parties to be registered in the 1990s, Abu Doaa registered a new party. He was promptly arrested and tortured—and had to escape from Iraq as a consequence.

We got to know each other in the four or five days he was

there—and one thing I quickly established was that he was a strong chess player. As we talked, it emerged that he knew my family and had actually played chess against my father. He told me stories about my father playing against ten people at the same time. Abu Doaa himself was an extremely experienced player—he beat me in something like 70 per cent of the games we played!

He was in solitary confinement for some of the same reasons as me—the detention centre was a hotbed of discontent, rumour and intrigue. Under those conditions, a lot of personal animosities built up and it wasn't unusual for detainees to report others for perceived or entirely fabricated misdemeanours. I lost touch with him after that and I have no idea where he ended up or what happened to him.

I spent a lot of time studying my medical textbook, which I read from cover to cover several times. With the benefit of hindsight, that period in solitary confinement served me well. It helped me master the subjects that would be the basis for my future and eventually helped me get a job in Australia and pass my exams to become an orthopaedic surgeon—which, trust me, are some of the most difficult exams anyone can undertake.

To this day, I still have that book. In fact, it contains the names, phone numbers and email addresses of many of the people who were crucial in helping me through the detention centre ordeal.

Almost as soon as I had returned from the court case, I started hearing rumours that detainees were being granted visas and were leaving Curtin. Doha would come in to see me for twenty minutes or half an hour every second day and she would tell me the camp was emptying. I'm sure this included Ali and Hussein, the two companions who'd shared this journey all the way from Amman. We hadn't spent a great deal of time together during our detention in Curtin. Naturally, I saw them around the camp each day but they were quiet and mostly kept to themselves. I lost touch with them after they left the detention centre and I have no idea where they ended up.

Of course, being in solitary confinement, I had to rely on Doha's reports of the number of detainees being released into the community. I couldn't see it for myself.

Even so, I was encouraged by the news and my attitude changed. As the days passed, I began to realise that it was only a matter of time before my ordeal would be over. I was phoning Dr Al Jabiri regularly to find out what was going on and he was updating me on the latest developments.

Events were unfolding rapidly by now and, within a couple of days, I was instructed to undergo a blood test and chest x-rays. When I heard that, I knew the end wouldn't be far away for me, either.

In mid-August, Doha came in and told me that all of her family had been granted visas and were being flown to Brisbane. She said she wouldn't see me for a while, but would phone when she could.

The next few days were some of the toughest for me because I had no definite indication of my fate and I was genuinely on my own. Doha and her family had been a lifeline and constant confidantes. My existence in the detention centre was much harder without them.

On 25 August I spoke to Dr Al Jabiri, who delivered the best news—my visa had been granted. But, unlike the rest of the detainees who'd been allowed legal entry to Australia that day, I wasn't released immediately. In fact, the day passed as most others had over the last month.

I was becoming increasingly frustrated that I'd heard nothing while everyone else seemed to be packing their bags and leaving. I determined that the next day I would start asking questions to find out when I'd be released.

Then, late at night, Greg Wallis, accompanied by one of the guards, pushed open the door to my cell.

For the first time, he called me by my name rather than my number.

'Munjed,' he said. 'I thought I'd come myself to give you your visa!'

It was some of the most welcome news I've ever heard. An incredible relief.

As usual, though, there was a catch. He went on with words that I interpreted as meaning: 'Your visa has been issued, but I've decided I want to keep you here another day and, because you have money and speak good English, we didn't think you'd need to be transferred. We'll give you the money and you can look after yourself. I'll get one of the officers to take you out onto the main road. There'll be a bus coming from Derby around six o'clock in the morning. That's the bus which will take you to Broome.'

To my knowledge, I was the only person who was ever simply dumped on the roadside rather than formally transferred to another city or town.

Perhaps Wallis believed this was the crowning glory, the ultimate way to show me how insignificant I was. To be honest, it was of very little consequence—a small inconvenience to me. In my mind, it merely confirmed what I had always thought about him.

But rather than dwelling on anything Wallis could dish up, I was thrilled that, after nine months, I would be getting out of Curtin Detention Centre in a matter of hours. And could, after all the turmoil, get on with the next chapter of my life.

# 15

# THE NEW BEGINNING

There was an early morning knock on the door of my room in The Hotel. The guard handed me my bag of belongings which had been held in storage since the day I'd arrived at Curtin. Gruffly, he told me: 'You have fifteen minutes to get ready.'

I was escorted out to a ute, wearing my own green shirt and grey pants which had been in storage. They weren't clean, but they felt great.

A single guard drove me to the main road. He dropped me off shortly before 6 a.m. and, within a few minutes, the bus arrived. I was free for the first time in nearly ten months. I had arrived on Christmas Island on 8 November 1999 and I was leaving Curtin Detention Centre on 26 August 2000, less than a month before the Olympic Games were held in Sydney.

The relief and excitement was indescribable. I wanted to tell the handful of people who were sharing the bus with me that I was finally free and allowed to stay in Australia.

The 220-kilometre journey south-west to Broome took more than three hours. I remember a couple of teenagers on the bus were playing card games. It was refreshing to be in a society and situation where that could happen freely and openly.

I clambered out at the bus station and took a breath of the hot northern air—for the first time happy in the knowledge that no one would be dragging me back to Curtin.

At the detention centre, they'd told me to catch a plane from Broome to whatever destination I chose. I had different ideas. I thought it might be the only chance I'd get to see this part of Australia, so I decided to take the bus all the way south through rural Western Australia to Perth. I exchanged my US dollars for Australian ones in Broome and then hopped on a bus to Perth.

First Port Hedland, then Karratha. I distinctly remember the odd feeling as we drove through Karratha. Of course, this was familiar territory—I'd done that part of the trip a few months earlier, without actually appreciating the passing scenery from inside the police wagon, and my mind went spinning back to my time in jail in the town.

Then we took the coastal route. All 2300 or so kilometres of it. Through Exmouth, Coral Bay, Carnarvon, Dongara, Jurian

Bay, Cervantes, Lancelin and finally Perth. It's a marathon trip of more than thirty hours, but you certainly get to see Western Australia!

During the journey, I'd also slept—but only as much as anyone can sleep on a bus. All the same, when I arrived in the centre of Perth in the middle of the day, I decided to straightaway get stuck into the process of finding work as a doctor.

The first point of call was the Royal Perth Hospital. I approached the receptionist and, purely on speculation, asked if any Iraqi or Arabic-speaking doctors worked there. I hit the jackpot. There was one—and he was on duty. Before long, he came out to the reception area, shook hands with me and we started talking. We'd both trained in Baghdad, but he was about four or five years older than me. All very optimistic to that point. But that was where the encouragement ended.

The doctor, who was there as a resident, asked what sort of work I wanted. I told him I planned to be a surgeon and specialise in orthopaedics. He shook his head and told me I was dreaming.

He asked whether I had qualifications in orthopaedic surgery. I explained I had qualified in general surgery, but nothing more. The doctor furrowed his brow and informed me that my current qualifications wouldn't be accepted and that I should go and pick grapes at a winery while I obtained the Australian equivalents.

As for orthopaedic surgery? He was even more dismissive.

'You have to be the right colour and come from the right background,' he told me grimly. 'We're not.'

I thanked him for his advice and left the hospital, thinking to myself, 'Damn it! There must be a way.'

After the gloomy prognosis on my career prospects in Perth, I decided not to hang around. Instead, I went straight to the bus station and bought a ticket to Melbourne which, on a hunch, seemed to hold the potential of being a bigger city with more opportunities. Plus, I had relatives there who might have been able to give me some guidance.

I can't remember a great deal of the journey. The Nullabor is pretty relentless, but I guess everyone who's travelled it says that. Mostly, I slept. We had a brief stopover in Adelaide. Then again I slept between Adelaide and Melbourne. Largely, I was just delighted to be celebrating my freedom.

As soon as I arrived in Melbourne, I called my cousin Sam, who was living in a rented two-bedroom unit in Footscray. This time, unlike our earlier phone call, he was enormously positive and insisted I stay with him. His unit was in the middle of a three-storey block that had seen better days, and seemed to be home to a collection of Vietnamese and African refugees.

Sam lived with a young woman flatmate who used the second bedroom. But we hardly saw her during the week I was there. I slept on the sofa while I found my feet in my new country. It certainly wasn't luxurious, but that didn't worry me in the slightest. All my thoughts were focused on finding a job.

As well as giving me a roof over my head, Sam helped me through the administrative processes. On my first full day in Melbourne, he took me to register at Centrelink, fill out the appropriate forms and open a bank account—pretty standard procedures when you arrive in a new country, but it was a tremendous help to have someone with the local knowledge leading me through.

The next day, I went back to Centrelink to complete my CV so I could start applying for jobs. The grim advice from the Iraqi doctor in Perth was still hanging over me like a black cloud, though—so I contacted other migrant doctors to find out their assessment of my prospects. One was another boat person who was working in Ballarat in Victoria. He was much more encouraging and said, 'Just apply for as many jobs as you can. You never know what will turn up.'

With the job-seeking process underway, I needed to find somewhere of my own to live. I went to the main real estate agent in Footscray to see what was on offer and, equally as important, find out whether a refugee like myself would be accepted as a tenant. I needn't have worried. The real estate agent didn't seem at all concerned that I had no income and no history of renting accommodation. As I became more familiar with Footscray and its population, I could see why. Most of the people there were like me—from a migrant background and with little or no income.

In early September 2000 I moved into a rundown three-bedroom, single-storey house with a rusting tin roof at 7 Federal Street, Footscray. The location was hardly salubrious. The vacant block next door was being used as a car park. But the rent matched the location. I think I was paying about $170 per week for it.

I needed to buy some furniture for the place, but didn't have much money, so Sam took me to the nearest Savers—the equivalent of the Salvation Army shop. I couldn't bring myself to buy secondhand clothes there, but I did purchase a three-seater sofa, two chairs that didn't match, a couple of beds and mattresses, a kitchen table and chairs, plus some pots and pans. My biggest expense was a brand new desktop computer, which I thought was essential in my search for a job.

In those early days finding work occupied most of my time and I couldn't afford to see much of Melbourne, although I do remember being struck by the climate, which, even in spring, was cold and wet. A complete contrast to the heat and humidity of my home in Baghdad and the detention centre in the desert of north-west Australia.

Doha and her family were the only fellow detainees I kept in touch with after we'd left Curtin and, once I was established in the house in Footscray, I asked all five of them if they'd like to move from Brisbane, where most of the asylum-seekers from Curtin seemed to have ended up. Their future in Brisbane was uncertain and they accepted my offer enthusiastically. They flew down a couple of days later.

# The New Beginning

In the meantime, I'd printed hundreds of copies of my CV and was deeply absorbed in the process of finding work, spending most of my money on envelopes and stamps to send my details to every hospital I could locate around the country. On top of that, I'd spend many hours at Centrelink phoning hospitals here, there and everywhere to explore any openings for someone with my qualifications and relatively limited experience.

I guess I was following Woody Allen's advice that '80 per cent of luck is turning up'!

I received plenty of responses saying they weren't interested. But amazingly, within a fortnight, I had two expressions of interest—one from Shepparton Hospital in the fruit-growing area of the Goulburn Valley in north-eastern Victoria, the other from Mildura Hospital on the Murray River on the Victoria–New South Wales border.

The administrator at Mildura Hospital was first out of the blocks and called my mobile, asking me to undergo an interview on the phone a few days later with the Head of Emergency, Dr Fiona Russell. Our conversation lasted only about fifteen minutes. It was the first job interview I'd had in Australia—so although Dr Russell was delightful, I had absolutely no idea whether I'd performed okay.

The next day, the administrator called me back and offered me the job.

Someone from Shepparton Hospital also interviewed me on the phone. And I then got a call from them offering me a position, too. Two job interviews! Two job offers! My confidence was on the rise after the humiliation of the detention centre.

Now, at this stage I had no idea which was the better of the two hospitals. But I had found out that six of the seven doctors working in Emergency at Mildura Hospital were Iraqis and the seventh was Turkish. So, as you do in such circumstances, I opted for the comfort of cultural familiarity and accepted the offer from Mildura.

Within days the hospital sent me an official written offer and I went through the process of applying to the Medical Board of Victoria for a temporary registration. I was interviewed by two officials at their offices in Melbourne. The whole process went smoothly and lasted no more than half an hour. They simply went through my CV, talked about my experience, checked that I hadn't experienced any professional problems and made sure I spoke good English. Once I had jumped that hurdle, I could register with the Federal Department of Health and receive a provider number as a medical practitioner.

I flew up to Mildura, because at that stage I didn't own a car, and started work on 1 November 2000, just a week short of one year since I'd arrived on Christmas Island.

Life as a doctor in the Emergency Unit in Mildura Hospital was pretty hectic. At the time it was a base hospital with about 150 beds, serving a major agricultural region, so there's a constant flow and variety of cases. And as well as working in Emergency, I was taking every opportunity possible to observe the surgical procedures. While I was beginning to form the foundations of my new life in Australia, I was being approached by the media, which had established me as a key contact after the breakout from the detention centre. In early December 2000, I was interviewed by Geoff Parish for a story about boat people and conditions in Curtin on ABC Television's *7.30 Report*. The story, which was a serious examination of conditions for asylum-seekers, did have another side. I was living in a studio apartment in the doctors' residential quarters about 500 metres from the hospital and part of the interview was carried out there. As the ABC team was leaving the area, the camera operator tripped, injuring his ankle quite badly. I had to treat him in Emergency before he could leave.

Amid the work, my personal circumstances were also changing. Doha flew up from Melbourne and joined me in Mildura that summer, a couple of months after I had moved there, while the rest of her family stayed in the Footscray house.

Mildura was an interesting introduction to working life in Australia. The Iraqi and Turkish surgeons were a lively bunch, each with their own foibles. One of them, for example, ended up in a bizarre fist fight with a patient in Emergency. The patient was an addict who'd come to the hospital demanding a hit of morphine. He got a hit from the doctor all right—but it wasn't morphine!

I worked as a resident in Mildura until the middle of 2001, gaining invaluable experience along the way. The senior registrar at the hospital took long spells of leave while I was there, which allowed me to fill in for her. Much of the time, I was busy working the night shift, operating on emergency and trauma cases, many of them road accidents.

Then, out of the blue, the Clinical Director, Ian McInness, told me an opening was available for a surgical registrar—a resident RMO1 position—at Austin Hospital in Melbourne. Now, although an RMO1 is above an intern, it's not far from the bottom of the surgical ladder; in fact, largely a punching bag for the nurses! I would be paid as an intern, but I would perform my duties as a resident—seeing, assessing, managing and treating patients, the majority of the time unsupervised in my work. And from my first year intern status, I would effectively jump a few levels to Registrar 1. It would be a big promotion.

The Austin is a major teaching hospital attached, among other things, to the University of Melbourne's Department of Surgery. So it was ideally suited to my career aims. And the duties would include a term in orthopaedics, which was another extremely attractive proposition.

It seemed they were having difficulty finding someone to take up the post. I'm not sure what had happened, but my impression was that a doctor had accepted the job but had withdrawn at short notice. Ian McInness was generous enough to say that he would recommend me and act as a referee if I was interested. Mildura Hospital's orthopaedic surgeon and

# The New Beginning

Dr Fiona Russell, the Head of Emergency who had initially interviewed me, also agreed to act as referees.

Some of the other Iraqi doctors in Mildura advised me against applying for the position, warning that I was trying to run before I could walk and was likely to fall flat on my face. Regardless, I thought it was a once-in-a-lifetime opportunity— a case of being in the right place at the right time—and I jumped at the chance. Again, I was interviewed by phone and a day later, I was offered the job. Obviously they were desperate to fill it!

My first three-month rotation at Austin Hospital was the nightshift in general surgery; the next rotation was at Bendigo Base Hospital in country Victoria, a brilliant experience. Built on the wealth amassed during the gold rush of the mid-nineteenth century, the city of Bendigo is a substantial and historic regional centre, 150 kilometres north-west of Melbourne and with a population of more than 100,000. The people there were most welcoming and made me feel very much at home.

The hospital has nearly 700 beds and was busy and challenging. One of the most valuable parts of my stay in Bendigo was the opportunity to work with senior surgeons and learn from them. In my previous posts, I had been largely unsupervised and left to my own devices. At the same time I was studying for the Medical Board of Victoria exam so I could achieve full accreditation and registration in the Australian medical system.

By chance, an old acquaintance from my days as a university student in Baghdad, Louay, was also sitting the exam. We had arrived in Australia around the same time, but by different methods. He came in officially by plane as a migrant backed by the United Nations High Commission for Refugees. Louay and I worked together and supported each other through the exam. Of the 531 candidates sitting the exam, he finished seventh. I finished 34th.

In addition, I sat the initial exam for the Royal Australasian College of Surgeons, which I completed by the end of 2001. That meant I could apply for the advanced training program. With the fresh qualification, I was spurred on to achieve my ultimate aim of becoming an orthopaedic surgeon.

While I was in Bendigo Doha gave birth to our first son, Adam. He was born at the Sunshine Hospital in Melbourne on 25 October 2001.

For all the rapid advances in my life, I was still tiring of Melbourne and Victoria. The weather and general atmosphere didn't suit me. I just didn't feel comfortable there. So I applied for an orthopaedic registrar position at Wollongong Hospital, south of Sydney, on the coast of New South Wales. I started there in January 2002 as a junior unaccredited orthopaedic registrar. It meant I was being trained as an orthopaedic surgeon, although not through the Australian Orthopaedic Association's (AOA) official four-year training and accreditation program. That was another matter entirely.

# 16

# WALKING TALL

My experiences in Wollongong changed my life. Nearly as dramatically as everything I'd been through over the previous three years. But my time in The 'Gong didn't start well.

At full strength, there was a team of four orthopaedic surgeons at Wollongong Hospital. Because I had arranged to sit my primary Royal Australasian College of Surgeons (RACS) exams as a general surgeon at the same time I was due to start at the hospital, I asked to take my first two weeks at work as study leave. Another new member of the team was due to arrive from the UK, but his visa hadn't come through. This meant that only two of the surgeons—one who was due to sit the RACS exam at the same time as me—were carrying the burden for the whole team. The two absentees weren't popular.

To make matters worse, I passed the exam and my colleague, who'd been forced to work through the lead up, failed. That put me even further down the pecking order.

To be honest, by this stage I was a bit of a lost soul. I'd had a sheltered upbringing in a privileged family, but subsequent events had brought me into the real world with a massive bump. I knew I wanted to be an orthopaedic surgeon, but I didn't quite know how to go about it.

Three surgeons I met in Wollongong were crucial in shaping my future. Between them, they helped me lay the foundations to become a successful orthopaedic surgeon. The first was Sham Deshpande, a most gifted surgeon and one of the first orthopaedic surgeons in Australia not to come from an Anglo background. He's a really delightful person and an outstanding teacher. Sham taught me how to be an orthopaedic surgeon.

The other two were young orthopaedic consultants, Stuart Jansen and Greg Stackpool. Both were typical boys from The 'Gong—surfers who drove ridiculously fast Subaru WRXs. Stuart was extremely harsh with me; he never let me get away with anything. Greg was equally tough, but he delivered some of the best advice and guidance I've ever received. They both taught me how to be a consultant.

I also received enormous help from Yiu Key Ho, who guided me through the first research paper I published.

One incident stands out in my mind. My senior registrar at Wollongong Hospital was a woman who would regularly embarrass me in front of other surgeons by asking questions I couldn't answer. After one of these incidents, Greg took me to one side and told me in no uncertain terms that I needed to get my act together. He knew I was good with a scalpel, he told me, but if I was ever going to make it as an orthopaedic surgeon, I had to knuckle down and master the clerical donkey work as well. He told me I needed to be at work before all the other orthopaedic surgeons and there after all the others at the end of the day. If I could do that, when the time came he would support me in applying for the AOA training course.

The advice from all of them was invaluable. And over the two years I was in Wollongong, I took heed of it.

After a few months, Doha and Adam came up from Melbourne and we rented a house in the city. Our second son, Dean, was born on 6 February 2003.

I applied to join the AOA training program, but I was still very junior and, my first application was knocked back. After a couple of years, I felt I had achieved as much as I could professionally and was in danger of becoming stale. I believed my chances of getting on the AOA training program would be improved by moving on. The next step was to Canberra Hospital. With the backing of the surgeons there and the support of some excellent referee reports, I again applied for the AOA training program. This time I was successful and

I started in 2005. This heralded a whole new chapter in my professional career.

Surgeons on the four-year orthopaedic training program move hospitals every six months, so you can be based virtually anywhere in New South Wales, Adelaide or Darwin. I was shifted from Canberra to the Women's and Children's Hospital in Adelaide, to Nepean Hospital on the western fringes of Sydney and then to Lismore Base Hospital in northern New South Wales. By the time I was working in Lismore, the hectic schedule and concentration on my work was taking a toll on my marriage, and Doha and I separated.

Subsequently, I completed my training at the Royal Prince Alfred Hospital in central Sydney, Westmead Children's Hospital in Sydney's west and at Hornsby Hospital in the city's northern suburbs. While I was at Westmead in 2008, I sat the final exam of my AOA training program—and passed first time.

Passing the orthopaedic surgery exams was the beginning rather than the end. My natural curiosity dictated that I wanted to continue studying and look for the latest technological advances in orthopaedic surgery.

I had become fascinated by the potential of osseointegration. Through tooth implants, the technique had revolutionised dental treatment and was being applied by a couple of surgeons in Scandinavia and Germany to replace amputated limbs. The first osseointegration operation for amputees was carried out in Sweden in 1995, and the Germans followed with a different approach based on existing hip replacement technology in 1999.

To many people osseointegration sounds like science fiction. It's based on the discovery in the 1950s that implanted titanium rods fuse with human bone. A handful of surgeons are now using this technology to treat amputees. We implant titanium rods in what remains of the bone, then attach adaptors that protrude a small way from the amputated limb. We then clip on a high-tech robotic prosthesis. The results can restore more natural mobility, allowing the patient to walk with a near normal gait and substantially improving their lifestyle.

In 2009 my life underwent more significant changes.

On the personal front I married my Russian-born wife, Irina, whom I had met while we were both working as junior doctors in Lismore. Irina now works as a GP in Sydney.

On the professional side, Irina and I moved to Berlin where I undertook a post-graduate fellowship in hip and knee replacement surgery. I also carried out extensive research into osseointegration and formed my own thoughts on the next stages of its development. In particular, I was determined to build a team who could analyse and support every aspect of the patient's experience. Previously, these professionals would have worked in relative isolation from each other.

When Irina and I returned to Sydney with our daughter Sophia, who was born in St Petersburg on 14 July 2009, I set about building the team, including surgeons, orthopaedic fellows, PhD students, anaesthetists, prosthetists, physiotherapists, rehabilitation physicians, pain management specialists, biomechanical engineers, perioperative care specialists, psychologists and amputee representatives. We consult on every patient from start to finish. We have extensive criteria before we accept a patient and everyone on the medical team has the right of veto.

Having set up the team, one crucial component was still missing—a patient!

In 2010, I was contacted by Brendan Burkett, an outstanding paralympian and Professor of Sports Science (Biomechanics) at the University of the Sunshine Coast in Queensland. Brendan had always been an accomplished sportsman, captaining his local Rugby League team and representing Queensland Country on a tour of New Zealand. But tragedy struck in 1985 when, at the age of twenty-two, he was knocked off his motorbike by a hit-and-run driver. His left leg was so badly damaged that it had to be amputated above the knee. After recovering, Brendan turned his attention to swimming and went on to win gold, silver and bronze medals at successive Paralympic Games. He carried the flag for Australia at the Paralympics in Sydney in 2000 and he's also set world records and won the world championship in his category.

Brendan was an ideal candidate for osseointegration. He was fit, determined and, from his work as a sports scientist, had a thorough understanding of the procedure and its potential to change his life. I operated on him at Macquarie University Hospital. The surgery and rehabilitation went smoothly, and Brendan has become a shining example of what osseointegration can achieve. His lifestyle is now much the same as yours and mine, although he does need to clip his artificial leg on and off each morning and night. It's a process that takes no more than ten seconds.

Other patients followed, including a young Sydney amputee also injured in a motorcycle accident who has now resumed his career as a gym operator and personal trainer, and a woman who was once confined to a wheelchair but now regularly plays eighteen holes of golf. And then there's Michael Swain, the British double amputee I saw receive an MBE from the Queen at Windsor Castle on that April morning in 2014.

In early December 2013, Michael arrived at my clinic in Sydney to undergo the osseointegration procedure. Over the next three months, I operated on him twice: the first to fit the titanium rods into the remains of his thigh bones, the second to attach the adaptors. The robotic legs were specially designed and built to meet his needs and, on 28 February 2014, Michael was fitted with his new legs. With the help of two crutches, he took his first steps in a small gym room at Macquarie University Hospital in Sydney's north.

It was an instant success and, because of his enthusiasm and determination, we actually found it difficult to stop him walking! The prosthetists in charge of Michael's robotic legs were certainly in no doubt.

'You're a bloody champion,' they told him as he insisted on leaving the gym and walking fifty or more paces down the corridor.

It was only a matter of days before Michael had progressed to using a single crutch. Ten days later, he strolled onto a Qantas plane at Sydney Airport, ready for the flight back to London. A few days after that, I was emailed footage of him walking unaided outside his home in Luton in the UK. Naturally, after such a success, I was delighted to be invited as Michael's special guest to watch him receive his MBE.

The results we've achieved through osseointegration are remarkable and have given dozens of amputees a completely new lease of life. And while osseointegration transforms the lives of people who've suffered the most awful traumas, my work also has reinvigorated—in a slightly less dramatic fashion—the lives of many hundreds of patients who've undergone hip and knee replacements. My patients are my primary motivation. The transformation of their lives is one of the greatest rewards of my work.

Nothing gives me greater satisfaction than knowing I can provide positive changes for them, helping restore a healthy, active lifestyle. The smiles on their faces and their love of life when they return to a pain-free, expansive existence are priceless. I have seen patients in their fifties and sixties transformed from a sedentary existence where they struggled to walk 100 metres, to a vibrant lifestyle where they have confidently trekked in the mountain ranges of Nepal or on the Inca Trail to Machu Picchu, and even cycled around Cuba. Life-changing, life-enhancing experiences.

But there is so much more that can be achieved and Australia, if governments are serious about it, can capitalise by establishing world-leading osseointegration facilities in this country. Only a handful of surgeons around the world have the training to perform these operations and already, as well as Australians, amputees from Europe and the United States are coming here for treatment, because they believe we set world-class standards and offer their best chance of achieving a virtually normal life. There is an opening for a world's best-practice osseointegration clinic, operating on patients, researching new technology and techniques, training surgeons from across Australia and around the world. I would like to think that federal and state governments will see the massive potential osseointegration offers.

Now and then, I reflect on my journey from Iraq, the dangers and traumas I encountered along the way. From a humanitarian point of view, there are a number of lessons which could, and should, be learned.

Of course I understand the raw popularity of the 'Stop the boats' catchcry. But I believe politicians should take a much more compassionate approach to asylum-seekers rather than attempt to portray them as the evil enemies of the state. Mostly, they're not. To my knowledge, thirteen qualified doctors were in detention at Curtin while I was there. Twelve of them are now working as medical professionals in Australia, many of them specialists. Plenty of others were engineers, trained craftspeople and skilled tradespeople.

Long periods of incarceration are simply inhuman. Certainly, refugees should be detained at least until they have passed all the necessary medical checks to ensure they're not carrying communicable diseases. But even during that detention, they should be known by a name rather than a number and should be afforded the standard levels of respect we apply to other human beings in our day-to-day lives.

After that, they should be educated and rehabilitated, including attending classes about Australian history, culture and lifestyle and how to assimilate into their new country's society.

Certainly, they could be housed in detention centres at night, but during the day they should be electronically tagged and allowed to work in jobs others don't want, like fruit picking or agriculture-related work in regional centres, where they can mix with locals and learn to speak English.

Children should be allowed to attend the local schools to gain an education, establish friendships and learn Australian values while they're young and their brains are like sponges. The current approach is simply traumatising them. Often for life.

All of this would create an opportunity for individuals and families, by the time their visas are granted, to feel comfortable in their surroundings and want to stay and become part of the community, rather than be drawn to ethnic ghettoes in the major cities.

The current system alienates asylum-seekers. And if they're alienated at the start, they'll remain alienated. When they're released from detention they're scarred and disaffected, they've lost their skills and don't speak English. So, too often, they fall into the arms of the waiting fundamentalists and are merely more fuel to the fire. They end up on the fringes of Australian society. The fundamentalists feed off their isolation to create even greater divisions in our community. It's sad—for everyone.

I would like to think decision-makers of all political persuasions and the people who do their bidding could come up with smarter solutions.

Sure, I realise the mass popular appeal of offering simple answers to complex problems. But it's an utterly shallow approach. Don't forget, we're dealing with real human beings—unlike the treatment I received in Curtin, people are not just numbers or statistics. Every human being deserves something better than having their lives dismissed in a flood of simplistic rhetoric, posturing and crass political point-scoring.

# ACKNOWLEDGEMENTS

It had long been on my mind to write a book detailing the experiences that have helped shape my life. But, for a number of reasons, it remained a dream. Like most busy professionals, finding the time was always going to be problematic. I also had to face the reality that my primary skills are not in the literary sphere.

Then fate intervened, as has so often happened throughout my life.

In 2009 I graduated as an orthopaedic surgeon at a black-tie dinner during the Australian Orthopaedic Association's Annual Scientific Meeting in Hobart, Tasmania. As the graduates relaxed after the presentation, I was approached by Patrick Weaver, an accomplished journalist who was, by then, running his own public relations consultancy. We talked about my experiences, initially with the idea of writing a magazine story. Patrick then suggested the tale was so powerful that it was worthy of a book. And he wanted to write it.

Over the next five years, we met when and where we could to piece together the disparate elements of the story. Patrick tirelessly drove the project. It is because of his determination and dedication that my dream of producing the story of my life has now become a reality.

We've also become firm friends.

Subsequently, Claire Kingston from Allen & Unwin has provided an intelligent and enthusiastic rudder to steer the book through the publishing process. Sarah Baker and Susin Chow also made important contributions and, with quiet efficiency, smoothed the rough edges.

Alongside most successful men, of course, stands a surprised woman. In this case, it's my wife Irina. She has been a tower of strength. My work involves long hours in the operating theatre, monitoring patients and developing prostheses with engineers and technologists. Then there are my international professional commitments. Working on this book has even further reduced the hours available to spend with Irina, our daughter Sophia and my sons Adam and Dean. I would like to publicly thank Irina for being such a rock and for her constant support, patience and tolerance, and also the children for their understanding.

I thank Doha Fahmi for adding her recollections of events and for providing photographs that illustrate some of the deprivations we went through.

Professionally, I am surrounded by an outstanding team which strives to deliver the very best in patient care. Like me, their aim is to change people's lives for the better through improved mobility and a healthier lifestyle. I thank all of my staff for their contribution and commitment.

The backbone of my practice is Belinda Bosley, who not only ensures the smooth running of its day-to-day activities but has also made a valuable contribution to this book.

# ASSOCIATE PROFESSOR MUNJED AL MUDERIS

Munjed Al Muderis is a world leading osseointegration surgeon and Adjunct Clinical Associate Professor at the University of Notre Dame Australia in Sydney. He practises as an orthopaedic surgeon at the Norwest Private Hospital, the Seventh Day Adventist Hospital and the Macquarie University Hospital in Sydney's northern suburbs.

He lives in Sydney with his wife Irina, who's a GP, and their daughter Sophia.

# PATRICK WEAVER

Patrick Weaver is a highly regarded writer and public relations consultant who runs his own public relations and creative writing business in Sydney. He was previously a senior executive with an international public relations firm and with the Australian Broadcasting Corporation.

Patrick is a former journalist with extensive experience in radio and newspapers in Australia, New Zealand and the United Kingdom.

He was born in the UK, migrating to New Zealand in 1975 and to Australia in 1978. He lives in Sydney and has two adult children.